Wanderer on the American Frontier

Wanderer on the American Frontier
The Travels of John Maley 1808–1813

Edited by
F. Andrew Dowdy

University of Oklahoma Press · Norman

On the title page: Frontispiece from Maley's journal, presumably a self-portrait. *Courtesy of DeGolyer Library, Southern Methodist University, U.S. West: Photographs, Manuscripts and Imprints.*

Library of Congress Cataloging-in-Publication Data
Names: Maley, John, approximately 1776–1819, author. | Dowdy, F. Andrew, 1950– editor.
Title: Wanderer on the American frontier : the travels of John Maley, 1808–1813 / edited by F. Andrew Dowdy.
Description: Norman, OK : University of Oklahoma Press, 2018 | Includes bibliographical references and index.
Identifiers: LCCN 2018004904 | ISBN 978-0-8061-6039-9 (hardcover : alk. paper)
Subjects: LCSH: Maley, John, approximately 1776–1819—Diaries. | Explorers—United States—Diaries. | Frontier and pioneer life—Northwest, Old. | Frontier and pioneer life—Texas.
Classification: LCC F484.3 .M26 2018 | DDC 910.92—dc23
LC record available at https://lccn.loc.gov/2018004904

The paper in this book meets the guidelines for permanence and durability of the Committee on Production Guidelines for Book Longevity of the Council on Library Resources, Inc. ∞

1 2 3 4 5 6 7 8 9 10

Contents

❦ *Illustrations*

Figures

Maps

Preface

Introduction

In 2012 Michael Brown, a Philadelphia dealer in rare books, found an old manuscript in a barn sale in Pennsylvania. The manuscript, 195 pages long, turned out to be the first half of a journal written by John Maley, an obscure explorer on the American frontier from 1808 to 1813. It was later acquired by the DeGolyer Library at Southern Methodist University (SMU).[1] The second half of his journal, a 184-page manuscript long known to historians, is included among the papers of Benjamin Silliman at Yale University.[2] It is not clear how the two fragments became separated. Maley reportedly sold his journal to Philadelphia publisher Isaac Riley for five hundred dollars.[3] Riley never published the book, but sometime between 1821 and 1822, he provided the journal to Silliman, a professor of chemistry and geology at Yale who was interested in Maley's description of meteorites in North Texas. Silliman apparently only had access to the second half of the journal,[4] which recounted details of the meteorites.[5]

We will likely never know how Maley's journal was separated, but the reuniting of both halves of this book, some two hundred years after it was

1. Maley, "Travels, Hunting Expedition, Trapping Discoveries, Trading, Etc., Etc."
2. Maley, "Journal of John Maley's Wanderings."
3. Tiffany Le, "SMU Purchases Explorer's 200-year-old Journal," *Dallas Morning News*, July 5, 2013, accessed November 30, 2015, https://www.dallasnews.com/news/news/2013/07/05/smu-purchases-explorers-200-year-old-journal.
4. Maley's account flows without interruption between the two volumes, but he flipped the orientation of his writing, from pages oriented in a portrait style in the SMU journal to a landscape style in the Silliman journal. Thus, it appears the journal was bound in two separate volumes from the beginning.
5. There is a notional table of contents scribbled in the initial pages of the SMU manuscript, which may indicate that Riley or a subsequent owner considered publishing the first half of Maley's book.

written, offers a new perspective on the author and his travels. The Yale manuscript, which has been studied by a number of historians, begins abruptly, in mid-sentence, during a trip to Natchitoches, Louisiana, and details Maley's adventures on the southwest frontier from late 1810 to 1813. These include his participation in a foray into Spanish Texas in 1811, an extended trip up the Red River in 1812, and, in 1813, his attempted return up the Red River and participation in a voyage up the Ouachita River. With the addition of the SMU journal, one discovers that Maley's adventures actually began in 1808 with his travel down the Ohio River to Illinois and Missouri. His stated objective was to explore the major tributaries of the Mississippi, and the SMU journal contains accounts of a number of excursions in 1809–10, including voyages up the Missouri, Tennessee and Arkansas Rivers, and the exploration of the Ozark Plateau and western Arkansas.

Unlike the journals of some of his contemporaries, Maley's book is not a diary, with detailed descriptions of where he went and what he saw on a day-to-day basis. Rather, it was written for publication several years after Maley's travels were done. While writing about his arrival in Cape Girardeau in March 1810, for example, he commented on the damages incurred at New Madrid due to the earthquakes that occurred in 1811 and 1812. Similarly, into his account of his visit to New Orleans in 1811, Maley interjected a long description of the Battle of New Orleans, which ended in 1815. His journal also refers, at two points, to steamboat traffic on the Mississippi and Ohio Rivers, which appears to date the work to 1817 or afterwards. Most of the book is a fairly straightforward recounting of events, but at several points, it takes on the tone of a travel brochure, as Maley exhorts his "readers" to take advantage of the various opportunities along the frontier. At other points, he drifts into a soliloquy on the hardships he faced in an effort to dramatize the narrative a bit.

Maley does not inform his readers why he began his journey, but he was likely motivated, at least in part, by the Louisiana Purchase. With that 1803 transaction, the United States gained sovereignty over much of the continent west of the Mississippi, and despite the expeditions of Lewis and Clark, Dunbar and Hunter, and Freeman and Custis, the new lands remained largely unknown. Although his exploration included a few excursions on the east side of the Mississippi, Maley focused on examining commercial opportunities in the newly acquired Louisiana Territory, from the Missouri to the

Red Rivers. Maley's account does not provide the specificity (or accuracy) of the various scientific expeditions. What it lacks in depth, however, it makes up for in breadth, providing a relatively contemporaneous snapshot across much of the American frontier at the beginning of the nineteenth century.

A number of historians have studied the Yale manuscript, and it has met with considerable skepticism. In his 1967 work "Exploration and Empire," William Goetzmann noted that it was impossible to confirm the veracity of Maley's "incredible and hitherto unknown adventures," warning readers to accept his story "only on the most tentative basis."[6] Dan Flores in his 1971 study concluded that the journal was probably an authentic account of conditions on the southwest frontier, but acknowledged that Maley could have invented all or parts of his account.[7] However, by the time he published his 1985 book on the journal of Anthony Glass, Flores believed that Maley's accounts of his two expeditions onto the plains were probably "fabrications"; the "product of interviews and research," instead of personal experience.[8]

The Yale account was also cited extensively by Steve Wilson in his discussion of treasure in Oklahoma.[9] While he didn't pass judgment on the validity of the document, Wilson clearly had difficulty in reconciling Maley's tale with the known topography of the Red River region. Wilson concluded that Maley's discovery of gold diggings might match accumulations in the Wichita Mountains of southwest Oklahoma, possibly Spanish-era works in Devil's Canyon, in the mountains north of Altus, Oklahoma. However, the author didn't speculate on the location of a Spanish silver mine that Maley reported finding on a "mysterious" sugarloaf mountain in north Texas, and closed by noting that Maley's stories of his "bizarre" discoveries would lure adventurers up the Red River for years to come.

The Author

Compounding the question of authenticity is the fact that we know very little about Maley himself. One of the few public records found is an 1819 obituary published in Charleston, South Carolina, which appears to be Maley's.

6. Goetzmann, *Exploration and Empire*, 54–55.
7. Flores, "The John Maley Journal," 7.
8. Flores, *Journal of an Indian Trader*, 137.
9. Wilson, *Oklahoma Treasures and Treasure Tales*, 78–85.

According to that notice, John Maley died on July 16, 1819, at the age of 43 (which would put his birth circa 1776); he was a native of New York, had lived in Charleston for three years, and left behind a widow. There appears to be no record of Maley in any U.S. census, but we now know that he was somewhere up the White River in Arkansas when the 1810 census was conducted. As noted by other researchers, what little we do know about him comes from correspondence between Supreme Court justice William Johnson of South Carolina and Benjamin Silliman at Yale.[10] Johnson met Maley by accident, and after hearing of his travels, considered him a "wanderer." Johnson's letter also confirms that Maley died sometime before 1821. For his part, Silliman referred to Maley as an "erratic adventurer" and a man "with a roving disposition . . . (and) . . . a strong and inquiring, though uncultivated, mind."[11] The Yale professor, however, appeared to accept his journal as legitimate, citing it in the 1824 paper he wrote about the meteorites of north Texas.[12]

One doesn't learn much more about the author by reading his journal. Maley makes no reference to his education. He appears literate by the standards of the time, but he was by no means a polished writer, and his writings suggest he had no more than a grammar school education. He does appear to have experience in mineral prospecting, regularly commenting on the minerals encountered in his travels and explaining how to use mercury to test ores for silver content (a skill that he may have honed while working in the Missouri lead mines during the winter of 1808–9). Finally, it seems clear that Maley was a businessman of some means. Not a destitute wanderer, he had the resources to buy a horse, gun, or trade goods as the situation demanded. Much of his journal focuses on business opportunities on the frontier, and Maley provides commentary and analysis on the profitability of various ventures, ranging from salt manufacturing in Illinois to the economics of slave-cultivated cotton in Louisiana.

A bit of Maley's personality also emerges from his writings. If he were alive today, he would be an exemplar "type A" personality. In his letter to Silliman, William Johnson described him as "one of those troubled spirits that find rest only in motion," an assessment that seems borne out by his

10. Flores, "The John Maley Journal," 4–6.
11. Silliman, "Malleable Iron of Louisiana," 219, 221.
12. Ibid., 218–25.

journal.[13] For example, when faced with the prospect of playing billiards during a winter in Shawneetown, Illinois, Maley instead rounded up a crew to explore the Tennessee River by keelboat. Later, with a few weeks to kill following that expedition, he rented a horse to wander across Tennessee and Kentucky. He also exhibits little patience for the indolence of others, including many of the men he encounters on the frontier. In his journal, Maley expressed pity for the Kentuckians who squandered all their money in Natchez grog shops and bordellos and contempt for the "dissapated characters" hunting buffalo and beeswax up the Red River.

Finally, the journal reveals a transformation in Maley over the five years he spent on the frontier. Early in his journal, he reflected on the fear he felt in spending his first night out alone in the southern Illinois countryside, with howling wolves and screeching owls keeping him awake. By the end of his story, however, Maley seems transformed into a prototypical long hunter, with a bit of adrenaline junkie thrown in for good measure. Only weeks after he and his companions were robbed by the Osage and almost starved to death along the Ouachita River bottoms, we find Maley joining an excursion up the river to Hot Springs and then borrowing a gun for a twenty-one-day solo walkabout in the Ouachita Mountains. By the end of his journeys, he had truly become the man with the roving disposition described by Silliman.

Authenticity

The discovery of the first half of his journal provides historians an opportunity to reassess the authenticity of Maley's account. As noted earlier, the Yale account of his travel up the Red River has raised legitimate concerns on the part of historians, and it remains difficult to reconcile that account with what we know about the geography and native tribes of the region. The SMU journal, covering his earlier travels, exhibits a few similar problems. For example, he makes errors in describing the locations of the Cache River in Illinois and the White River in Indiana. There are also internal inconsistencies as to how long Maley traveled in his various journeys. For example, based on his recitation of events on his exploration up the Arkansas River, one would calculate that the trip lasted a minimum of eighty-nine days.

13. Johnson to Silliman, August 18, 1821, Silliman Family Papers.

However, based on the dates he departed and returned to Arkansas Post, Maley was gone only sixty-eight days.

Notwithstanding these problems, with respect to the first half of his journal, one is left with little doubt that Maley traveled where he said he did. For many of the settled areas along the frontier, his descriptions are corroborated by the accounts of other contemporary writers. Beyond the settled frontier, Maley's observations are generally confirmed by later visitors. His accurate description of Big Spring, Missouri, for example, provides the earliest known written account of the area. Similarly, Maley's 1810 observation of lead ores on the headwaters of the White River, near Springfield, Missouri, was confirmed a decade later by the geologist Henry Schoolcraft.[14] Even where there are inconsistencies, such as his excursion into western Arkansas, Maley's observations appear to confirm that he actually visited the region. Finally, the people he met, from Governor William Henry Harrison to Chickasaws George and Levi Colbert, are real historical figures, and his account fits comfortably into what historians know about them and their affairs.

The key reason historians have questioned Maley's veracity is the account of his 1812 trip up the Red River, contained in the Yale journal. That story remains a confusing mess. One can reasonably reconstruct Maley's travel up the Red to the Kiamichi River. After that point, however, it becomes difficult to reconcile the chronology of Maley's account—the apparent distances traveled—with his observations of the geography of the region. As a glaring example, based on a straightforward reading of the account, a reader would expect to find Maley's "New Potosi"—a sugar-cone shaped mountain topped by a Spanish silver mine—somewhere around Dallas, Texas. No such feature exists. The problem is compounded by Maley's reported location of a Pawnee village, which he appears to have encountered much further up the Red River than earlier explorers.

Given these inconsistencies, some previous researchers have suggested that Maley's Red River account was a fabrication. That theory—a reasonable one at the time—seems much less credible with the discovery of the first half of his journal. If, as the SMU journal indicates, Maley had already traveled the Missouri, Gasconade, Wabash, Tennessee, Current, Spring, White, and Arkansas Rivers, why would he hesitate to ascend the Red? It

14. Schoolcraft, *Journal of a Tour into the Interior of Missouri and Arkansaw*, 55–56.

would seem less perilous than his earlier travels deep into Osage country. Furthermore, if Maley's objective was to write a popular adventure book, he had already collected more than enough material prior to his Red River jaunt. Finally, as pointed out by Flores, if Maley was relying on published sources to write a fictional account, why did he get so many details wrong?[15] Not only does Maley misspell the names of places and people, but for several of his excursions, the number of days he reported traveling is not consistent with the dates he reports beginning and ending the trip. If Maley's account is a fabrication, it seems a sloppy one.

Rather than being a fabrication, the inconsistencies in Maley's account are likely due to his reliance on memory, rather than notes, to recount his adventures. We don't know how extensive his notes were, but the only mention he makes of writing materials is a "pocket book," which he apparently carried on his person. Moreover, a careful reading his account suggests that Maley recorded notes only sporadically. In some passages, such as his trip from Natchitoches to a Coushatta village up the Red River, he provides a day-to-day account of what he saw, what he ate for dinner, and how he slept, so one presumes that he was working from diary entries. In other passages, however, one suspects that Maley only recorded an occasional date and relied on memory to fill in weeks of activity. Adding to the challenge is the fact that Maley appears to have written his book in 1817 or later, which was years after the events he described.

Even if we conclude that Maley's Red River account is not a work of fiction, it remains so jumbled as to be of questionable value to historians. There are several clues, however, which may provide new insights into his travel. For example, if we focus on Maley's description of "New Potosi," instead of his recollection of how he traveled to the site, there is strong evidence that he was in the copper-bearing red beds of north Texas, much further west than his journal implies. The mountain he described may, in fact, be Big Mound, in Hardeman County, Texas. Another clue has to do with the location of a Pawnee village visited by Maley on his expedition. Some researchers have assumed that this was a well-known village site near present-day Spanish Fort, Texas, an assumption that makes it quite difficult to reconcile other details of his account. It appears, however, that there was

15. Flores, "The John Maley Journal," 7.

no village at that site when Maley ascended the Red in 1812, because the tribe had abandoned the location in 1811.[16] It is still not clear where Maley's Pawnee village was located, but it was likely much further west, probably on the North Fork of the Red.

Relevance

Maley's journal recounts his travels across parts of thirteen states and on sixteen rivers. Because of the breadth of his explorations, however, many historians may find his account to be frustratingly skimpy on details of specific regions of the country. In his 1819 travel up the Arkansas, for example, the naturalist Thomas Nuttall wrote almost fifty pages describing Arkansas Post and his travel to Cadron, about three hundred miles up the river.[17] Maley's journal covers the same material in a page and a half. Despite its lack of detail, the manuscript does provide interesting historical snippets. As an example, Maley's exploration for copper in Indiana, at the behest of Governor William Henry Harrison, illuminates an interesting aspect of Harrison's negotiation of the Treaty of Fort Wayne. Similarly, his description of Ste. Genevieve, Missouri, gives readers a firsthand account of the lively social life of French residents in the territory. Finally, Maley's manuscript provides a rare blue-collar view of the frontier, with better insights, perhaps, into the daily life of the traders and trappers on the frontier than the journals of his better-known contemporaries.

Maley's book, of course was not written for historians, but for the broader public. That audience today will find no great literature here, but a fascinating tale. It also records the remarkable achievement of a man who, by himself or in the company of one or two companions, covered more territory than any of the more famous expeditions of the time. We don't know what drove Maley to undertake this effort, but, if nothing else, he should be recognized as one of the great wanderers in American history.

16. Garrett, "Dr. John Sibley and the Louisiana-Texas Frontier, 1803–1814," 403.
17. Nuttall, *A Journal of Travels into the Arkansas Territory*, 73–122.

Acknowledgments

As neither a historian nor a writer, I had no thought of producing a book when I first stumbled across a reference to John Maley. Instead, I was intrigued by his claim of finding a silver mine in North Texas and thought it would be an interesting geological puzzle to solve. The search turned out to be more complicated than I had assumed, and it led me to transcribe Maley's journal from the transcripts held at SMU and Yale. At that point, I realized that the silver mine was only a small part of a pretty interesting yarn, a tale that someone should publish. Egged on by my daughter, I concluded that researching a book would, at the very least, provide a useful excuse for buying a few interesting books and taking a couple of long road trips across the country.

The more I researched Maley's travels, the more confident I became that he was recounting actual experiences—real people and places. My research also revealed how woefully ignorant I was of the history and geography of America in the early nineteenth century. Fortunately, I discovered a number of sources to help educate myself. I found the work of Dan L. Flores, including his 1971 master's thesis on Maley and his other writings on the history of the Old Southwest, to be particularly relevant in framing Maley's Red River travels. I also appreciate the encouragement he gave me as I undertook this project. A number of online tools were also useful. The Internet Archive[1] proved to be a wonderful source for out-of-print books, including contemporaneous accounts of the American frontier. Online map tools, such as Google Maps and the U.S. Geological Survey's National Map,[2] made it possible to quickly examine large areas of terrain, estimate distances,

1. At www.archive.org.
2. At https://nationalmap.gov.

and follow Maley's excursions. Finally, the David Rumsey Map Collection[3] provided access to a host of historical maps of the areas traveled by Maley.

I was also fortunate to receive the assistance of a number of individuals I met in my travels. Dr. James Price was particularly helpful in understanding Maley's exploration around Big Spring, Missouri. Neal Pankey at Fort Massac State Park, Illinois; Erik Ditzler at Arkansas Post National Memorial; and the staff at Fort Osage National Historic Landmark were all generous with their time when I visited their sites. Similarly, I was fortunate to meet Emily Smithey at the Natchez Trace Visitor's Center, who provided a copy of her master's thesis with information on George and Levi Colbert. I am also grateful to John Crain, Alton Hoke, and Jim Hance of the Summerland Foundation for facilitating my visit to the Medicine Mounds, in Hardeman County, Texas.

We would know nothing about Maley, of course, absent the efforts of Yale University Library and DeGolyer Library at Southern Methodist University to acquire and preserve his manuscripts and to make them available to the public. George Miles, Curator of the Western Americana Collection at Beinecke Library at Yale, provided a critical review of an early draft of the text and suggested a number of areas for improvement. Similarly, I am grateful to Russell L. Martin III, Assistant Dean for Collections and Director of DeGolyer Library at SMU, for his suggestions on the draft, as well as providing information on SMU's acquisition of the first half of Maley's journal.

Kent Calder, at University of Oklahoma Press, has been extremely supportive in guiding me through the publication process, and I am grateful to Emily Schuster, Steven Baker, and Ariane Smith for their help in turning my drafts into readable prose. I also want to thank my cartographer, Bill Nelson, for producing a series of maps illustrating Maley's travels.

Finally, I want to thank my family for their support. My daughter, Katherine, encouraged me to produce this book, and my sister, Ann Bowers, provided encouragement along the way. The history buffs in my family—my brother, Ruskin Dowdy, and son, Daniel—provided critical reviews of early drafts of my manuscript. Finally, I want to thank my wife, Jeanne, not only for her support on this project, but for the various other ventures I've undertaken over the years.

3. At www.davidrumsey.com.

Editorial Procedures

Maley's journal consists of two manuscripts. The first part of his travels are covered in a 195-page manuscript that was discovered in 2012 and is now held at DeGolyer Library at Southern Methodist University. The second half of his travels, described in a 182-page manuscript obtained by Professor Benjamin Silliman in 1821 or 1822, is currently included in his papers at Yale University Library. The two manuscripts appear to be written at the same time, as the text flows seamlessly from one to the other. However, the document was apparently bound in separate ledgers from the beginning; the SMU manuscript was written with pages in a portrait orientation, while the Yale manuscript was written in a landscape orientation. These two volumes were apparently separated at an early date. A title page in the Yale manuscript indicates that it was examined in 1822 by Silliman, who paginated it as a separate document. Similarly, the SMU manuscript contains a notional table of contents, written by someone other than Maley, indicating that it had been reviewed by someone who only had access to that volume.

Despite their different provenances, the two manuscripts appear relatively complete. There is missing text in the Yale manuscript, but it is likely only one page, and one page in the SMU manuscript is also out of sequence. Furthermore, there are only a few unintelligible words in the manuscript. He wrote in a clear hand and, while he used rather creative spelling for many words and place names, almost all can be clarified using their context in the account. Similarly, although Maley often chooses the wrong word, substituting, for example, "their" for "there" and "where" for "were," his intended meaning remains clear.

The greatest challenge in editing Maley's manuscripts is that he used no uppercase lettering or punctuation to indicate the division of sentences. The text therefore requires careful deciphering at times, to understand where he intended one sentence to end and another to begin. Maley also had a penchant for long, run-on sentences and sentence fragments, which defy normal punctuation rules. In presenting Maley's work to a broader audience, the editor has concluded that a strict diplomatic edition of the manuscript, without punctuation, would offer a frustrating experience for even the most determined reader. On the other hand, producing a completely modernized version of Maley's journal would require significant rewriting to produce grammatically correct text. This, in turn, would require a greater level of interpretation of Maley's words, risking misinterpretation.

Instead, the editor has chosen a compromise intended to offer as much of Maley's original journal as possible, while allowing readers to get through the text without stumbling over it. To this end, only a minimum amount of punctuation has been added to separate the text into sentences and to otherwise clarify Maley's prose. The editor has also organized the journal into paragraphs, chapters, and sub-chapters (chapter and sub-chapter headings are not part of the original text). Similarly, the transcription incorporates, without overt indication, the many corrections and interlinear write-overs made by Maley to his original text. Maley's spelling of words has also been maintained, with an editorial interpolation provided in italics where needed, and footnotes where some elaboration is required. Hopefully, these changes will meet the needs of most readers. Also, in addition to standard annotation provided in notes, the editor offers more extended historical comments on Maley's world in italic text interspersed in the author's narrative. For those wishing to study the unvarnished original documents, facsimiles of Maley's journal are available from SMU (online at the DeGolyer Library site) and Yale (on microfilm).

Wanderer on the American Frontier

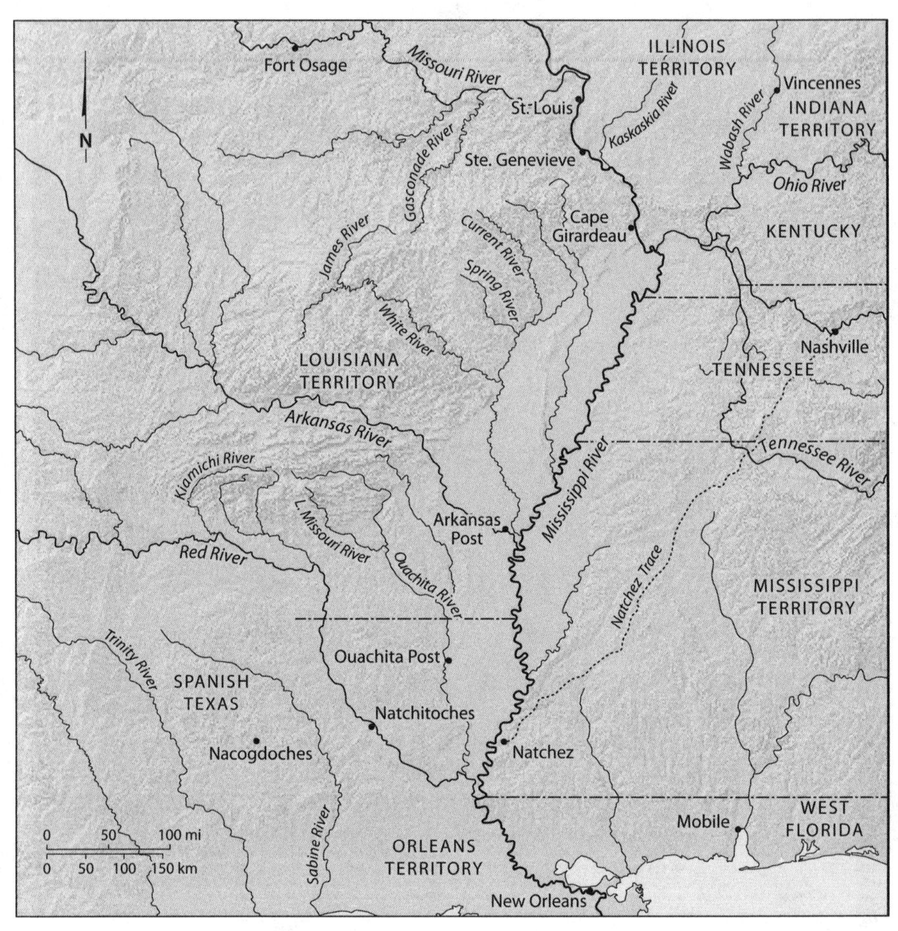

The American frontier in the early nineteenth century.
Map by Bill Nelson. Copyright © 2018 by the University of Oklahoma Press.

PROLOGUE ❦ *A Time of Transition on the Frontier*

THE HISTORY OF ANY ERA is a story of transition, but, in retrospect, the period of Maley's wanderings, from 1808 to 1813, was a time of particularly rapid change on the American frontier. American expansion—the inexorable westward flow of American settlers, entrepreneurs, and adventurers—had been the basic plot line for the history of the American frontier, and would remain so through most of the nineteenth century. With the 1803 Louisiana Purchase, however, the boundaries of the American frontier leaped hundreds of miles west in a single bound, from the Mississippi to the Rockies and Texas. This not only dramatically increased opportunities for Americans, but it increased pressure for the removal of indigenous tribes from east of the Mississippi to new lands in Louisiana Territory. The sale of Louisiana was also a signal event on the continent, formally ending France's colonial ambitions in the Americas and undermining Spain's ability to protect its interests against American expansion. The period also witnessed the beginning of the War of 1812, which would redefine Britain's presence in North America. Finally, the period marked the beginnings of the industrial revolution, which would dramatically alter the economy of the region.

The decline of French culture and influence on the western frontier was one of the more obvious transitions occurring at the turn of the nineteenth century. The French began settling along the Mississippi in the 1600s, but following the French and Indian War, France ceded its lands east of the river to Britain, and those west of the Mississippi to Spain. Even with its loss of sovereignty, France's influence was deeply imprinted on the cultural and commercial life of the region. With few exceptions, the settlements that Maley would visit had been founded by the French. In Missouri, French businessmen still dominated key areas of commerce, including lead mining and the peltry trade; in the south, French planters were growing cotton on their Louisiana plantations; and French voyageurs and trappers still roamed the rivers and forests of the territory.

Changes were occurring, however. The first shift occurred after France's 1763 cession of lands to Britain. In Illinois, this triggered a migration to communities on the west side of the Mississippi. Towns such as Kaskaskia, Prairie du Rocher, and Cahokia were replaced as centers of commerce by Ste. Genevieve and St. Louis. By the time of Maley's travels, the old French towns east of the Mississippi were being resettled by Americans. As he observed, Kaskaskia was beginning to flourish as the county seat of Randolph County, and the American population of Vincennes had grown to comprise one third of the total. The 1803 Louisiana Purchase stimulated a similar shift west of the Mississippi. Maley noted the predominance of Kentuckians working in the lead mines of Missouri and the establishment of new American settlements, like Alexandria and Prairie Mer Rouge, west of the river. The decline in French influence was not a welcome development to many French residents. Maley found some Louisiana planters to be quite hostile to Americans, presumably due to uncertainties regarding their land claims. On the whole, however, it appears that French influence was not so much displaced but diluted by the surge of Americans migrating to the territory.

For Spain, the transition was more abrupt. With the 1762 Treaty of Fontainebleau, Spain gained sovereignty over French lands west of the Mississippi, and at the beginning of the nineteenth century, it controlled most of North America: not only Louisiana, but Florida and the U.S. Gulf Coast, Texas, Mexico, and the American Southwest to California. However, under pressure from Napoleon, Spain returned Louisiana to France in 1800 and then witnessed its sale to the United States three years later. The loss of the 828,000 square miles of Louisiana Territory was only the first of several blows that the Spanish Empire would absorb. By the time Maley arrived in Natchitoches in 1810, Father Miguel Hidalgo y Costilla had issued his *Grito de Dolores,* which marked the beginning of the Mexican Revolution and the beginning of the end of New Spain.

However, Spain did not surrender its interests without a fight. Maley's 1810 foray into Texas to buy mules, and the resulting shootout between royalists and republicans, was just one small skirmish in a war that would last another decade. Also, while the boundary between Texas and Louisiana Territory was not defined, Spain had not hesitated to defend what it considered to be the borders of New Spain, sending a military force in 1806 to block the Freeman and Custis expedition before it had ascended halfway up the Red River.[1] Furthermore, in 1807 Spanish forces arrested Zebulon Pike and his men in Colorado. Spain had begun to refrain from punishing American traders along the frontier, but it remained concerned over American influence with the tribes along the Red River.[2] Spanish authorities undoubtedly would have objected to Maley's 1812 wanderings south of the river, but they had their hands full at the time defending Texas from an armed invasion, referred to today as the Gutiérrez-Magee filibuster.

Maley also witnessed the impact of American expansion on indigenous tribes. In the Northwest Territory, which comprised present-day Ohio, Indiana, Illinois, Michigan, Wisconsin, and part of Minnesota, there was growing resentment against American demands for new land concessions; Maley arrived in Vincennes in 1809 as William Henry Harrison was wrangling additional concessions from the tribes through the Treaty of Fort Wayne. Opposition to that treaty may have contributed to the hostile reception Maley received on his attempt to prospect for copper up the Wabash River. More importantly, it would ultimately lead to Tecumseh's War and would be a contributing factor to American Indian participation in the War of 1812.

In the Southeast, tribes were also being coerced into selling their lands. Some responded by adopting white lifestyles: raising cattle instead of hunting, buying slaves to grow cotton and other crops, and engaging in commerce. Maley noted the success enjoyed by two prominent Chickasaws, George and Levi Colbert, and chronicled the Chickasaw and Choctaw merchants who provided food and lodging to travelers on the Natchez Trace. Other tribes chose emigration in response to the pressures of American expansion, and Maley encountered a number of tribes west of the Mississippi—Shawnee, Cherokee, Coushatta, Pascagoula, and Choctaw—who had migrated far from their original homes in the Southeast.

West of the Mississippi, the Osage Nation remained a formidable barrier to American expansion and proved to be Maley's principal nemesis. With

1. Flores, *Southern Counterpart to Lewis and Clark*, xi.
2. Flores, *Journal of an Indian Trader*, 23.

their villages centered in southwest Missouri, the Osage had expanded their domain by 1800 to include much of the land between the Missouri and Red Rivers, and west across much of present-day Kansas and Oklahoma. They also acquired more enemies that any other tribe; to the south and southwest, they could count among their foes the Quapaw, Caddo, Wichita, Comanche, and Kiowa. The United States attempted to address the Osage challenge in the 1808 Treaty of Fort Osage, persuading the tribe to relinquish its claim to most of Missouri and Arkansas. On paper, this was an enormous cession, but the treaty was largely ignored by the Osage, who resented the emigration of tribes from east of the Mississippi onto lands they previously occupied.[3] The ensuing conflict between the Osage and various eastern tribes, such as the Cherokee and Choctaw, continued well into the nineteenth century. The treaty did little to limit Osage attacks against white hunters and traders, which continued for years to come.

In comparison to the Northwest Territory and the Osage heartland, Maley found the Red River to be a relatively peaceable kingdom. Due in part to the Great Raft, an enormous logjam that blocked passage on the river, there had not yet been significant white settlement above Natchitoches, and the Americans were heirs to the friendly relations established by the French with the Caddos and Wichitas. Maley even had an amicable encounter with the Comanche, who, in years to come, would become the most feared tribe in Texas. There were changes on the river, however. In the decades before Maley's arrival, several southeastern tribes had migrated to the Red. More importantly, in 1811, the year before Maley paddled up the stream, the Wichita/Taovaya had abandoned their village complex on the Red River near Spanish Fort, due to concerns that they could no longer defend it from the Osage. As noted by Flores, "this village complex had been the most important EuroAmerican trade base on Southern Plains, and its disintegration deprived the Americans of their most important Indian contacts there."[4]

Finally, Maley's 1808–13 journey occurred as the first ripple effects of the industrial revolution were being felt on the American frontier. In his travels, Maley searched out, and commented on, the commercial opportunities presented by minerals, salt springs, timber and crops, livestock, and the fur trade: the same activities that French and Spanish explorers would

3. Ingenthron, *Indians of the Ozark Plateau*, 61.
4. Flores, *Journal of an Indian Trader*, 92.

have taken an interest in a century earlier. However, Maley also witnessed the beginnings of the cotton boom in the South, driven by the invention of water-powered spinning machines and looms in Great Britain and the cotton gin in America—a transition that was occurring at a remarkable pace. The cotton gin, which made the cultivation of upland varieties of cotton commercially viable, had been invented only sixteen years before Maley's travels in Louisiana, but in that time, it had become the dominant structure on most plantations. His comments on the lucrative economics of slave-cultivated cotton help explain its rapid growth.

Maley also witnessed a transformation brought about by another development of the industrial revolution—the steamboat. His own travels relied on human-powered navigation, and his journal provides a good picture of the arduous task of paddling, rowing, poling, or towing canoes and keelboats upstream. It also provides insights on how travelers took advantage of cutoffs and bayous to shorten those voyages. By the time Maley sat down to write his journal, however, the steamboat was altering the economy and culture of the entire region. The change not only fostered commerce and industry on the rivers, but also gave rise to new towns like Vicksburg, Cairo, and Paducah, which hadn't existed when Maley paddled past. Steamboats also replaced the Natchez Trace as the primary option for travelers to return back up the Mississippi.

Maley's account provides a snapshot of a relatively short period of history—the time between the acquisition of the Louisiana Territory by the United States and its subsequent transformation by Americans. From a frontier that had appeared relatively stable for decades under French and Spanish rule, Maley witnessed the seeds of change that would redefine the landscape within a generation. His excursion into Texas presaged not only Mexico gaining its independence from Spain but also Texas gaining its from Mexico. The nascent cotton industry he observed, and its reliance on slave labor, would within decades forever alter the face of the land and the politics of the new nation. The Indian tribes he encountered would continue to be pressured by American expansion and ultimately face extinction or removal to Indian Territory. The upper Red River would remain the one area on the frontier where change would come slowly; it would take forty years, until the Marcy expedition, before the United States would have an accurate description of its headwaters.

THE JOURNAL OF JOHN MALEY

Travels, Hunting Expeditions, Trapping, Discoveries—Trading, etc., etc.

An account of four years travels through the Illinois, Indiana, Louisiana, Missouri and Mississippi territories with a true and accurate account of every principal river west of the Mississippi from the Missouri down to Red River explaining their different lengths and courses, the white inhabitants and towns, with an account of the natives inhabiting on these rivers from their sources to their confluence; also an account of the mines and mineral salines and natural curiosities, soil productions and staple commodities showing the advantages and disadvantages of trade both among the whites and natives of the country, intermixed with an account of the author's wonderful sufferings and fatigues during the expedition.

By John Maley

Author's Preface

A country that is new and unexplored creates in every man of an interprising spirit a desire to become acquainted with its soil and productions and the natives of that productive heart of the earth which has so long been unknown to that part of the civilized world who are the general promoters of arts and sciences which ignorance leaves them blind in these unknown parts which the author from his perfect knowledge of the country is induced to call the garden of America on account of the superior excellency of the soil and the luxuriancy of its vegetation. The readers who are induced from motives of interest or curiosity to obtain a knowledge of that part of America on the

Mississippi, particularly on the west of it, also of the natives trade and soil, will find this work very interesting. No one has hitherto been so able from experience as the author to give so diffinite an account of that country, of the manners modes and customs of the natives, there staple commodities and manner of trade peculiarities of which the traveler through them parts will find worthy of his attention.

CHAPTER I ❦ *1808*

Down the Ohio, Pittsburgh to Shawneetown

When I first set out with an intention to explore those parts of America which will one day become the emporeum of wealth and commerce, it was on the 29th day of May, 1808. I left Brownsville or Red Stone Old Fort on the Monongahala River in the state of Pensylvania, thence down that river 30 miles to Pittsburg, the capital of Alleghany county Pennsylvania.[1] It is seated on a point of land formed by the confluence of the Alleghany and Monongahela rivers. There it forms the Ohio opposite the town. The Ohio is a quarter of a mile wide and in dry seasons is navigable only by small crafts. In freshes it will carry vessels of 2 or 300 tons. Topsail vessels have been built and launched at Pittsburg. It contains a courthouse, a jail and churches, an academy, three banking houses and a library of 2000 volumes. The manufacturers of this town are flourishing. It has a rolling and slitting mill, another for flour and other for paper, a cotton, a woollen, and a wire factory all conducted by steam, likewise two white and three green glass houses, three extensive air founderies, two white and one white and red lead factories.[2] Its population at present is estimated at rising 8000. The distance from Pittsburg to the junction of the Ohio with the Mississippie is 1188 and to New Orleans through the various windings of both rivers about 2000 miles. To Carlisle 180, to Philadelphia 290 and Washington 253. N Lat 40–31, W Lon 80–12.

1. Brownsville, Pennsylvania, was at this time a principal point of embarkation for goods coming by wagon from Virginia and Maryland from the head of navigation of the Potomac River at Cumberland, Maryland. Cramer, *The Navigator*, 7.

2. Maley is referring to developments that occurred significantly later than his passage through Pittsburgh. The first steam engine used for milling flour in Pittsburgh went into operation in 1809, but it apparently wasn't until 1816 that steam engines were used for the other manufacturing processes listed here. Buck and Buck, *The Planting of Civilization in Western Pennsylvania*, 316.

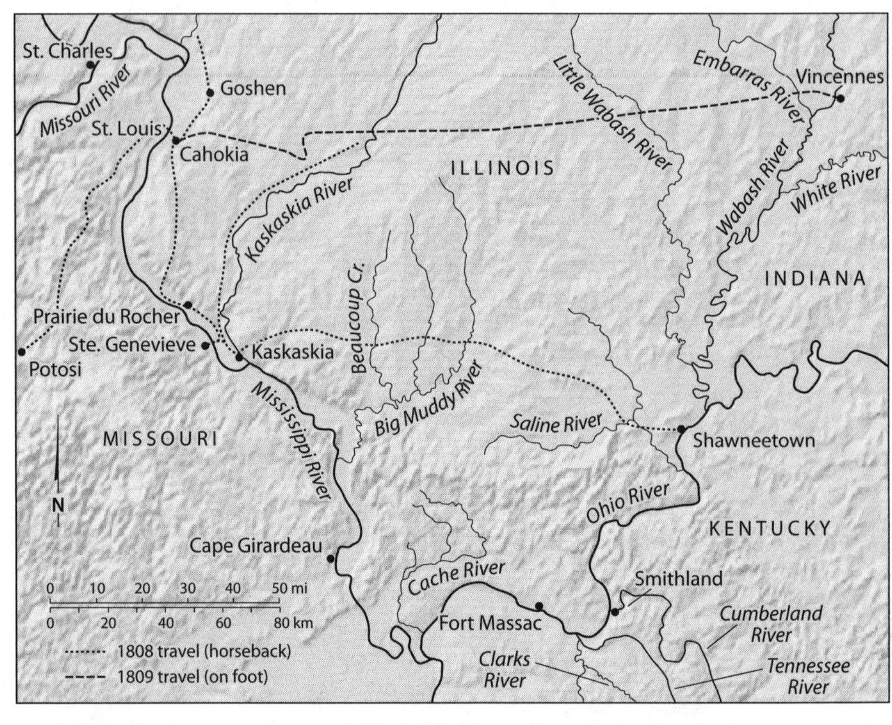

Maley's Illinois travels.

Map by Bill Nelson. Copyright © 2018 by the University of Oklahoma Press.

After leaving Pittsburg, I proceded down the river to Wheeling, a small town 73 miles SW of Pittsburg. It lies on the E side of the Ohio River and is the capital of Ohio County, Virginia and 302 miles from Washington. The settlers are chiefly Quakers and their staple commodity is flour and bacon.

Staying a few days at Wheeling, I steered my course down the river and made a stop at Marietta, a post town of Ohio, Washington County. It is situated on the W bank of the Muskingham River near its junction with the Ohio. It contains a court house, jail and academy and 1400 inhabitants, distant from Washington 317 miles. N Lat 39–24–21. Their staple commodity is flour and bacon. Ship building has formerly been carried on there but at present there is very little if any thing done at it. The immigrants are chiefly from N England.

I made but a short stay at Marietta and made my way down the river to Newport, a post town and capital of Campbell County, Kentucky, situated on the E side of the river at the junction of Licking River, 513 W of Washington and immediately opposite to Cincinnatti, Ohio, population about 260. N Lat 39–7, W Lon 84–15.

After leaving this place I made no more stops till I got to Louisville, a town of Kentucky in the county of Jefferson. It is seated on the Ohio opposite the grand falls, 95 miles SW of Lexington. It is a post town 639 miles W of Washington and contains 1300 inhabitants. W Lon 85–30, N Lat 38–3. At these falls is a portage of three miles for the goods brought by the steam boats. One runs from their to N Orleans and one to Pittsburg.[3] All the other boats go down at any stage of water, but to the stranger looks very dangerous. There is a pilot appointed by the state who takes sole possession of the boat and generally takes them over safe. His salary is $2 for every boat he takes over.

When I left this place I proceded down the river to Shawnee Town, 10 miles below the Wabash River, which was 295 miles below Louisville and 963 miles from Pittsburg. It is situated on the west bank of the Ohio River. It is a place of portage and deposits of salt. It is 12 miles from the United States [Saline in the Illinois territory.[4] Shawnee town is built on United States

3. The first steamboat on the Ohio was built in 1811, and the first regular passage of steamboats on the Ohio and Mississippi began in 1817. This is another example in the journal where Maley interjects into his contemporaneous observations developments that occurred much later. Lloyd, *Lloyd's Steamboat Directory and Disasters on the Western Waters*, 41–45.

4. Text within brackets is from an earlier page in the SMU journal and has been placed here in what appears to be its original context.

territory on the right of the Saline, the buildings are of small round logs and very low altho a place of a great deal of business. Provisions generally sell very high here and cash very plenty.

Across Illinois on Horseback

After a few days stay at that place, I sat out by land in order to reach Kaskaskias on the Mississippi River. The route I had to go was only a foot trace and no inhabitants on stages that might be] reached at night by very industrious traveling. I started on horse back by way of the United States Saline, tarried there two days, looked around and took all the necessary observations I could.

The original discovery of this saline was a spring where the Indians used to make there salt when they were there convenient and afterwards the United States had it occupied for a number of years, but men of experience and skill soon found out that this natural spring was not salt enough for much profit even to derive from it. At a distance of three miles from this spring were dry licks where the bufaloe had formerly licked away the earth in great holes the clay being strongly impregnated with salt. Therefore they made an attempt of sinking a well which proved successful. By encountering several difficulties they obtained a well of the best of salt water which water makes one to twelve. The difficulties are these: By digging anywheres on such a bounty, they obtain water by going the depth of forty five feet to fifty. When they get through to the water, it gushes up with the greatest rapidity which then runs in with a quicksand from every side, which is then very troublesome to sink. They make salt on a very extensive scale. I was informed that they make six thousand bushels per week. Congress leases those works to the highest bidder for the term of three years at a time and also fixes a price on the salt which is seventy five cents per bushel and also has an agent their to superintend. All mechanism is carried on at these works for the good of the United States.

The United States Saline

Maley's visit to the United States Saline (later known as the Ohio Saline) in southeastern Illinois, provides insight into a long-forgotten industry that was important to development on the American frontier. Salt was an essential commodity in the early nineteenth century, particularly due to its role in food preservation. Early settlers west of the Alleghenies paid considerable attention to the location of salt licks, where game was plentiful, and also sought out salt springs, where salt could be produced by boiling off the water. Notably, it was on a mission to procure salt that Daniel Boone and his colleagues were captured by the Shawnee at Kentucky's Lower Blue Licks in 1778.[5] *The importance of salt on the frontier was reflected in its price. In 1808, when Maley traveled through St. Louis, salt was selling there for $4.00 a bushel.*[6] *By comparison, as noted by Maley, prime farmland at Kaskaskia cost only $2.00 per acre at that time.*

The importance of the Illinois salt springs had been recognized for some time. Early settlers found an enormous salt lick near present-day Equality, Illinois, where buffalo had eaten away the soil to a depth of twelve to sixteen feet, and the presence of numerous mammoth and mastodon bones indicated the site may have been frequented by animals for thousands of years. The site also contained remnants of large kettles, made of non-fired clay, for boiling the saltwater from nearby springs.[7] *It is not clear whether these activities had been carried out by Indian tribes or by the French, but at the time the territory was acquired by the United States, salt was considered so important that exploitation of the resource was enshrined in the early legal framework of the territories: in 1796 the United States required its land surveyors to record the location of "all mines, salt licks, salt springs, and mill-seats" so that they could be reserved for the federal government. Later, when the various states composing the Northwest Territory were admitted to the Union, the enabling acts generally prohibited the states from selling the properties or offering them under long-term leases.*[8] *To ensure that workers would be available for the southeast Illinois salt works, the first constitution of Illinois even provided an exception to the state's ban on slavery, permitting "bound labor" to continue at the salt works until 1825.*

5. Lippincott, "The Early Salt Trade of the Ohio Valley," 1039.

6. Ibid., 1036.

7. The Goodspeed Publishing Company, *History of Gallatin, Saline, Hamilton, Franklin and Williamson Counties, Illinois*, 17–18.

8. Lippincott, "The Early Salt Trade of the Ohio Valley," 1031.

The ostensible purpose for public ownership and regulation of salines was to ensure that salt was provided at reasonable prices to the public. However, governments also saw the salines as a source of revenue. At the time of Maley's visit, the price of salt from the United States Saline was set at 75¢ per bushel, but during the War of 1812, the saltmakers were allowed to raise the price to $1.25 per bushel to increase lease payments to the government.[9] *Following their transfer to the states, the salines continued to be an important source of income. In 1819 the Ohio Saline generated $9,600 a year to the State of Illinois, equal to more than one third of the state's budget.*[10]

Although an enormously valuable asset in the early part of the nineteenth century, the profitability of the Illinois salt works declined over time. One factor was the enormous amount of wood required to boil the water, which resulted in clear-cutting the forest within the vicinity of the springs. Ultimately, rather than hauling wood from further and further away, the operator used pipes bored from tree trunks to move the saline water to furnaces closer to the timber.[11] *While this increased output for a time, with the introduction of steamboats and falling transport costs, the Illinois salt works had difficulty competing with salt that was imported via New Orleans or produced on the Kanawha River in present-day West Virginia. The brine on the Kanawha was stronger and required boiling off only a fraction of the water needed to produce a bushel of salt at the Equality salt works. The Kanawha springs also had the advantage of using locally produced coal and employing slave labor.*[12] *As a result, between 1810 and 1850 production of salt from Kanawha County, Virginia, rose from 740,000 to more than 3 million bushels a year, while Illinois production fell from 150,000 to 20,000 bushels. The salt works in Illinois were finally shut down in the 1870s.*[13]

I LEAVE THIS and pursue my journey for Kaskaskia, which is now one hundred and twenty miles travel. On the first day, and did not reach a house to stay at, this being a new scene to me having no company and in

9. Ibid., 1043.
10. Ibid., 1034.
11. Smith, *A History of Southern Illinois*, 473–74.
12. Lippincott, "The Early Salt Trade of the Ohio Valley," 1046.
13. Ibid., 1051.

the wilderness wild and unknown to me. Shortly after the sun had dropped the horizon, I took up camp by a stream of water although a slow current and a dismal looking bottom, the timber very lofty and overspreading. I tied my horse and cut grass for him with my pocket knife and then struck fire, gathered some wood and sat down and eat my biscuit, but the water I could not drink. I cut myself some grass and weeds to make myself a bed and laid down thinking to forget my fears and take my repose, but behold soon after I laid down, I was alarmed by the tremendous howling of wolves who inhabit this swamp and they advanced toward me with great rapidity. A hero from the north then dropt his courage. I kept a good fire, which repelled them. They came that near that I had to throw chunks and brands of fire at them, which after a few hours left me as it were, in great rage went off howling and making the woods ring and echo like so many savages. Thus I passed the night without closing my eyes, for even the owls make such screaching with so many tones of voice that a person unaquainted with these things would be daunted at this uncommon music. As soon as daylight approached, I was overjoyed.

I repaired for my journey, which I pursued and in about ten miles I reached a small prarie and a house presented to my view, which agitated my feelings with agreeable sensations. I made a stop there that day as the day being so far spent that by going on I should again have found myself in the same unpleasant situation. The nourishment that, as on the preceding night there being no town within 30 miles, I could get here was but very indifferent. The soil here is good and fertile.

Next morning I started early and went with great anxiety to get through to the first house, which I reached a little before sunset, but before I got to the house, I had a stream of water to cross called Little Muddy which proved to be muddy sure enough when I came to it. I was frightened to see it, as I could see no bottom the water being very muddy, but I had to venture across which almost proved fatal to myself as my horse sunk deep into the mud and it was with difficulty that he extricated himself and that I saved my life but providentially escaped and got safe to the opposite shore. After having crossed the stream, I had 3 miles to travel before I reached the home where I got feed for my horse, but as for myself the fare was hard: nothing but some dried venison and some whiskey. My bed was an earthen floor with a few dear skins under me, and so passed the night.

Started early the next morning, went about a mile. There I was surprised with the sight of an extensive prarie. All the beauties of nature opened to my eyes, the grass almost to its highth and all the flowers proud of their gaudy looks and sweet perfumes that enchants the traveler as he breathes the zephyrs that pass over these extensive plains. Nothing there escaped my eye to see the fertility of this country, a new thing to me. The man whom I stayed with that night had a large field of corn here, which shewed the productiveness of the land which in appearence was very great and so I passed on for another days journey, and when I got in the middle of the prarie looking north and south, could see no timber nor a twig of any kind but east and west it was about twelve miles across, then got into a beautiful grove of post oak timber very level and open. This continued for about three miles and entered another prarie still larger than the former and so on the day, through then a prarie then a grove of timber. By sunset I reached a creek called Buchooe [Beaucoup Creek], crossed it and came to a house on the edge of an extensive prarie. This man by the name of Cox was well provided for. I got a good supper of coffee and biscuit, cheese, etc., and my horse well provided for. He raised plenty of corn and cattle. I slept comfortable in a good feather bed, was then but twenty six miles from Kaskaskia.

Kaskaskia

Took breakfast before I started next morning and then entered this beautiful plain and crossed it then rode through an open level woods till I got within five miles of Kaskaskia. It was then thick inhabited and so pursued until I got to the descent of the bluff that surrounds that extensive country, the American bottom, so called which being the low lands of the Mississippi. On this eminence, I had the view of the Mississippi and Okaw[14] Rivers then descended the bluff which was nearly a mile before I got down. There came in sight of that ancient town Kaskaskia, came to the Okaw River on the south side and crossed over into the town. This ancient place has for some years past been rather a deserted village and the buildings are in a great measure gone to decay, but at present is in quite a flourishing way, it being the seat

14. Maley refers to this stream as the Okaw River, which, as noted by Bateman, was an alternative name for the Kaskaskia River. Bateman et al., *Historical Encyclopedia of Illinois and History of Hancock County*, 247.

of justice of Randolph County, Illinois, the governor and judges inside at their place. The old French made flat roofs, a porch or plaza all around the house. The work must have been bad; some were built of stone and others framed and filled-in with mud and white washed outside. There are a few fine buildings here built by the Americans. It contains no place of worship but a Roman chapel. It has about three hundred and fifty inhabitants and is situated on the north bank of the Okaw River three miles from its junction with the Mississippi and six from St. Genevieve, a village on the west side of the Mississippi in the Missouri territory.

Kaskaskia is settled principally by the French inclosure; it is said there that who hold this land in one common. They have five thousand acre within one fence. The soil is very fertile; indeed this field has been every year planted with corn for upwards of one hundred years and still is as productive as ever. They hold their land by Spanish rights obtained before it was ceded to France.[15] Such rights may be bought for two dollars per acre. The climate is suitable for wheat, rye, Indian corn, oats, flax, and corn yields from seventy five to eighty five bushels per acre and wheat from thirty to forty.

Ste. Genevieve

After making some remarks at this place, I undertook to cross the Mississippi to St. Genevieve. When I came to the river, I was struck with amaze: a water running with great fury as it were turning in whirlpools and forcing its way on with great rage and mixed with half loam which never settles. The river was about one mile across with a sand bar in the middle. Therefore, I had to cross in two different boats. I was landed on the sand bar and had to lead my horse across the bar to the other boat. As soon as I got on the bar, all the earth moved under me, seemingly like the waves swelling around me. Thinking every minute of sinking down to a better foundation but got safe over and landed into an extensive corn field which appears more to me like a cane brake, the corn so lofty that it would take a tall man to reach an ear. I traveled on three miles before I got through it. I then came to a gate which was opened to me by a keeper placed there for that purpose who is

15. There is no record of Spanish land rights at Kaskaskia. Maley probably meant to say that the landowners held French rights before Kaskaskia was ceded to Britain following the French and Indian War.

imployed by the company that owns this large enclosure, then rising a small ascent, entered into the town of St Genevieve.

It was on Sunday; every thing seemed to be a stirring. I stopped at the hotel which was a very commodius building. The house was full of company, seemingly gentlemen of the first rank and different denominations. I soon discovered all kinds of vice and imorality carried on: music and card playing, baiting and horse racing. Even the priest had to be called upon by a messenger to go; the people were waiting for him to go and perform his sacred functions. He but soon returned to the liew[16] table again. I walked up and down the village and saw the billiard rooms open and the people busily employed at the game.

This is a town of considerable business, cash seems to be very plenty. About thirty miles from this place lead ore is found in great abundance, and this being the principal place of deposit of this until from where the traders from Orleans take it and leave goods or cash in exchange. Makes it quite flourishing because lead sells generally at five dollars per long hundred. There is but two small stores in the place. Dry goods sell very high. It is supposed to contain about five hundred inhabitants. The buildings are all after the French form, very low and rooves flat. The Americans have made no alterations yet as to building. Traders here think nothing else but making a fortune which they, if industrious, accumulate in a short time.

I took dinner which was served in the gentlest manner, good cookery and different dishes and a great many partakers after dinner. I took my horse and went to the salt works which was five miles out of town. Salt can be made here in any quantity. It sells at the works at seventy five cents per bushel. There was one well in operation which made sufficient for the consumption of the country. After viewing these works I returned to the town. It was then almost sunset. Behold, to my great surprise when I came to the inn, they were in the ball room a dancing and grand music. The ladies were all French and looked very captivating, most elegant figures and make a fine appearance in dress, although going home from the ball with their gallants,

16. This is apparently a reference to "loo," a trick-taking card game also known as "lanturlu," which was popular in the eighteenth and nineteenth centuries. Based on its description, it appears similar to "bourré," a Cajun French card game still enjoyed in Louisiana. *Encyclopaedia Britannica Online*, s.v. "Loo," accessed June 7, 2016, https://www.britannica.com/topic/loo-card-game.

if the streets are muddy, they pull off their elegant slippers and stockings and carry them in their hand. In that way you see them next day barefooted.

I'll give a small sketch how strangers are taken in when they come to the place where a ball is to be. He gets an invitation. As soon as the ball is opened, the king and queen of the evening, so called, makes their adress to the stranger, tells him that he is to be crowned King; that being their custom at their balls to bestow that honour on a stranger. After crowning him they take him through the room and give him an introduction to the ladies and then undauntedly to choose the queen. Out of all those figures before him, they never refuse so great an honour as to be crowned queen. When this is performed, they are joined hand and hand and sit down in a seat provided for them. They dance when they please; they then go on with the performance of the evening, cakes served round at different times with some good hot coffee and wine occasionally.

Before the dismission, the King of the evening pronounces these words: "your royal highness has been endowed with all the honour that we thy subjects can bestow, and thou hast made choice of a queen, and thy person excepted now, we wish you to see her safe to her place of abode, their to guard and protect her person, and we thy subjects shall have provisions made to have the honour of being once more in his Majesties company." All those crowned heretofore paid the expenses of the evening so their next evening have their bill at the expense of the King which sometimes amount to a hundred dollars. This is the way they take in a stranger. Some give them the slip, leave town before the ball comes on, and leave their queen in despair.

This town is healthy with good spring water.

Ste. Genevieve

According to a historical marker erected by the state historical society, Ste. Genevieve, named for the patroness saint of Paris, was founded about 1735 as the oldest permanent settlement in Missouri.[17] *Other sources place its founding at about 1750.*[18] *Whatever the date, initially the town was little more than a satellite of*

17. Historical marker placed in Ste. Genevieve by Missouri Historical Society, 1953.
18. Eckberg, *French Roots in the Illinois Country*, 88.

Kaskaskia, on the other side of the Mississippi. Following France's 1763 cession of lands to England, however, both Ste. Genevieve and St. Louis witnessed an influx of French from communities on the east side of the Mississippi. Originally located close to the Mississippi River, the town suffered a series of floods in the 1780s and was relocated approximately three miles west following the flood of 1785.[19] *As noted by Maley, at the time of his visit, the principal sources of commerce in the town stemmed from lead production at the mines west of town, and from salt produced at Saline Creek, approximately six miles downriver.*

Maley also noted the enormous enclosed field east of Ste. Genevieve, "Le Grand Champ." Estimated to contain seven thousand acres, it was dedicated principally to the cultivation of corn, pumpkins, and spring wheat.[20] *While many Americans, like Maley, assumed that the field was owned in common by the village, Le Grand Champ actually comprised a number of strips of land, each held and cultivated by individual families. In the French tradition, the plots were typically two arpents (380 feet) wide, and ran from the river to the line of hills west of the river. While the land was not owned in common, each landowner was responsible for maintaining a portion of the common fence, and there were strict rules on when livestock could be turned into the field after harvest.*[21]

At the time of Maley's visit, Ste. Genevieve was a prosperous and growing town. Maley noted that the town had two stores and about five hundred inhabitants; less than a decade later, Brackenridge reported six stores and fourteen hundred inhabitants. Maley's description of the ball he attended in Ste. Genevieve also seems consistent with the lively social life enjoyed by many French communities in America. According to an early observer, the French were "passionately fond of dancing." They conducted themselves with considerable decorum, however, and the priest would frequently attend the early part of the balls to ensure good behavior.[22] *A mural in Ste. Genevieve's post office depicts a French New Year's Eve tradition, "La Guignolée," that has been observed since the 1700s. According to the custom, a group of male revelers in period costume travels from house to house, dancing and singing "La Gui-Annee (Happy Year)."*

Ste. Genevieve today is not a large town, but its historic district boasts some of the best examples of French colonial architecture to be found anywhere, including

19. Ibid., 88–92.
20. Brackenridge, *Views of Louisiana*, 228.
21. Eckberg, *French Roots in the Illinois Country*, 128–34.
22. Reynolds, *Reynold's History of Illinois*, 38.

Greentree Tavern (Janis-Ziegler House).
One of two taverns in Ste. Genevieve at the time of Maley's visit.
Photograph by the editor.

several vertical-timber buildings that were a unique French style of construction. We don't know where Maley stayed while in the town, but several buildings in the town date to before 1808, including two buildings that served as inns or taverns at the time of his visit.

Exploring the Kaskaskia River

I tarried here all night and returned in the morning to Kaskaskia. There I was encouraged to take a route up the Okaw river as the Indians has frequently brought down to this place several curious stones of an imperial kind and ores of lead and copper which they said they got high up the river. There is a nation of Indians here that formerly owned a large tract of land. Congress has purchased it from them, and their yearly emoluments amounts to a thousand dollars. Their tribe is but small, only fifty souls. They have a chief among them who calls himself Jefferson after Thomas Jefferson, our former president. The nation is called the Kaskaskias. The chief has a commodious house built for him in town where he resides. All this was done at the expense of the United States. He rides about in state, talks good English, can read and write. His dress is scarlet leggings trimmed with blue ribbands, a callico shirt and a callico gown or mantle. These Indians dare not hunt up this river any distance for the Sutawatamies[23] are their enemies and kill them when they come across them.

I proceeded up the river. The first day's journey I had a road to travel an found some inhabitants. The face of the country a good deal broken and intersected with small praries, the soil not so good. I got to stay at a house the first night and spent the time very agreeable. There had been a corn shucking there that day and diverted themselves in dancing and different kinds of plays, seeming all an innocent amusement. They treated me very hospitable. It was a Scotch settlement. Next day I proceeded up the river, got out of the settlement but reached another small settlement that night where I found a man that offered his service to go with me to the head of the river, as he was acquainted with the woods.

We started next morning. He equipt himself with a good rifle, a side knife and tomahawk and so went on. He took me chiefly through prarie, it being better traveling. The grass chiefly burnt off, the soil is very fertile. The grass grows very spontaneously. Some places where the grass was not burned, I had the curiosity of seeing the operation, the wind being a head which other wise would not have answered for with the wind it runs so fast that a horse could scarcely keep before it. We dismounted, struck fire and put the blaze to it which, in a few minutes, was dreadful to behold. Roared like falls of many waters, the blaze rising seemingly to the clouds so we pursued on our journey riding through an extensive plain, barely burnt and very level, the wind NW very piercing cold and a very clear atmosphere.

Behold, in ten steps from us, we saw a prarie wolf a laying in a hold fast

23. Transcribed as spelled. Maley may be referring to the Potawatomis.

asleep in the sun but before the hunter could get his rifle down, the wolf jumped up and ran with all speed. Two dogs which we had with us saw him as he started and immediately ran after him in a close pursuit which give a fair race, the ground being so level. We kept them in view, and after running a mile as we suppose, they caught him. One of the dogs was very stout. He buckled him first and with the assistance of the smaller one they had him almost dead before we got to them. The prarie wolf is a size smaller than the common wolf.[24] Their is a fowl here called the prarie hen. They are very plenty, they are a size larger then the fezons [pheasants] of the northern states and resemble them very much as to feathers, but much better eating. We got through the praries and traveled in the bottom lands of the river all very level and fertile. We killed an elk which we feasted on that night.

Next day we got to our journey's end and found what I was in pursuit of. Came to a place on the bank of the river where there was an appearance of ancient works. There was a hole dug in the earth formed a conical shape about 4 feet deep and from the bottom a hole or conductor out of that into another of the same size there was fall enough for the lower one to receive the full of the upper through this conductor. There laid a large pile of calcined stone here which appeared to be very rich. The stone were easy broken to pieces and inside there was an appearance of pure gold and silver but behold it was nothing but a light substance like an ising glass.[25] These men have often been deceived who were not judges. I viewed the banks of the river which were high and stony. There I discovered the natural cinnabar that proved to be the calcined stone that lay at that place before mentioned and holes for the purpose of extracting the quicksilver.[26] I found pirites of all descriptions, sulfur and copperas. I went no higher up the river but struck my course back to Kaskaskia where I returned in four days.

The American Bottom: Kaskaskia to Cahokia

I came to Kaskaskia on the sixth of October, tarried one day and then fitted myself for to take a route up the Mississippi through that beautiful country

24. What Maley refers to as a "prairie wolf" is likely a coyote, which is smaller than the gray wolf that also inhabited the region.

25. Isinglass, another name for the mineral mica.

26. Cinnabar is an ore of mercury, which is also known as quicksilver.

called the American Bottom. This is the richest soil in the known world beyond any doubt. The soil is twelve feet deep. There is a bottom on the river for about two miles wide, well timbered and then takes a rise of about ten feet that is called the second bottom. It is most part prarie intersected with beautiful groves of timber, making it convenient for the inhabitants. They have nothing to do to make an improvement but to make their rails and fence their ground. How soon may a man have a farm to his land! This bottom is from ten to thirteen miles wide. Everything looks pleasing to the eye. To take a view of the bluff that surrounds this bottom exceeds all scenes ever beheld before, where you may see the distance of ten miles. This lofty eminence, a ledge of limestone not less them five hundred feet perpendicular, which surprises the stranger with the appearance of a town in his imagination to see huge rocks in forms of cones and spires standing as it were in minature.

The first days journey was but fifteen miles to a French village called Peraderouge [Prairie du Rocher]. One mile below this town is this great curiosity an ancient fort and fortifications that the inhabitants to can give no true account of it being very strong and the inside very extensive it appears to have been difficult to enter by windings from the entrance gate. There has been several implements of war found here such as cannon, aspantoones, etc.[27] These were got by digging. I started early in the morning in order to make a good days journey and got to another village called Peradesio,[28] four miles further a larger village by the name of Kahokia [Cahokia]. Here I found some Americans. This was about five miles from St Louis on the Mississippi. I stayed that night in Kahokia at the hotel kept by a man formerly from the state of New York.

Next day I still continued up the river, no alteration as to the face of the country or soil. I reached that day to an extensive settlement called Goshen which was after the land of Goshen where Joseph's brethren dwell. Well might be so called; it was a land flowing with milk and honey, fruit very plenty such as apples and peaches. This is all settled by Americans emigrated from Kentucky and Tennessee. They have most beautiful improvements and

27. Brackenridge, *Views of Louisiana*, 273. "Aspontoon" is apparently a reference to "espontoon" or "spontoon," a pike-like weapon. There is no record of a fort one mile below Prairie du Rocher, but Maley is apparently referring to the ruins of Fort Chartres, 3.7 miles west of the town. Brackenridge describes visiting the "noble ruin" in 1810 and seeing broken cannon buried in the ground.

28. The editor has been unable to find any record of a village by this name.

not titles for their land, as Congress never had any survey made in that part of the territory. They only settled promiscuously, but they have obtained a preemption by Congress that they have the first right to purchase their land. No person can purchase without paying them for their improvements. I continued my route up to Wood River. Here this bluff encloses the American Bottom, points down to the Mississippi River, then above that comes in the waters of the Illinois River so I returned back to Kahokia. From there crossed the Mississippi River to St Louis, which makes a very majestic appearance as you are crossing the river, the river nearly a mile and a half wide.

Kaskaskia and the American Bottom

During his 1808 travels in Illinois, Maley traversed the "American Bottom," an area stretching more than eighty miles south from Alton, Illinois, to Kaskaskia. The area, which encompassed the floodplain bounded between the Mississippi River on the west and steep bluffs on the east, is three to nine miles in width and comprises more than 350 square miles of some of the most fertile farmland found anywhere on the continent. Those soils had long attracted settlers, and the bottom was the home of the largest Mississippian-era culture in North America, at the Cahokia Mounds site, east of St. Louis. That site held a population of as many as 30,000–40,000 at its peak, but had been abandoned by the time of seventeenth-century French exploration in the region.

With France's 1763 cession of lands east of the Mississippi to England following the French and Indian War, there was a movement of the French population from the American Bottom to communities west of the river. The movement was not immediate, however; the first British census of Kaskaskia in 1767 indicated 903 residents, considerably above the French census of 1752.[29] *By the 1780s, however, Kaskaskia had suffered a major exodus of inhabitants.*[30] *Fort Chartres, which had been the center of French military power in the territory, was occupied by British forces in 1765, but the location was abandoned in 1772 due to encroachment by the Mississippi River, which caused the collapse of the south wall.*[31] *In 1778, during*

29. Eckberg, *French Roots in the Illinois Country*, 152, 155.
30. Ibid., 55.
31. "Fort de Chartres State Historic Site," accessed April 14, 2016, www.fortdechartres.us.

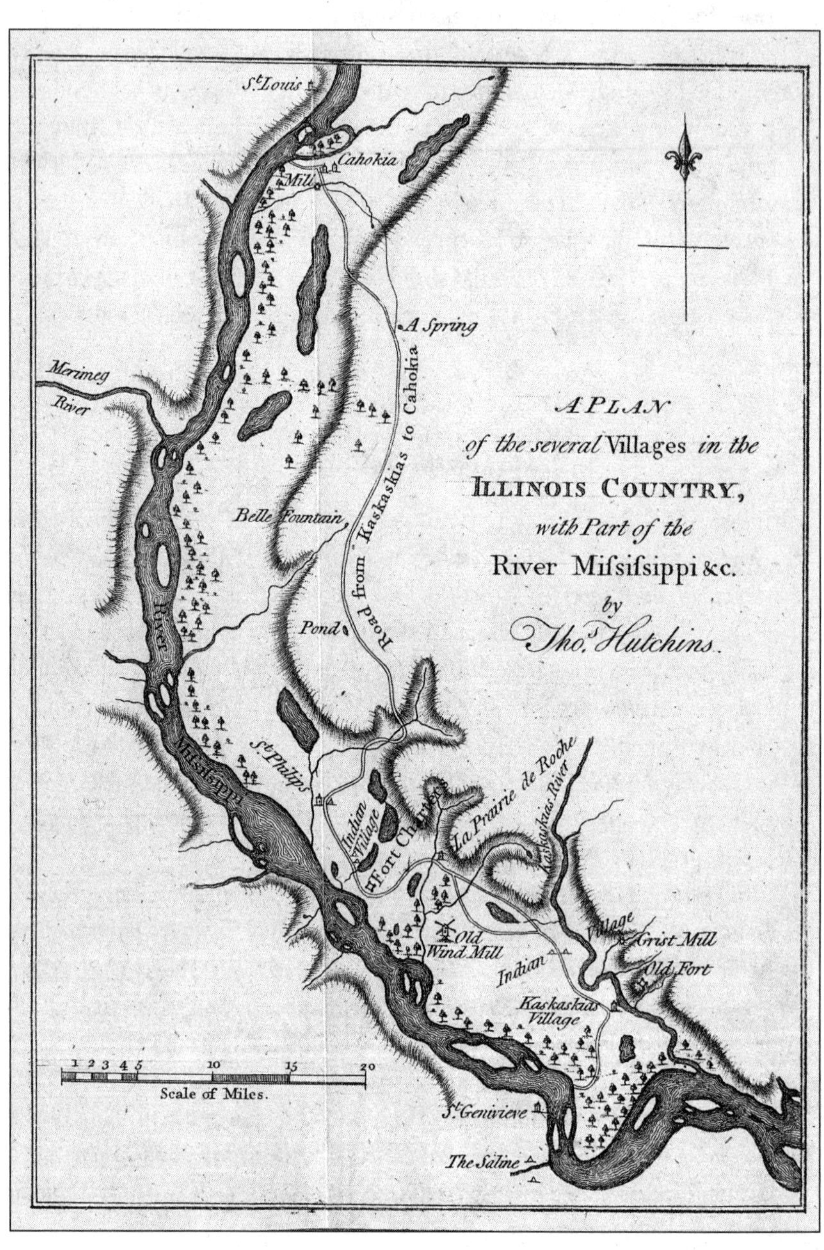

Map of Illinois Country—the American Bottom, Thomas Hutchins, 1778.
Courtesy of the David Rumsey Map Collection, www.davidrumsey.com.

the Revolutionary War, Kaskaskia, Cahokia, and Vincennes were captured by Virginia militia under the command of George Rogers Clark, and the territory became part of the United States following the end of the war.

By the time of Maley's visit, American immigration into the American Bottom had resulted in a dramatic growth in population. As he noted, Kaskaskia had been designated the seat of Randolph County and was a booming place. Following his visit, in 1812 it was named the territorial capital of Illinois, and became the state capital when Illinois was admitted into the Union in 1818. At that time, the town had an estimated population of seven thousand. However, the state capital was moved to Vandalia in 1819, and Kaskaskia began a long decline. Damaged by a flood in 1844, the Mississippi changed course in 1881, destroying much of the remainder of the town and leaving it on the west bank of the river.[32] *The village was moved approximately three miles south of the town's original location, but the only remnants of this once-thriving community are a historic church and a few houses.*

❦ ❦ ❦

St. Louis and the Lead Mines of Missouri

The town stands on a high eminence. The bank of the river is perpendicular rock. The houses built on the very brink though have steps made to go down to the water. They make use of the river water altogether, for it is considered very healthy altho not fit for use until it stands and settles. It is never clear in the river. This town is eighteen miles below the mouth of the Missouri, thirty miles from St. Charles up the Missouri, a post town and the only town on that river. There was a few traders there that traded with the Indians that come down the river, but St. Louis takes the lead, as this was the only place of deposit of all that came from the northerd and westard. It was well fortified with four forts or round houses built in the rear of the town on an eminence that commands the town and river in front and an extensive prarie in the rear. Thus is the town secure.

St Louis contains about seven hundred inhabitants; is in the Missouri Territory. The governor lives in this place which is that undaunted hero Lewis

32. "Illinois in Focus: A Photographic Tour of the Land of Lincoln," accessed April 14, 2016, www.illinoisinfocus.com.

who explored the Missouri but unfortunately afterwards killed himself by some misunderstanding that took place betwixt him and Congress.[33] The houses here are nearly the same as the other villages but larger. There are several stores in this place; dry goods are very high. The Americans flock in daily, this being in November, the weather getting cold.

I fitted myself for the lead mines and there to take my winter quarters which was seventy five miles from this place. Next morning took my leave and started for Mine a Breton,[34] the first digging where I arrived in two days. This seemed to me like a home immediately. I was received with all the hospitality imaginable, a smart village and chiefly all Kentuckians that came to this place for the purpose of making lead, which is a very profitable business.

One man has as good a chance as the other. He raises the ore, cleans and hands it to the smelting house and there gets two dollars per hundredweight in cash. I have seen as many as three hundred hands at one digging at a time but it is very uncertain. The miners move about where most ore is to be found. There is always new discoveries made by man that follow nothing else but digging in different places which when they find a rich place of ore they sell the discovery to others and then search again. There are men their that have accumulated great wealth by following the lead, maling [mauling?] and digging of ore which he does by owning some slaves and also by hireing hands at the extravagant price of thirty dollars a month. There are several diggings. There is Mine Arno, Mine Lemot, Mine Afoe, Mine a Breton, new diggings and Brown's digging and several others. These diggings take in the scope of forty miles square.

I made it my business to explore them all and I go in company with a chemist from Saxony who instructed me in the art of refining different kinds of ore that might come to my view and also the smelting and fluxing ores. We had a furnace in operation all that winter smelting and separating the silver contained in the lead but found it not a profitable business. The production in silver was but small, so we quit it and agreed on an exploring voyage in the spring. The country here is exceeding healthy altho broken and abounds in

33. Meriwether Lewis was governor of Louisiana, residing in St. Louis when Maley arrived there. He died of gunshot wounds at an inn on the Natchez Trace the following year. Debate continues to this day as to whether he committed suicide or was murdered.

34. Mine à Burton, located at current-day Potosi, Missouri.

limestone. Springs water, large bodies of good land as well as poor. People are imigrating very rapid to that country and several religious societies forming some Presbiterians some Baptists and some Methodists here.

The Lead Mines of Missouri

When Maley arrived in southeast Missouri, the lead mines there had been worked for almost a century. Father James Gravier first noted the potential for lead mining on the Meramec River during a voyage to Missouri in 1700, and mining in the area was initiated by Phillippe Francois Renault in 1721.[35] *Renault, the son of an iron founder, had been engaged by the Royal Company of the West to exploit the mineral resources in Louisiana. He left France in 1719 with two hundred workers and mining tools and, en route to America, bought five hundred slaves in St. Domingo.*[36] *Although Renault discovered copper near the head of the Mississippi and on the Illinois River, the company did not find precious metals. Renault therefore concentrated his efforts on developing lead mines in Missouri,*[37] *including a number of small deposits north of present-day Potosi, Missouri, and at Mine La Motte, near Fredericktown. Although these mines produced as much as fifteen hundred pounds of lead per day,*[38] *the venture appears to have had limited financial success. Renault sold his slaves and with a number of workmen, returned to France in 1742. He apparently died on the passage home or shortly thereafter.*[39]

Following Renault's departure, very little mining appears to have been done, due possibly in part to an inability to protect the operation from Indian attacks. The principal achievement that took place under Spanish authority, following France's cession of the territory in 1763, was the discovery of Mine à Burton, located at current-day Potosi.[40] *In 1797 the Spanish provided a land grant to an American, Moses Austin, to work the deposit at Mine à Burton. Austin, who had previously operated a lead mine in Wythe County, Virginia, erected a furnace to extract lead from the ashes left behind from the smelting processes, built a*

35. Seeger, "History of Mining," 10. Renault is also variously spelled Renaut and Renaud.
36. Schoolcraft, *A View of the Lead Mines of Missouri*, 15.
37. Brackenridge, *Views of Louisiana*, 256–57.
38. Seeger, "History of Mining," 10.
39. Brackenridge, *Views of Louisiana*, 257.
40. Schoolcraft, *A View of the Lead Mines of Missouri*, 18.

tower to produce lead shot, and began manufacturing sheets of lead. Several other Americans followed Austin's lead, moving to Spanish-controlled Missouri.

Following the Louisiana Purchase, American immigration surged and, at the time Maley arrived at Mine à Burton, in the fall of 1808, business was booming. Production at the mine averaged 800,000 pounds per year from 1804 to 1808,[41] *and the smelting furnaces that Austin built were so efficient that many other miners paid him to smelt their ore.*[42] *As noted by Maley, however, the mining process remained unsophisticated, with almost all the ore recovered from shallow pits on the surface using shovels and pickaxes. Furthermore, much of the ore smelting was rudimentary. Miners would build a stone-lined hearth into a hillside, fill it with wood and lead ore, and after burning the wood, collect the lumps of lead that had been melted out of the ore. According to his account, Maley worked with a chemist from Saxony to extract silver from the lead produced in the region. They likely used a process called "cupellation," which had been used with some success in Germany, but there wasn't enough silver in the Missouri lead to make it economically viable.*[43]

After Maley departed the Missouri mines in 1809, production from the region continued to rise, but Moses Austin faced a series of financial problems.[44] *The price of lead, apparently fluctuating with developments in the Napoleonic wars in Europe, had plummeted by 40 percent in 1807, and several of Austin's shipments to New Orleans were delayed. In addition, production from Mine à Burton fell as miners were attracted to newly discovered deposits. In an attempt to address his financial problems, Austin founded the Bank of St. Louis, but it failed in the Panic of 1819. Austin was jailed for indebtedness in 1820, and Mine à Burton was sold to settle part of his debt. In his final business venture, in 1821 Moses Austin secured a land grant from the Spanish government to bring colonists to Texas, but he died before he could carry out the venture. His son, Stephen F. Austin, assumed responsibility for the project and is now remembered as the "Father of Texas."*[45]

41. Ibid., 49.

42. "Moses Austin," accessed April 15, 2016, http://shsmo.org/historicmissourians/name/a/austin/.

43. Schoolcraft, *A View of the Lead Mines of Missouri*, 111.

44. "Moses Austin," accessed April 15, 2016, http://shsmo.org/historicmissourians/name/a/austin/.

45. Stephen F. Austin, born in 1793, spent time at Mine à Burton as a boy and later served as manager of the mine. However, he was apparently away at school at the time Maley was there. Barker, "Austin, Stephen Fuller," accessed April 18, 2016, https://www.tshaonline.org/handbook/online/articles/fau14.

Lead production from many of the shallow deposits declined in the first half of the nineteenth century, but deeper mines began operating in the area in the 1860s. Many remained in production until the 1960s and 1970s. In the latter half of the nineteenth century, new mines were opened in southwest Missouri, and the Viburnum Trend in southeast Missouri began production in the 1960s. Today, Missouri still accounts for more than 90 percent of the nation's lead production.[46]

46. Missouri Department of Labor, "The Importance of Mining in Missouri's History," accessed April 18, 2016, https://www.visitmo.com/missouri-travel/the-importance-of-mining-in-missouris-history.aspx.

CHAPTER 2 ❦ 1809

Up the Missouri and Gasconade Rivers

We spent the winter very agreable and prepared ourselves for a Missouri trip. Left the mines on the first of March to St Louis, there bought a pirogue, very light and handy, each a good rifle, plenty of ammunition, and all other things that we thought necessary. Our objective was up the Missouri as far as the Gasconade, then up that river to the headwaters in pursuit of mines and minerals. We took leave of St Louis on the 29th of March 1809 and so pursued our journey. Got to the mouth of the Missouri the first day of April. There camped and proceeded up the Missouri the next morning. Had hard puling; the stream is very swift, went but fifteen miles that day.

The Missouri bottoms are very fertile, much like the Mississippi, a timbered bottom next the river and off praries, the banks perpendicular. Very dangerous to land at places for the banks are continually caving in by the rapidity of the stream. The water always cold and very healthy. The cause of the immense snows that melt from the Rocky Mountains, the high waters of the Missouri are generally the last of May and first of June. This day we got to St. Charles, a French village much after the form of the other towns, not much business done here. They raise plenty of Indian corn which is a white flour corn.

Next day we made a halt after going about ten miles as we found a safe harbour to lay in. Took a hunt and and soon killed a deer and two turkeys. Game here was plenty. Went to our boat and then lived sumptuously on our venison, slep unmolested that night, rose early in the morning and made a kettle of soup of one of our turkeys. Took breakfast and started. Found nothing worth noting that day but passed two islands well timbered and plenty of game on them. We did not kill any thing as we had to be saving of our ammunition; only wanted to kill when necessity required. We only went about fifteen miles that day. Struck camp and broiled our venison. We felt much fatigued, mosquitos very troublesome and owls make a great noise, also howling of wolves altho they kept their distance. Did not rest well that night. It had the appearance of rain which about the middle of the day it began. We had to strike camp and make us a shelter to keep our baggage dry, especially our powder. We had a large bear skin, which by stretching tight in a slope, was sufficiently large enough to shelter all. We were weather bound two days, the third day the wind NW and clear.

We pursued our journey, the current hard to stem, got about eighteen miles that day, saw the first bufaloe but got no shot at him. Struck camp, had to keep a great deal of smoke to keep away the mosquitos. We were disturbed in the night by something scratching in a tree right above us throwing down large flakes of bark. We judged it to be some large animal but could not see it. Had to wait in suspense till morning. We could not sleep for fear of it coming down and making a prey of us. We kept a good fire and watch about till day light. As soon as we could see, we tried to find him but it was a long time before we discovered any thing. At last saw him laying on a limb, very little of his body to be seen but he was very anxious to look down. His head was very fair, but the tree so lofty that I thought it would be a chance shot, but I took courage to try him a shot. I thought perhaps I might move him to a more advantageous place, went a little distance from the tree and took aim at his head which proved to be fatal. I shot him right in between the eyes and fetched him down soon enough. Behold, it was a she panther which the first of the kind I had ever seen. We did not take off his skin but started on our journey.

The river winds in continual bends the general course of the river about W an by N, current not so strong as usual. Made a good days journey, had a good camping ground that night. Nothing disturbed us; we rested well. In the morning, took a hunt, found nothing but a couple of turkeys which we killed and so went on for another day. The bottoms still fertile. Timber very large. The growth is cotton wood, over culp and piquan [pecan].[1] Made another good day's journey. The weather clouded up for rain. It was fair in the morning and so we continued day by day without much difficulty till we arrived at Fort Osage.

1. Maley is apparently referring to "overcup" oak, also known as swamp post oak, swamp white oak, and water white oak. U.S. Department of Agriculture, "Overcup Oak," *USDA Plant Guide*, accessed December 14, 2015, http://plants.usda.gov/plantguide/pdf/pg_quly.pdf.

Replica of Fort Osage, Sibley, Missouri.
Photograph by the editor.

There were about sixty regular troops who keep the garrison. They informed us of the danger of going up the Missouri as the Osage Indians were troublesome at that time, as they were laying wait for that party of men that were sent by Congress to take home the Mandan chief whom Clarke and Lewis had fetched down to treat and be friendly, but the party had passed up the river unaware to them. I still ventured on thinking that the Gasconade would not be dangerous. Went unmolested till we got about thirty miles up the Gasconade River. There, to our sorrow, we saw five Indians well armed, but we made the opposite side of the river from them. They shot at us immediately but proved to no effect. We laid down in our pirogue and, the current swift, we soon got out of their reach, but they cut us off at another point and had another shot a piece at us, but we providentially made our escape and made down the river again as swift as we could go. It was not many days before we reached Fort Osage again.[2]

2. If Maley's account is accurate, it is not clear why he and his companion would have returned to Fort Osage, which would have been a considerable paddle back upstream from the mouth of the Gasconade River. Given his subsequent discussion, presumably they had trade goods that could be best exchanged there.

Let this not dishearten others from trading up this river with the natives. They are all peaceable now and this is the country for men of means and enterprise to adventure. Dry goods are the articles wanted among the natives is which they take in exchange for their furs is chiefly the beaver and otter, beads, silver broaches and rings. Red vermilion is a good article. The dry goods to consist of Indian and pointed blankets, calico shawls of different colours and quality, chintses, and common callicoes, blue plains very saleable, small cased looking glasses. The way most expedient for traders that should wish to try their fortune who reside in the northern or eastern states take their route by the way of Philadelphia then to Pittsburg on the Ohio river, which is about three hundred miles west of Philadelphia. From there you have water carriage to the Missouri. The best way to trade to that country is to go into the Missouri as high as Fort Osage and their wait for the Indians that come down the river, and he may also sell abundance to the inhabitants; the immigration to that country is very considerable. Let me mention jewelry and cutlery of all kinds also to be articles.

I leave Fort Osage and return to St. Louis and their my partner resigned his commission of traveling any more where Indians might be found. I was then at a loss for a companion and could find none that would join me, as I was determined to explore all the country, land and water west of the Mississippi, but could not go alone. I then set my resolution to explore the Illinois River, as I understood that there was a great prospect up that river of mines and minerals which was my main object and from that to the Wabash River. This route I fixed upon to go by myself.

Fort Osage

In 1809 Maley and his unnamed partner ("a chemist from Saxony") ascended the Missouri River to Fort Osage, located about twenty miles east of current-day Kansas City. The site for the fort had been identified by William Clark on his 1804 expedition up the Missouri with Meriwether Lewis, and construction began in the fall of 1808.[3] *At the time of Maley's visit, the fort was just being completed.*

3. "Fort Osage National Historic Landmark," accessed April 19, 2016, http://www.fortosagenhs.com.

Unlike many other frontier posts, Fort Osage was a substantial military structure, with a stockade that enclosed almost two acres and five blockhouses. The fort was manned by a company (nominally eighty men) of regular troops and had several small cannon that could be used in defense or to command traffic on the river below.

The key mission of the post was to manage relations with the powerful Osage tribe, and the fort was built pursuant to an 1808 treaty between the United States and the tribe. In that treaty, the Osage ceded all their territory east of a line running south from Fort Osage to the Arkansas River. In return, the United States agreed to build the fort and a trading post on the site, and to provide the tribe the services of the fort's blacksmith. In addition, the government agreed to provide $1,500 per year in trade goods and indemnified the tribe for up to $5,000 in claims that Americans might bring against the Osage for theft or destruction of goods since the Louisiana Purchase.[4] *To carry out trade, the United States established a "factory" at the fort under the management of a "factor," George Sibley, who arrived in 1808.*[5] *He began trading with the Osage almost immediately, but the factory, where trade goods and furs were stored, was still under construction when Maley visited the post in 1809.*[6]

As noted by Maley, he arrived at a time when the United States was attempting to return the Mandan chief, Shahaka, to his home following a visit to Washington. This was one of the more problematic episodes in the history of the region. On their expedition to the Pacific, Lewis and Clark had been hosted by Shahaka, and on their return, they invited the chief and his family to accompany them to Washington. Shahaka did so, meeting with President Thomas Jefferson and spending the winter of 1806–7 in Philadelphia. However, in 1807, when the United States military was escorting the chief and his family back to their village, the expedition came under attack by the Arikaras and had to turn back to St. Louis. In response, in 1808 Meriwether Lewis, then governor of Louisiana Territory, persuaded the War Department to pay $7,000 to a newly organized company, the Missouri Fur Company, to return the chief to his village.[7] *The Missouri Fur Company comprised a veritable "Who's Who" of prominent individuals in St. Louis, including William Clark, who was superintendent of Indian affairs; Reuben Lewis, Meriwether*

4. Kappler, *Treaty with the Osage*, 95.

5. George Sibley was the son of John Sibley, the U.S. Indian agent at Natchitoches, Louisiana, whom Maley would meet in 1812.

6. Smith, *Seeking a Newer World*, 96.

7. Wallace, *Jefferson and the Indians*, 264–67.

Lewis' brother and sub-agent to the Osage; Pierre and Auguste Chouteau; Manuel Lisa; and other prominent traders. This expedition, which included 350 men, stopped by Fort Osage in July 1809 and is the group referred to by Maley.[8]

Although the Missouri Fur Company was successful in returning Shahaka to his village, the venture generated controversy. By the time the second effort to return the chief was undertaken, Jefferson had been succeeded by James Madison as president, and in July 1809, Madison's secretary of war, William Eustis, chastised Lewis for paying so much to a private company, with its own commercial objectives, to return the Mandan chief. Lewis fired back a letter in August, promising to come to Washington to explain his actions. It was on this trip, in October 1809, that Lewis died under mysterious circumstances (possibly suicide) at Grinder's Stand on the Natchez Trace, southwest of Nashville.[9]

Following his aborted trip up the Gasconade, Maley apparently returned to Fort Osage to barter his trade goods, then returned to St. Louis. With the exception of a period during the War of 1812, George Sibley continued to operate the trading factory at the fort until 1822, when the United States abandoned the factory system. The post was permanently abandoned in 1827. Beginning in the 1940s, Jackson County, Missouri, undertook a project to locate and reconstruct the fort. A replica of the fort and a modern museum are currently open to visitors at Sibley, Missouri.[10]

❦ ❦ ❦

Venture on the Illinois River

I prepared myself with every necessary I could think of with as much not to overload myself as I had to pack horse myself. After being ready, I took my leave of St Louis, had a perogue and two men to take me up the Mississippi as far as the Illinois River. I left St Louis the third day of August 1809, started and on the fourth day landed on the east bank of the Mississippi above the

8. According to Maley's account, he was told that Osage warriors were lying in wait to ambush this group. This is certainly possible, but since the group included officials and traders who were key to the tribe's trade with the United States, it seems unlikely. Perhaps Maley or his interlocutors were confused as to the identity of the Indians who intended to ambush the expedition.

9. Smith, *Seeking a Newer World*, 92–93n29.

10. Fort Osage National Historic Landmark, accessed April 19, 2016, http://www.fortosagenhs.com/.

mouth of the Illinois. There we camped together that night and my company took leave of me in the morning. All I had to support myself was what I could kill with my rifle. Traveled on that day. I had chiefly a thick timbered country, the soil very fertile but the next day I got into extensive meadows with abundance of grass and tall weeds. I had to encounter a great deal of difficulty in traveling, went on that way for several days but found no game and begun to be in want of something to eat as I had had none for two days. Could see no end to the meadows up the river, traveled on and shot a turkey which had flew over the river from the opposite side.

As there was appearance of a timbered country, which obliged me to try to get over the river but this was a difficult piece of business without a boat. The only way was I had to hunt for drift wood on the river and make a raft and so cross it, which I at last effected, found wood enough and made me a raft. I had to paddle it over as the water was too deep for me to reach the bottom with a short pole, so I got on and laid my rifle down on the raft and I went to paddling my craft across the river which was sluggish indeed and my paddle only a round stick of wood. My raft being very tottering, by walking from one side to the other, the raft opened and lost my rifle and sunk which for a moment put me in despair.

My whole dependence; what could I do without it. Why, I could get nothing to eat, had nothing then but a turkey that I had killed before I crossed the river, which I could chiefly eat all that night as I had been two days fasting already. No other ultimatum but to return to the nearest inhabitants which was Goshen settlement in the American Bottom, which I did. I was not destitute of making fire to comfort myself, for I had a knife that would strike fire so I could keep away the vermin. I began to get very weak the second day, but finally weathered the cape. On the third, I got safe to a settlement where I found plenty of nourishment their. I rested two days and started for the town of Kahokia from there to take a new start. When I got their, I tried to purchase a rifle but it was out of my power to prevail on them that had one to part with it, so I was in a bad fix.

Crossing Illinois on Foot

I then took another resolution thinking I could go from that to Fort Vincinnes on the Wabash River without a gun by carrying enough on my back. The route was about one hundred and sixty miles and an Indian trace all the way. By enquiring, I found that I could, by travelling thirty miles the first day, come to a house and also the second and third day from that to carry three days provisions would bring me to inhabitants. Again fitted myself for the journey, took with me to travel on the first day fifteen small crackers, got my directions, which I had to go to such a mentioned place to rise the bluff out of American Bottom and there to take the plainest trace and pursue my journey. I found every thing to answer the directions, found the passage up the bluff, but when I got there, there was a half dozen of paths. It put me a good deal to a stand but I was then five mile from the nearest house and hated to turn back.

I made my own choice of road. I took a good start in order to reach the thirty mile house, traveled through an open country and some broken soil but light chiefly post oak timber. I traveled on till night found no house still anxious to pursue a little further thinking every minute the house to present to my view but I tried so long that I had dark to fix my camp, so I made a halt and struck fire and kindled it. As it happened, wood was easy come at although it was dark. I made me a good fire and laid down by it being very tired of walking so fast. I then had to study what to do next, knowing then that I had not the right trace. It also was not as plain as it was in the morning. Still, in the morning I kept on further, thinking it might lead me to a house but in vain I pursued. The path come to nothing by taking off in different directions up water courses. It proved only to be the hunters that made it.

I stood a long while and held a counsel what to do, and so concluded by striking a right angle to the left, I would be sure to hit the path on my left, as I had taken notice when I started on the top of the bluff there was a plain left hand path which I threatened to take but made choice of the wrong one. I set my pocket compass and took my course, which was nearly a north course, traveled on and found it very disagreeable traveling. The course, being parallel to the Mississippi River, had a great many small water courses to cross which run towards the river and they all have steep hills to go up and down in traveling that direction. I kept on that day until night and found no path, still continued some after night. I was so anxious to find it but in vain had to make a halt and strike my fire which I did now.

I was in a study again what to do next. I could not decide in my mind that night. I ate my last bisket, which was but a light meal, as I had been on short allowance before my belly called for more, but no relief could be found. I therefore comforted myself in a good fire, laid down by it, and slept well that night being so fatigued and hungry. I arose in the morning and considered what to do, and sat my resolution and started in an oblique direction to the right thinking I might have crossed it after dark by not seeing the path when I came to it. Therefore I fell off to the right but discovered nothing traveled in that direction till middle of the day then made a halt called a council and by the voice of a majority, gain the day to go on strike a strait course for the Wabash River. I being very well acquainted with the geography of the country as to the course, I knew the direction.

I sat my compass and started. Put my trust in a Providence who is able to support life in some unknown and mysterious manner still thinking that I might fall in with some inhabitants, but hard was my fate. Had nothing to eat, traveled without my dinner and took up camp that night and went to bed without my supper. Slept easy, arose in the morning and pursued my journey before I took my breakfast for why—because I had none to get, which gentlemen is a good reason. This was the fourth day that I started with fifteen small biscuits. In that time, I begun to feel very weak, the days very warm sunshine. At night I found no relief but had to repeat the old thing over again.

Ordeal on the Prairie: Hazelnuts and Grapes

I started the fifth day and about the middle of the day I got into an extensive prarie which was the first I met with on that route. The face of the country was now altered from a broken country to a level one and the soil exceeding fertile. The growth of timber after I got through the first prarie was chiefly shellbark hickory and post oak undergrowth, a great deal of the hazelnut bushes. It was just in the time of this fruit being fit to eat altho in a green state. I found great relief by them. I spent that night under the hickory trees and spent my evening in cracking of them. Laid down and felt sick at my stomach by eating too many of these nuts upon an empty stomach but felt better in the morning.

Started but found myself very feeble which was the sixth day and entered another prarie. In the heat of the day, I was compelled to lay down and rest my body, as I could not stand traveling in the sun. After leaving this prarie, I found a great growth of some grapes. I filled myself with them and took a hankerchief full with me for fear I might not meet with any more, but I was agreably disapointed, found them plenty betwixt every prarie. When I entered a prarie and did not get through by night, I traveled after night. It was the pleasantest traveling. The days being warm and I being weak caused the nights the best traveling to one in a prarie. I could steer my course by the north pole[11] in clear weather which I was blessed with. The moon began to give light in the forefront of the night that made the evenings pleasant but sometimes found many difficulties, the grass and weeds being sometimes so tall that it was like traveling through a hemp field. It was far above my head and after getting through into the woods I could find no way to kindle a fire on the account of getting wood. I was then exposed to the mercy of the wild vermin and was often disturbed by them by the howling of wolves and other uncommon noises and some would approach very near to me but still never hurt me.

I brought over another night in the dark and started in the morning which was the seventh day. Still found grapes which preserved my life but still was very weak. Laid down in the middle of the day and traveled after night. That night I was traveling through a prarie and the moon on my back. I saw before me something alive of a grayish appearance, which seemingly animated my feelings with joy, the sight of something alive, altho I knew not what it might be. I approached towards it to see but it squat down in the grass. I advanced wthin a few steps and looked. I saw it to be a lengthy animal and a long tail resembling the panther only much larger. I walked round and round it and as I walked round it turned its head still towards me and swung its tail up and down and kept a padding with its fore feet on the ground. These uncommon motions I did not like so well so I sheared off without shaking hands. After I started away from it I began to be apprehensive of the danger I had been in. Still kept looking behind me for fear he might pursue me, but saw nothing of him and so traveled on till I got through the prarie, struck fire and laid down by it and slept unmolested.

I arose in the morning, eat my grapes and few nuts and started the eighth day. When night came on I entered another prarie. After night I was about in the middle of the prarie, it clouded up and got very dark. I could not see to steer my course only by the wind on my left side so traveled on in that

11. Maley is presumably referring to the North Star.

posture till at last it began to rain and blow enough to sweep me away. The wind was N West which caused it to be prodigious cold. I thought then was I only in a hermits situation; a cave to take shelter in and I would have been contented, but behold I had no where to put my head and shivered of the cold. I at last got through in to the woods and it was so dark that I could see nothing. The rain still continued but not so fast as it had. I was shivering like one having an ague, my teeth snapping together, not a dry thread on me. I leave to the reader to think what situation I was in. My firework I did not dare touch as long as it rained for fear of getting wet if it was not so already.

I took in the woods the underbrush being very thick I went through the brush feeling and kicking with my feet to find something till at last I found a large tree laying down and felt along the body with my hands. I found it was burnt out hollow on the under part and a shell above. Under that shelter I found dry leaves and other dry trash. I took off my knapsack and put it under the shelter wiping my hands with my freshest handkerchief till I got them dry keeping my hands under the shelter and got out my fire works and found my punk dry and struck fire and kindled it with the dry leaves I found there. After having a blaze I hunted around by feeling for see I could not and providentially found an old tree top much broken in pieces by the fall. I went to work lugging of wood and made me a large fire which was a great comfort to me. I got myself in a sweat by carrying of wood. I got wood enough to last all night but it still continued raining. I could not lay down for I had no shelter stood before the fire. Turning then one side to the fire and then the other, so I continued till nearly midnight then the rain abated. I then cut some brush and made me a kind of shelter. It still rained some.

I was very weary, laid down before the fire and soon got in a doze but had not laid down long before I was disturbed by something walking in the brush very heavy footed in appearance like a horse making right towards me. I jumped up in fear trying to see it but could not make out. It kept round and round, seemingly as if it wanted something and still kept in the brush so that I could not discover what it was. It kept me from my rest which I stood much in need of. To stand guard a man living on so light a diet as sour grapes and a few nuts was too fatiguing but I thought it dangerous to lay down and perhaps get asleep and if I laid down I was sure to drop asleep for all the fears. I at last thought to drive it off by throwing brands of fire at it, to throw at random in the brush where I heard it. Finally I took the resolution, tryed it, flung and immediately it made a great spluter and jumpt off very heavy like some very large animal, but behold it approached again. I then felt more stouter as I had one throw at it and made off. I got me a couple of brands, stept towards it and threw both chunks as fast as I could one after the other. It made off in great fury. I heard it jump for a great distance and heard no more of it. I stood a long while and listened. I presume I hit it with the fire.

I laid down and soon dropped asleep. It was not long till daylight appeared, which I was not sorry to see. I still took a nap. After daylight, I awoke and behold it was a pleasant morning fine sunshine weather. I got up and looked around for something to eat and soon found some grapes and very good ones, the best I found yet. I struck my course and started my ninth days journey. Traveled about one mile, came to a large creek and apparently very deep. Could not cross it there, but took down stream and soon found a ford, crossed it very conveniently.

The soil here is very fertile, well timbered for use, the country beautiful and level. I found no more praries that day, but a fruit full country. How many thousands there are that want lands to cultivate let them come to these countries and live! Congress will give them a good chance land, the first rate only two dollars per acre. Now is the time to go to that most beautiful country. Let it not be a wilderness any longer, let not the traveler be at a loss like myself. This country must be healthy, good cold winters and the air very pure. I am no more at a loss for grapes but not quite so pleasant traveling as the praries.

Wolves on the Wabash

I got before night, I thought, in river bottom land very rich timber very tall which revived my spirits, thinking to be near the Wabash River. I took camp by sunset in order to provide wood for the night. I thought it might be dangerous in such dark woods as wolves always inhabit such places. I gathered my wood and made a fire, laid down and fell asleep and awoke. It was dark and my fire out. I got up and made up a good fire and laid down again but was soon alarmed by desperate howling of wolves. I heard them a long while a great distance off but still they approached nearer to me till at last by the echoing noise they made caused the neighbouring dogs to be alarmed and fell to barking which seem to be a great distance off. I jumped up overjoyed to think there might be relief once more. I listened which way these dogs were so that I might strike my course that way. Sleep and fear left me I felt myself much revived. The wolves by this time began to be troublesome they came in sight of me but dared not approach the fire. I saluted them once and awhile with fire brands they made off a small distance but increased their howling and still renewed their attempts so I had to fight them off all night.

As soon as daylight appeared I made an attempt to start as my anxiety was so great that I did not mind the wolves but behold they pursued me in great rage had no fire brands then to make them retreat therefore I thought it prudent to climb which I did. I got into a sapling. Their they came under me, looked up and made a great noise and held me there till almost sunrise. Then they walked off and I came down and pursued my course this being the tenth day since I came on the Mississippi bluff. Walked about one mile, I saw an improvement. I soon advanced towards it and came to a corn field, the corn then was ripe. I got over the fence and fell to eating the corn and found some pumpkins, cut one of them. The corn was very tall had no chance to look around me for a house. I took across another fence and their found a turnip patch. I fell to eating but was cautious of not eating too much. I could see no house as yet. I got out of the enclosure on an imenence that from there I discovered a smoke at a distance. Went that way and found a cabin.

When I came to it, I was saluted by the watchful domestics that piloted me their. They shewed all respect and joy they could towards me. I entered this homely cottage and found an aged old man sitting by the fire side and a young girl churning which appeared to be very laborious her churn seemingly was full up to the brim. I sat down in a few minutes but no person spoke to me. Then I thought I'd make my complaint and introduce the subject, but the old man seemed to pay no attention to my discourse. With this the girl told me that her father could not hear unless speaking very loud, which I tried and the old man paid attention to my distressed story. He soon ordered me something to eat, which was some butter milk and corn bread and butter. I eat some but it did not lay long on my stomach, but still tried again, eat some more and it seemed to revive me a little. This old gentleman was not very intelligent. I then made my enquiries where I was. He told me that I was only seven miles from Post Vincennes on the

Wabash, half a mile from a stream called Embrau,[12] a fork of the Wabash, and three quarters of a mile below the ferry on the Embrau, the path that I was in pursuit only three quarters of a mile to my left hand.

See to what disadvantage I travelled and a path so near me! What does it seem like to travel such a distance through an unknown wilderness and not much accustomed to it? Consider my feelings, how they were at different times, but fortitude and a good resolution was the thing. Otherwise my carcass might have been devoured by the ferocious animals that I so courageously fought with my fire brands and saved my life to come and tell you the news and give an information of the country. I escaped, but I would not advise a stranger to run the same risk. If you miss your road, turn back and take a new start.

Vincennes and Indiana Copper

Now it was the middle of the day, and seven miles to a place where I could get any nourishment I required. I told the old gentleman I wanted my directions to the Wabash. He tried to prevail on me to stay two or three days with him and recruit myself; it should cost me nothing. I thankfully refused the offer thinking that I might get more of a nourishment in town then I could by staying there, as my body actually required it, so the old man gave me my directions, which I followed and got to the Wabash river a little before sunset, in sight of the town of Vincennes. Now I leave the Illinois territory and enter the Indiana. I got safe over the river and walked half a mile and got once more where there was hopes of life.

This is a smart lively village about one third Americans and the remainder French. I went to an American house to put up at and was hospitably received and good care taken of me for a man in my situation. All nourishments procured that the town and country could afford. After being there about one week I broke out in boils that I could neither stand, sit, nor lay with any ease and continued on one for three weeks and then began to recruit and got healthy. Formed an acquaintance with the governor of the territory, which

12. This is a reference to the Ambraw River, currently known as the Embarras River, which joins the Wabash south of Vincennes. By his description, the old man's farm was likely in the vicinity of Lawrenceville, Illinois. U.S. Geological Survey, Geographic Names Information System, "Embarras River," January 15, 1980, accessed July 27, 2016, geonames.usgs.gov.

William Henry Harrison, by Rembrandt Peale, c. 1813. Oil on canvas. *Courtesy of the National Portrait Gallery, Smithsonian Institution; gift of Mrs. Herbert Lee Pratt, Jr.*

was our General Harrison. He gave me all the information of the country laid in his power. He fixed upon a route for me to take which was up the Wabash River in pursuit of ore which the Indians had brought him a sample of. He shewed me the ore and it proved to be the rose coloured copper ore.

I fixed on the day to start. The governor got one of the Muscoe Indians to pilot me up the river.[13] We started on the sixteenth of November. The route was about fifty miles, had a settlement for about twenty eight miles, the country very beautiful land, rich and fertile. It appeared very productive. I never saw corn so plenty in any country before and wheat in abundance, the river a gentle current, from sixty to one hundred yards wide. The second day we got into the new purchase made by Governor Harrison in behalf of the United States. This tract is about forty miles square, it is still uninhabited. It would be impossible for me to describe as to the beauties of it, the pleasant situations on the river, the extensive views in these praries which all are impregnated

13. A reference to the Muscoe tribe of Creeks. According to Governor Harrison, between twenty and forty or fifty members of this tribe resided in Indiana Territory, generally in the neighborhood of the Ohio and Mississippi Rivers. William Henry Harrison to Secretary of War William Eustis, February 10, 1810, in Harrison, *Messages and Letters of William Henry Harrison*, 398–99.

with beautiful groves of timber suitable to the planter for fencing and other uses for that is all the farmer has to do in this country to make his fence and plow his field and plant his corn. Then he may expect seventy to eighty bushels to the acre and stock will raise themselves giving them no more then to gentle them and keep them together. This is a true account. Lands now may be purchased at two dollars per acre from Government with four years credit to pay by paying one fourth down. This river is always navigable at all seasons of the year. They go down it into the Ohio and so on to Orleans. They also go up and down it to the Detroit by a small land carriage.

We camped the second night and lived sumptuously on a fat buck the Indian shot. Next morning we started after eating some breakfast. We traveled on till about the middle of the day. We met two Indians of the Miama [Miami] tribe who were hostile with the Muscoes. The Indians stopped and talked a long while. Together with that, they made motions to me to go back, that they would allow nobody to go that way, so finally the pilot told me it was dangerous to go any farther. He would turn back and left the two Indians and we struck our course back. After we were away from these two Indians, he apprised me of the danger we were in, that they might go and get assistance and pursue us. So we traveled with all speed nor did we lie down that night nor next day till night we got to the inhabitants again and next day safe in town. The governor recommended us for traveling all night after turning back.

I spent a couple of weeks in this town in riding through the country and seeing its situation. The town of Vincennes lies ninety leagues up the Wabash, a thriving place and an extensive prarie around the town. The French have a large enclosure according to custom which takes the most part of the prarie, and the remainder lies out in common for the good of their stock and also the citizens of the town find great benefit by it. It contains about four hundred inhabitants now, about one third American. It commands a considerable trade. The country around is thick inhabited land, very productive and settling very rapid. It is twelve miles from the town a north[14] course to White River, a branch of the Wabash and this all will improve. This river holds the best of land. There is a post road through from there to the falls of the Ohio which is one hundred and seventy miles and all a body of land that is tillable and fertile game in that country very plenty.

14. The White River is actually eleven miles *south* of Vincennes.

❦ ❦ ❦

Copper and the Treaty of Fort Wayne

John Maley arrived in Vincennes, Indiana, at a pivotal point in relations between the United States government and Indian tribes in the Northwest Territory. His trip up the Wabash in November 1809 occurred as Governor William Henry Harrison was negotiating the Treaty of Fort Wayne, which ceded approximately 2.9 million acres of Indian lands to the United States. Negotiations were contentious, with the Miamis initially refusing to cede a single foot of territory. Ultimately, Harrison persuaded the Miami, Delaware, and Potawatomi chiefs to sign the treaty on September 30, 1809, ceding territories east of the Wabash River, as well as relinquishing rights to a tract west of the Wabash, west of current day Terre Haute.[15] *In December, the Kickapoo ceded their rights to that tract west of the Wabash, as well as an additional tract between the mouth of Raccoon Creek and the Vermilion River, in an area including current day Newport, Indiana.*

Harrison's negotiation for lands east of the Wabash had been authorized by the president in July 1809,[16] *but the governor exceeded his instructions in also negotiating the cessions west of the Wabash. Harrison justified his negotiation for the Kickapoo tract in a December 10 letter to Secretary of War William Eustis,*[17] *in which he stated that it was "believed to contain a very rich copper mine." Harrison noted that he had received several examples of copper ore from the region, but added that the Indians were "extremely jealous of any search being made for this mine." Harrison further suggested to Eustis that the Congress consider reserving rights to any copper mines in the cession, as he was concerned that there were individuals who were scheming to have the Indians show them the mine and conceal it from the government so that they could buy the property cheaply after land sales were permitted on the tract.*

Maley's account of his meeting with Harrison fits in well with the events unfolding at the time. Maley was an experienced prospector, and it seems likely that the governor viewed his arrival in Vincennes as an opportunity to find out

15. Journal of the Proceedings at the Indian Treaty at Fort Wayne and Vincennes, September 1 to October 27, 1809, in Harrison, *Messages and Letters of William Henry Harrison*, 362–78.

16. Secretary of War to William Henry Harrison, July 15, 1809, in ibid., 356–57.

17. William Henry Harrison to Secretary of War William Eustis, December 10, 1809, in ibid., 396.

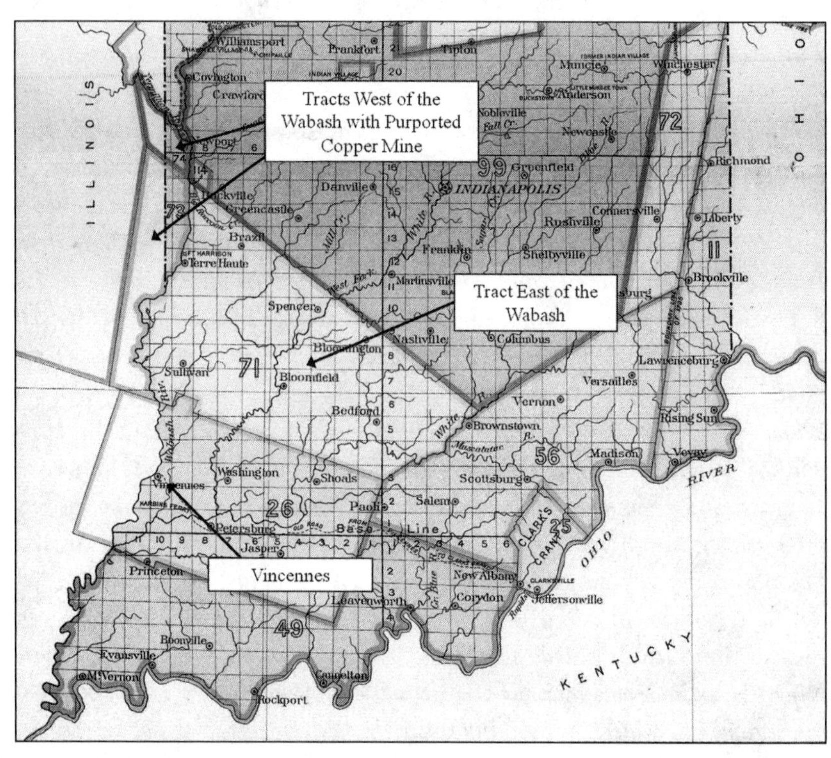

Indian Land Cessions under the 1809 Treaty of Fort Wayne.
From Charles C. Royce, Indian Land Cessions of the United States, in Eighteenth Annual Report of the Bureau of American Ethnology *(Washington, D.C.: Government Printing Office, 1899), Map 19, https://archive.org/details/annualreportofbu182smit.*

where the mine was located. According to Maley, Harrison showed him a sample of copper ore, proposed a route up the Wabash and identified a Muscoe Indian to accompany him. In any event, Maley and his guide were turned back by hostile Miami Indians before reaching their objective. Based on what his guide told him, Maley attributed the confrontation to hostilities between the Miami tribe and the Muscoes. The event, however, may have reflected a lingering resentment on the part of some Miamis to the recent treaty.

A few weeks after his aborted trip, Maley left Vincennes to continue his wanderings, but the events of 1809 would have repercussions for those remaining in the region. The cession of lands under the Fort Wayne treaty was adamantly opposed by the Shawnee leader Tecumseh, and bolstered efforts by his brother, Tenskwatawa (the Prophet) to unite the tribes against American expansion. Escalating tensions ultimately led to Tecumseh's War and Harrison's defeat of the Prophet at the Battle of Tippecanoe in 1811. Continuing British support for the tribes was one of the factors leading to the War of 1812, and Tecumseh was killed in 1813 while fighting with British forces against American forces led by Harrison at the Battle of the Thames. Harrison was elected U.S. president in 1840, but he died of pneumonia shortly after taking office.

Ironically, in spite of Harrison's interest in a potential "rich copper mine," no such mine was ever developed in the tract ceded by the Kickapoo, or indeed anywhere else in the state. There have been samples of copper found, but they all represent "glacial erratics": rocks delivered to Indiana by the continental glaciers that descended from the north during the ice ages.[18] *The samples that so excited Governor Harrison were, therefore, not an indication of an underlying copper deposit in Indiana, but more likely chunks of ore that had been scraped from the rich copper deposits in Michigan. In 1809 neither Harrison nor Maley would have been in a position to perceive this, as it wasn't until the 1840s that geologists began to develop an understanding of the effects of glaciers on the geology of the region.*[19]

18. Email, John C. Steinmetz, Indiana state geologist emeritus and senior scientist, to editor November 5, 2015.

19. Keith Montgomery, "The Development of the Glacial Theory, 1800–1870," Part 1: Introduction, accessed June 8, 2017, http://shipseducation.net/glaciers/Glacial-Theory-History.htm.

Down the Wabash to Shawneetown

Now I fixed myself to descend the Wabash River, bought me a small perogue and put my baggage aboard and took my leave on the fifth of December. I had no company but had procured myself a good rifle for a companion in the wilderness. The current and paddling took me at the rate of fifty miles a day. The first night I got to Coffee Island. A few French inhabitants where there. I made a halt and stayed all night. Soil good and fertile. There is a bluff that comes to the river, makes it a fine situation for building and an island in the river. I saw a number of Indians here of the Shawnee tribe who come here to trade and drink whiskey. A Frenchman here keeps some dry goods and takes their furs in exchange which consist chiefly of muskrat and racoon.

Next morning I started very early, left the high lands down nothing but low bottoms on both sides of the river and thick growths of cane. About an hour by sun, I found some high ground on the south side of the river, made a halt and took up camp in order to take a hunt. I took my rifle and walked round the bluff, found plenty sign of deer and also saw them, but could not get a shot at them. Continued till most night and killed nothing. I thought it prudent to return back, and in my retreat I met with a flock of turkeys and shot one. Took it to my camp and cooked it, had enough left for my breakfast. Laid down and after dark, I was again alarmed by my old companions, the wolves. I then wished them to come nigh so that I could show them the use of my rifle but they took care to keep out of the way. They did not come near enough to me. I tried to get asleep but even the owls made such a noise that it was late in the night before I could get asleep. I at last forgot the owls and knowed no more till daylight. I eat the remainder of my turkey and started, soon lost sight of the high ground.

The river makes no material changes in its current, no rapids but a gentle stream, the bottoms very rich soil. The growth of timber is the black walnut, over culp, hackberry, poplar and with the sugar tree in abundance. I saw nothing new till after the middle of the day, came to another bluff on the same side of the river. One came to it and discovered their to be stone, which was not common on the Wabash river. I made a halt and found the stone to be uncommon heavy. Broke one to see the inside and found there to be solid ore of sulphur intermixed with piritesy iron. I saw rocks of this description that would have weighed several tons. I walked down the river and found in the bank a strata of slate of about two feet thick and then a strata of an inferior kind of stone coal. I took some of the curiosities with me started after tarrying for about an hour, soon lost sight of the bluff again and found the river and bottom not much different, only heavier cane breaks.

Floated on till almost sundown. I came in sight of a plantation, came to it and made a stop. This man by the name of Robison seemed to enjoy himself there like a nabob, had plenty of every thing round him. He told me he had lived there but five years and all the stock of hogs was an old sow with six pigs when he first came to that place. He told me he has upwards of four hundred head. He shewed me some that would weigh nearly three hundred weight. I stayed there all night. I was then about one hundred and ten miles from the Ohio river. I rested very comfortable that night, took breakfast in the morning and started. Saw nothing uncommon that day but made the best of my way down the river, found several inhabitants that day but made no stop till night. I again camped at a home, the inhabitants of which were very friendly. I got plenty to eat and some spirits to drink and a good bed to lie in. Took breakfast in the morning and started down the river again. It was settled on the river for a good distance, nothing material to note that day.

Got to a house at night on a high bluff on the north side of the river made a halt and tarried all night. This was called the bone bank and well it might be for there were human bones there to be found in cart loads which washed out of the bank, the bank being perpendicular you could see the place where the bones washed from this bank was in a bend of the river where the whole force of the river runs against it still keeps washing away the bank with that the bones tumbled out and also different kind of vessels of different shape and sizes the rise of them we cannot account for some like foot glass and others like crucibles and the composition appeared to be of burnt oyster shells not pulverised very fine and a white clay. This bank was of a red colour and the spot where the bones were washed out was a black soil seemingly a hole dug about ten feet deep and twenty feet wide and in that space you could pull out the bones and by digging they are found in grate abundance, small bones, thigh bones, leg bones and finally every bone belonging to the human body. None of the natives or French can give any account of this circumstance.[20]

20. Maley here provides an early description of the "Bone Bank archaeological site," the location of a Mississippian village occupying the mouth of the Wabash, ca. A.D. 1400–1700. First identified in an 1807 land survey, Bone Bank was the first archaeological site excavated in Indiana in 1828. "Bone Bank Archaeological Research," accessed June 7, 2016, www.indiana.edu/~archaeo/bone_bank/.

Next morning I started for Shawnee Town, twenty miles to go, the first town I landed at when I came down the Ohio River. I got there safe that night, which was the fifteenth of December and weather cold. I then concluded to take my winter quarters there and in the spring start again in order to complete my journey which I was determined to fulfill, that was to explore the country in general west of the Mississippi to know the extent of every river emptying itself into the Mississippi as use is second nature. I then began to get used to traveling. I thought it no difficulty. I took my board in Shawnee Town for the winter. Billiards was the only thing I could amuse myself at.

Shawneetown, Illinois

John Maley passed through Shawneetown in 1808 on his way to Kaskaskia, and he returned there during the winter of 1809–10. The settlement, now referred to as Old Shawneetown, is located on the Illinois side of the Ohio River, approximately ten miles downstream of the Wabash. The site of a Shawnee village during the 1740s, it had been abandoned by that tribe decades prior to Maley's visit.[21] *It is not clear when the first white settlers moved to the area, but it was probably around 1800, and a ferry across the Ohio may have been established there as early as 1802.*[22] *Maley's description of the town is brief—a place of small cabins but considerable business, including at least one billiard table.*

Another traveler, F. Cuming, who passed through Shawneetown in 1808, provided a similar but more detailed description.[23] *He noted that there were only twenty-four cabins in the town, but that, with several trading boats at the landing, it was the busiest place he had seen west of Pittsburgh. Because both the town site and the adjacent salt works were owned by the U.S. government, the inhabitants did not own the land and were therefore unwilling to invest much in improving their cabins. Cuming suggested that if the residents were allowed to purchase their lots, Shawneetown would immediately become one of the most considerable towns on the river.*

21. Caldwell, "Shawneetown," 204.

22. The Goodspeed Publishing Company, *History of Gallatin, Saline, Hamilton, Franklin and Williamson Counties, Illinois*, 22.

23. Cuming, "Cuming's Tour to the Western Country (1807–1809)," 271.

Old Shawneetown.
Bank building *(center right)* is one of the few remaining structures.
Photograph by the editor.

It was not many years after Maley's stay that the town began to live up to its potential. The first bank of Illinois Territory was established there in 1816 by an act of the Illinois legislature, and Shawneetown was later the location of one of the branches of the State Bank of Illinois. The town was also prominent enough to host the Marquis de Lafayette during his tour of the United States in 1825.

Ultimately, the town's location on the banks of the Ohio served as its downfall. As early as 1819, one observer noted, "As the lava of Mount Aetna can not dislodge (the human animal) from the cities which it has repeatedly ravaged, so the Ohio, with its annual overflow, is unable to wash away the inhabitants of Shawneetown."[24] *Shawneetown suffered floods in 1832, 1847, 1853, 1858, 1859, and 1867. A levee was built following the 1867 flood, but it was breached in 1875, 1882, and 1883, when the waters carried away 108 houses in the town. In 1884 the levee was raised and extended four and one half miles following the work.*[25] *Despite continuing efforts to protect the city, it was completely inundated in the great flood of 1937, and the town was relocated several miles away on higher ground. Only a few buildings remain at the original site.*

24. The Goodspeed Publishing Company, *History of Gallatin, Saline, Hamilton, Franklin and Williamson Counties, Illinois,* 103.

25. Ibid., 103–5.

CHAPTER 3 ❦ *January–February 1810*

A Trip up the Tennessee

I being wearied of being confined their, I made up a party to go up the Tennessee River and so among the Chickasaw Indians to see what I could discover there. We prepared ourselves six men in number, took a keel bottom boat and every necessary that was wanted for a long voyage. We started on the seventh of January 1810, took down the Ohio River forty miles to Smithland, a small village at the junction of Cumberland and the Ohio Rivers. This town is a place for deposit for goods that come down the Ohio and also up the Mississippi as they cannot ascend Cumberland River at all seasons.[1] This is but twelve miles above the Tennessee River.

Went on next day and turned our course up that beautiful stream Tennessee River. This river is about two hundred yards wide at the mouth. It is in appearance the handsomest stream in the world for its gentleness of current, rich bottom lands on both sides of the river. This river runs mostly east and west. On the south side, the lands are held by the Chickasaw Indians and the north by the State of Kentucky. Eight miles up comes in a small river called Clarkes River on the south side.[2] We took up this river about twelve miles, then it was not navigable any further for our boat. We left our boat and took up it by land, found game very plenty. Killed several deer, turkeys also very plenty. We found in the banks of this river stone coal, sulphur and the kidney form pyrites of different kinds.

1. Cuming, who stopped in Smithland in May 1808, counted ten or a dozen cabins, two stores, two taverns, and a billiard table. He noted, "[O]n the whole, it is a miserable place, and a traveler will scarcely think himself repaid by a sight of the Cumberland, for stopping at Smithland." Cuming, "Cuming's Tour to the Western Country (1807–1809)," 275.

2. According to modern maps, Clarks River is only about four miles southeast of Paducah and two miles from the Tennessee's current junction with the Ohio.

Going one day's journey, we returned to Tennessee River, steered up, found the still gentle stream to continue and not many bendings. We discovered many signs of Indians and saw some. They told us they were Creeks. The third day came to another river[3] on the same side of the latter went up. That we knew no name for it; we called it Knife River for one of our men lost his pocket knife in it. Went as far as we could which was not over ten miles then struck camp rested that night and next morning we took it by land. Left some to guard the boat for fear of the Indians. We steered our course up Knife River the soil is but thin. We killed a very large bear the first day and feasted on him at night. Saw nothing worth taking notice of this day. Next morning started again soon killed another bear, they were very plenty, but deer we did not see so plenty. I found a mountain of iron ore which some day may be very valuable. There is a stream of water here sufficiently large enough for forge and furnace and well timbered.

We that day returned to our boat and next day took down Knife River again into the Tennessee and followed up that. Sometimes went into the country, found the soil vary from good to bad, cane brakes on both sides of the river, no inhabitants at all on this river, but saw plenty of Indians chiefly of the Creek nation, as this there hunting ground. They camped on the bank of the river and there dried their skins which they had very plenty, both deer and bearskins. They also had plenty of honey which they find in abundance in that country. They render the beeswax and bear's oil for market.

Still continued up the river, found a bluff came to the river on the south side. It had a perpendicular bank of about one hundred feet high and mineral water issuing out of the bank for a great distance along it. The virtues of this water was such that I saw whole trees petrified in a perfect stone bark and all stone. We split up a tree which was easy done, found it to be of an excellent bone grit found it to be the sycamore tree, by some called the buttonwood, and it was all one kind that was petrified. There also was plenty of copperas made by the sun's drying the water away, kidney form pirites in abundance, which tumbled out of the bank. We left our stone until we returned.

Went on several days, nothing more curious, passed the mouth of Duck River, which comes in from Tennessee. This river has great bodies of good land on it. Continued up Tennessee River until we got to George Colbert's on

3. Based on the number of days traveled, this was likely Big Sandy River, which currently forms a part of Kentucky Lake.

the great road from Orleans, Natchez and the Mobile country to Nashville, Tennessee. This George Colbert is a quarter-breed of the Chikasaw nation, lives in stile, has an excellent frame house well finished off inside and out and other out houses, keeps stores of all kinds suitable for the Indian trade. Keeps the ferry and entertainment for travelers, takes money by hands full daily, also cultivates an extensive farm, owns upwards of fifty slaves, has a full bred native for his wife, has daughters—one married to a white man whom he gives seven hundred dollars a year as an overseer and tend the bar. The squaws still dress in their Indian garb with their leggings and blankets round them. Colbert himself wears the best of broadcloth for a coat which is satoot [?] fashion altogether but will not wear breaches. Generally a good beaver hat on his head.

Seven miles out lives his brother Levi Colbert on a creek called Buzzard Roost. Lives in stile the same as his brother, still a larger house, entertains a great number of travelers, cultivates a larger farm and owns more slaves. He is a very sociable, conversant man, raises abundance of corn which is always a dollar a bushel to him. Keeps a good table, charges for a meals victuals twenty cents, has two wives in the house with him. This takes three beds to hold them. They all sleep separate but in one room. These women never trouble themselves with the affairs of the house no more than if they did not belong their. The cookery and management is altogether left to their slaves, who are very independent.

I returned to the river and next morning returned down the river. Stopped at the copperas bank, gathered a quantity of copperas and took in as much of these petrified stone as we could conveniently get and pursued down the river and in four days we got safe into the Ohio again.

George and Levi Colbert

Maley's trip up the Tennessee provided an opportunity to meet brothers George and Levi Colbert, two prominent figures in the history of the region and of the Chickasaw Nation. They were sons of James Colbert, a Scottish trader from the Carolinas, and Noe, one of his three Indian wives.[4] *James Colbert, who had begun*

4. Smithey, "Transformation," 34.

trading with the Chickasaw in the 1740s, assisted the Chickasaw and their British allies in confrontations with the Choctaw, who were allied with the French. In 1783, during the American Revolutionary War, he led a Chickasaw attack on Arkansas Post, which was under Spanish sovereignty at the time.[5]

George Colbert was born about 1764 and, at the time of Maley's visit, served as the "Tisho Minko" for the Chickasaw nation. In this role, he was advisor to the chief and played a central role in negotiating treaties with the United States. These included the 1801 Treaty of Chickasaw Bluffs, which allowed the United States to widen the Natchez Trace to accommodate wagon trade, and the 1805 Treaty of the Chickasaw Nation, which ceded lands north and east of the Tennessee River. George Colbert was considered a shrewd negotiator, not only on behalf of the Chickasaw Nation, but with respect to his own interests. In the Treaty of Chickasaw Bluffs, he successfully insisted that operation of inns and ferries along the Natchez Trace be reserved for Chickasaws, a move that both protected his own ferry business and provided commercial opportunities for Chickasaw-owned businesses, limiting American intrusion.[6] *George Colbert had two wives: one was from the prominent Minko clan and daughter of the previous Tisho Minko; the other was daughter of Doublehead, a prominent Cherokee war chief.*[7]

Levi Colbert, at the time of Maley's visit, had been more focused on commercial interests. He had four wives and a number of successful businesses. Two wives lived at his plantation in Long Town, where he also owned a salt spring and grist mill. Another lived in a home he built in present-day Okolona, Mississippi, where he raised livestock. His fourth wife lived at his house at Buzzard Roost, where he operated a "stand" or inn for travelers. Levi also operated ferries on Bear Creek and on the Tombigbee River.[8] *Levi would not emerge as an influential Chickasaw leader until after 1814, but he did play an important leadership role during removal of the Chickasaw to Oklahoma in the 1830s.*[9]

Although their father, James Colbert, had supported the British during the Revolutionary War, the Chickasaw were firm allies of the United States during the Creek War and the War of 1812. Following Maley's visit, the Chickasaws in 1811 rejected the request of the Shawnee leader, Tecumseh, to join his confederation

5. Arnold, *Colonial Arkansas, 1686–1804*, 111.
6. Smithey, "Transformation," 40–47.
7. Ibid., 35.
8. Ibid., 66.
9. Ibid., 65–69.

to fight American encroachment on Indian land. In 1813 George Colbert raised an army of 250 warriors to fight under Andrew Jackson, and recruited another 230 warriors in March 1814.[10]

Notwithstanding their support of the United States, the Chickasaw came under unrelenting pressure from Jackson and other American officials to cede their lands and remove themselves to west of the Mississippi.[11] *In 1816, in treaty negotiations carried out at George Colbert's house,*[12] *they agreed to sell 408,000 acres of land north and south of the Tennessee River and east of the Tombigbee. Subsequent treaties in 1818 and 1832 resulted in the cession of all Chickasaw lands east of the Mississippi and removal of the tribe to Oklahoma.*

DEPOSITED OUR STONE and crossed the river to the Illinois territory, entered up a small river called Cash River[13] about forty miles above the junction of the Ohio and Mississippi and twelve miles above Fort Massach [Massac], a garrison kept by the United States in pieceable times. Boats going up and down the river are all hailed at this place to give an account where they are from and which way they are bound, with an account of their loading and reported to the commanding officer.

Fort Massac

In early 1810, Maley and his companions stopped at Fort Massac in southern Illinois, to report their travel to authorities. The post, on a high bluff overlooking the lower Ohio River, had been a strategic site for more than fifty years. The French built Fort de l'Ascension on the site in 1757,[14] *and renamed it Fort Massiac,*

10. Ibid., 50–51.
11. Ibid., 76–86.
12. Ibid., 61.
13. Maley is referring to the Cache River, whose mouth was close to Mound City, approximately thirty miles below Massac, not twelve miles above it. It appears he may have conflated his notes—the Cache River is approximately twelve miles above the junction of Ohio and Mississippi, and Fort Massac is approximately forty miles up the Ohio.
14. *Fort Massac: An Historic Site.*

after the French Minister of the Marine, two years later.[15] *During the French and Indian War, the fort helped thwart British encroachment into French-held Illinois and served to secure French supply lines between Illinois and Vincennes and Fort Duquesne (at present-day Pittsburgh).*[16] *Illinois was ceded to Britain following the French and Indian War, but in 1765, before the British could take possession of the fort, the Chickasaw Indians burned the empty stockade to the ground. The British anglicized the name to "Massac" but never rebuilt the fort. That decision left British territories south of Detroit lightly defended, and during the Revolutionary War, American forces led by George Rogers Clark entered Illinois via nearby Massac Creek and successfully captured Kaskaskia, Prairie du Rocher, and Cahokia.*[17]

Following the Revolutionary War, Illinois came under control of the United States, and President George Washington ordered the fort rebuilt in 1794, in response to increased tension with Indian tribes in the region. Fort Massac later served to defend against Spanish and French efforts to reestablish their influence east of the Mississippi,[18] *and in 1796 the fort fired a cannon across the bow of a Spanish gunboat to halt its travel up the river.*[19] *In addition to its military importance, Fort Massac was a port of entry into the United States and served as a customs office for the growing number of goods moving on the Ohio River from 1799 to 1807.*[20]

At the time of Maley's visit, six years after the Louisiana Purchase, the fort no longer served as a buffer to Spanish and French influence in the Mississippi valley and had ceased collecting customs. As reported by Maley, however, the fort was still monitoring traffic on the Ohio, and it served as a base of operations for the region. Fort Massac had furnished volunteers for the Lewis and Clark expedition, as well as Zebulon Pike's two expeditions to the headwaters of the Mississippi and to Colorado. Also, Aaron Burr reportedly met with General James Wilkinson at Massac in 1805 to discuss their plot to set up a separate empire in the Southwest. In 1806 Burr and his "army" of a hundred men were temporarily detained at

15. Caldwell, "Fort Massac during the French and Indian War," 100–19.
16. Ibid., 109–10.
17. *Fort Massac State Park.*
18. Caldwell, "Fort Massac: The American Frontier Post, 1778–1805," 265–81.
19. *Fort Massac: An Historic Site*, 3. The Spanish government protested (the vessel was reportedly flying a flag of truce), but the fort's commander, Captain Zebulon Pike, considered the incident a test of the fort's defenses.
20. Ibid.

Replica of Fort Massac overlooking the Ohio River.
Photograph by the editor.

the fort.[21] *Based on the description of an 1808 visitor, the fort was in the form of a square, formed of pickets with a bastion at each corner. Approximately sixty acres of the surrounding plain was cleared to provide training grounds for the men stationed there, as well as to prevent a surprise attack. In addition to fifty men stationed there, Massac's defenses consisted of a small brass howitzer and a two-pound carronade.*[22]

Two years following Maley's visit, the fort would be damaged by the New Madrid earthquakes of 1811–12 but subsequently repaired. During the War of 1812, the post was reinforced in response to concerns of a possible British invasion of the Mississippi valley. By 1814, however, with the British loss of Detroit, the threat from the north had diminished, and the post was abandoned.[23] *Today, a*

21. Ibid., 3–4. Without any orders to arrest them, Burr and his men were released by the post's commander.

22. Cuming, "Cuming's Tour to the Western Country (1807–1809)," 276–77.

23. *Fort Massac: An Historic Site*, 4–5.

reconstruction of the fort is maintained next to the original site at Fort Massac State Park, near Metropolis, Illinois.

Exploring the Cache River

Going up Cash River, we found the soil exceeding fertile, several settlements on the river. Went up the river about fifteen miles and could get no farther. A party of us started by land to see the situation of the country and made discoveries. We left some to guard the boat. We traveled one day up the river, found deer very plenty. The river then got to be very small, nearly at the head waters and country very level and soil rich. Next day we shifted our course which was SW, traveled on through a beautiful country, found two large ponds or lakes and covered over with ducks, geese and swan, which is a snow white fowl much resembling the goose but three times as large. Their neck of an uncommon length. We could not get a shot at any of them. We killed deer and turkeys occasionally. Traveled two days and came to high grounds. Land not so good, only in creek bottoms, which was very good with thick cane brakes.

Traveling on a ridge, we found an ancient digging. It must have been done many years ago by the growth of the timber in the digging. They have occupied several acres, the shafts one against another as near as could be dug and some apparently very deep. By what I could discover it was a lead mine. Left this and traveled on still on extensive high ridges. We found a furnace in appearance, all tumbled to pieces but could not see the size of it but could perceive that the stone had been burnt. We still rose higher on ridges till at last we got sight of the Mississippi river. To go further on our course then was needless to go in the Mississippi bottoms so we shifted our course back to our own boat and the third day got safe back to our men. Brought a couple of good fat turkeys with us, which we feast on that night and next morning we started down the river and soon got into the Ohio again and crossed over and took in our stone and then made our way for Shawnee town where we started from. We got there the second day which was the twelfth of February.

Cache River

Following his return down the Tennessee, Maley describes a short trip up the "Cash River" in southern Illinois, "about 40 miles above the Mississippi and 12 miles above Fort Massac." There is no river fitting that description, but it seems clear that Maley has conflated his distances and is referring to the Cache River, which at the time joined the Ohio about one and a half miles south of present-day Mound City, Illinois, and about seven miles above the Mississippi. (It is Fort Massac that lies forty miles above the Mississippi.) With the construction of flood-control levees in the area, the Cache was diverted directly to the Mississippi south of the town of Cache, and the original lower river channel is now a quiet slough, connected to the Ohio via a culvert.

It is difficult to reconstruct exactly where Maley traveled up the Cache River. If his journal is accurate, the crew took the keelboat about fifteen miles upstream, which would be close to the mouth of Boar Creek, one and a half miles southeast of Sandusky, Illinois. Maley and his companions then went upstream on foot for one day where they approached the headwaters of the river, which may have been in the vicinity of current day Cypress, Illinois. They then turned southwest, passing by two large ponds covered with ducks, geese, and swan. There are several locations that fit this description, including Morgan Pond and Swan Pond, three miles east of current-day Dongola, or several ponds three miles southwest of the town, including Lenee Pond.

The "ancient digging" that Maley found is something of a mystery. He described finding several acres of shafts, some quite deep, on the top of a ridge, and concluded that they had been lead mines. The most likely explanation is that these were prehistoric chert quarries. From ca. A.D. *900 to 1500, Native Americans mined a particularly high-quality chert from pits in the area of Mill Creek, Illinois. This stone was highly prized because it occurred in large slabs and could be chipped into large stone tools. Mill Creek hoes and other stone tools have been found at archaeological sites across much of the eastern United States.*[24] *If Maley was describing these quarries, he and his companions would likely have been just west of the present-day town of Mill Creek.*

It is also possible that Maley found the remains of an old lead mine, particularly given his description of an ancient furnace. However, there is no record of lead

24. Email, Mary McCorvie, U.S. Forest Service, to editor March 8, 2016.

mines in this region of southern Illinois.[25] *In the 1840s several small lead mines were developed near Rosiclare, approximately forty miles east of Dongola.*[26] *There have also been reports of pioneer-era lead mining near the Delta Fault, a geologic feature about five miles west of Elco, but these reports cannot be confirmed.*[27] *If Maley, in fact, found a lead mine, it presumably would have been developed by the French and abandoned either in the 1720s, after richer deposits were developed in Missouri, or following France's cession of its Illinois territory to England at the end of the French and Indian War.*

Kentucky and Tennessee on Horseback

I rested a few days and took a notion of seeing Kentucky, as it was too early in the season yet to start on my Louisiana voyage. I hired a horse for one month and took across the river into the state of Kentucky, took my course for Russellville in Logan County, which was one hundred and twenty miles. Passed by a salt works called High Land Lick.[28] They draw their water out of a well about thirty feet deep, make beautiful white salt, sell it at one dollar per bushel. The country pretty well settled and very good land. I went by Muhlenburgh Court House, a small village containing about one dozen buildings, a good house of entertainment.[29] Stayed all night and in two days more got to Russellville, a smart lively town with three houses of entertainment, seven stores and some very full ones, about two hundred inhabitants. The buildings are good, some elegant brick buildings.

This is but forty miles from Nashville, Tennessee. I started and rode there in one day. Here I saw the most fashion I had seen since I left Philadelphia. Nashville is situated on the Cumberland River about one hundred and fifty miles up from the Ohio. It stands on an exceedingly high bluff which is a

25. Telephone conversation, Dr. Donald G. Mikulic, Illinois State Geological Survey, October 29, 2015.

26. Smith, *History of Southern Illinois*, 19.

27. Devera et al., from notes contained on "Geologic Map."

28. According to Meyer, this was an important salt lick about six miles west of Dixon, Kentucky. The road from Highland Lick to Shawneetown ran through Henshaw, Kentucky. Meyer, *Indian Trails of the Southeast*, 804–5.

29. The Muhlenberg County courthouse at the time of Maley's visit was a log structure located in current day Greenville, Kentucky. Rothert, *A History of Muhlenberg County*, 45–46.

solid ledge of limestone. The country adjoining Nashville is exceeding fertile and well inhabited. Streets are laid out in squares. The court house stands in the center of the town with the fronts of the buildings of three squares facing it. The buildings are elegant, chiefly brick, some very full stores and sell by the wholesale.

Stayed two days and started for Galantine twenty four miles from Nashville.[30] Got there the first day, rode through rich and fertile country, very thick inhabited. Galantine has but few buildings, but an elegant court house, it being the seat of justice for Sumney County. I left that and steered for Lexington, Kentucky, which was about one hundred and fifty miles all through an old settled country, elegant improved farms. Crossed Green River and Kentucky River both of them but small rivers. Kentucky River is worthy of remark. It is seemingly cut through a solid rock. It has no low grounds on it; the cliffs on both sides of the river are perpendicular not less than four or five hundred feet high, a solid limestone. It is difficult to get down to the ferry. There are but few places that are practicable for roads to the river. I crossed at a ferry, they call it Shawnee Run, where a creek comes in by that name.[31] After crossing I ascended that dreadfull cliff; it appeared as if I would tumble back every minute. Got safe up and got into a fine level country. Arrived at Lexington that day, put up at the hotel. I was much pleased with the town to see the order and regularity of the citizens, a place of industry and business. A large town and wholesale merchants. I shall not be so particular as to describe much about this place, as time will not admit of it.

I want to return so as to fit myself for my object in view, where I can be of service not to ever person but to thousands and to the curious agreeable passtime when they, thousands of miles off, read sitting comfortable by their fire sides. When, in one evening, they may know all that I have experienced in years with one fourth part of my time at the risk of my life and what is it worth to the rising generation. We all know that this new world will all be filled up and now is the time for youth to adventure, buy lands instead of paying taxes. It will be but a trifle of land, out of the body the United States holds, to pay the publick debt.

I returned to Shawnee Town, where I took my journey from, and I then began to look out to start for my Louisiana voyage. I wanted to take the

30. Gallatin, Tennessee, the county seat of Sumner County.
31. Mundy's Landing, about seven miles north-northeast of Harrodsburg.

best advantage of the country I could so as to take it all before me. Up the Missouri and at the lead mines, I have been seen the country, chiefly all as far as the head waters of the river St Francois [St. Francis]. Now my object was to see that river lower down, then every river below that emptying itself into the Mississippi, so I found a boat that was a going to start from that place to Cape Girardeau, a small village on the Mississippi about sixty miles up from the mouth of the Ohio. And so I prepared myself for to start with that boat. I bought myself some articles suitable for an Indian trade, thinking it might be of service to me. Perhaps the Indians might be more friendly to me by furnishing them with such articles as they stand in need of.

CHAPTER 4 ❦ *Spring of 1810*

Southeast Missouri and the Big Spring

So on the fifth of March 1810, I started down the Ohio to the mouth and took up the Mississippi and landed safe at Cape Girardieu, which we reached in five days from Shawnee Town. There I landed my baggage and looked around for information, mentioning my object in view. There I was informed that it was about seventy miles to the River Currents [Current River],[1] waters of White River, and that I would strike it in a proper place almost at the head of navigation. This place is situated on a high eminence, a great prospect of the Mississippi which makes it exceeding pleasant. It lies seventy miles above Lancely Grace or New Madrid where they have suffered much by the earth quake,[2] fifty miles below St Genevieve and about the same distance to the lead mines, and a rich and fertile country around it and thickly inhabited. This makes it a place of considerable trade. The country produces a great deal of wheat and the best streams for mills in the world, which is a rare thing in these countries. They manufacture a great quantity of flour, and pork and beef they have in abundance. This all comes to this place from whence it goes to different parts here.

I had to buy me a horse in order to carry my baggage, fitted myself and started. Had a very good road to travel. Had a good settlement to travel through, fared well. I found them chiefly all to be Dutch descendents from Pennsylvania, crossed several fine streams of water running rapid and very clear. Soil very fertile and the country very productive in wheat. I saw mills there with all necessary machinery in it for manufacturing flour. About thirty

1. Maley consistently calls this "River a Currents," presumably from the French name.
2. Maley is referring to the series of earthquakes that struck the region in 1811–12, almost two years after his visit.

miles my settlement gave out as there was only now and then a house. I had not to lay out at night. My road was only a foot trace. The fourth day, a little after the middle, I discovered ore of some kind which I examined and according to my judgement, I took it to be silver ore. Where I found this was in a branch, but not much water in it at present. By searching I found several pieces.

The country here was very broken, the timber chiefly yellow and pitch pine. I had rode all that day without a house, but according to directions, I thought I was near a settlement which was on River a Currents. There were three families there, the first settlers on that river, so I went on and in about two miles, reached the river and a house on the bank of the river. There I saw a river that exceeded all that ever I beheld before, the stream so clear and current so rapid without any thing to impede its progress. It runs down hill as it were at the rate of seven or eight miles an hour. Here I made a stop and, pleased with the prospect; this man that lived here lived in plenty. He raised plenty of corn, hogs raised themselves and game of all kinds in surplus even the buffaloe fish without end and fowl of all description. The soil is only good on the river and that over good and very large bottoms. This river abounds with bever, otter and muskrat. The woods abounds with honey, every thing to a man's hand. How could a man live easier than to live in such a country that five acres of land will bread a family of ten in number and the land only requires half the labour that lands in general do? How may a man enjoy himself, nothing to do but to recreate himself with his dogs and guns? This way he can both divert and support himself.

Here I fitted myself for to go down this river into White River and so up that. At this place, I fell in company with a man that followed the business of hunting, trapping of beaver. He was much pleased to take this route of discovery along with me, so I took him in as he was furnished with a good rifle and plenty of ammunition and a dozen of steel traps. We then set out and built us a pirogue, made it very light and thin that two hands could almost carry it. I sold my horse to this man that lived here, took pay in beaver skins. After we were all ready, in order to start I then had to go and see that great curiosity, the big spring, which is big indeed. Now I wanted to see that silver ore again to see if I could find out which course the vein run as this spring was five miles up the river and we had to go with the canoe.

I told the two men that I would meet them about five miles up the river and I would rather go by land and might perhaps kill something. It was

The Current River, near Big Spring, Missouri.
Photograph by the editor.

agreed on and I started with my rifle on my shoulder. I would not let them know my discoveries of this silver ore but I started immediately for this place, which was about two miles. When I came there, I viewed the place well and found some more of this ore. I discovered which way the vain run and followed it on across high hills and in every valley I could find plenty of the ore and I followed it in a strait direction three miles, which took me right to the river, in a tremendous mountain. The foot of it went down to the river but it was almost too steep to descend but still I had to venture which was difficult. I had to hold fast by the bushes so as not to tumble down the mountain.

When I got about halfway down I saw a large hole in the face of the mountain. I was curious to go and see it although it was difficult to get there. I made it out and, behold, it was a large and spacious cave and the entrance of it was about thirty feet wide and about fifteen feet high with an ovel roof cut in solid rock. It went in upon a level for a good distance and then made a short of set of down the river. I turned the elbow but turned again it being too dark to see to travel so strange a road. I went out and found some pine notts [knots], split them with my hatchet and went in with a torch in my hand. I saw numbers of beds of animals. After turning the corner again, I was met in a great surprise by three bears that ran with great violence in order to shun me. I suppose they never saw such a sight before as to see fire in that cave. I was very suspicious thinking there might be more. Kept a good look out and my gun in readiness, went on in that direction about a quarter of a mile, and the roof getting much lower and to look before me it appeared as if it was all in fire, the tags and icicles hanging down which was a hard composition of nitre and alum. The way they were formed was by the continual dripping of the water from the roof of the cave. It is only in places this composition is to be seen. By going a small distance farther, I had to stop for I came to a lake of water which seemed to be a general thing over the cave. I took stones and flung as far as I could but I could hear it sound in the water. The sound went a great distance in that cave so I had to give out my journey and turned back. Saltpetre may be made here in any quantity.

I got out safe and took down to the river. Got there I hollowed for my men who were waiting in suspense. They answered, thought I would come down to them, but it was out of my power for the bank was so that I could not walk down the river. I stayed a long while hollowing before they would come. They at last came to me. They thought some accident had happened to me but I told them my discovery and my meeting those bears. They then had to go and see the curiosity but they found it a difficult piece of work to get up that bank but they gratified their curiosity.

We took boat and started down the river to see that great curiosity called the big spring. It was about two miles down which did not take long till we got to another part of the river as large as the one we came down but by looking up the stream I saw the source. I saw tremendous spouting and foaming of water that it was dreadfull to behold and a perpendicular cliff of not less than five hundred feet high and the spring rushing out at the bottom of this cliff.[3] Dreadfull to draw nigh to it, the water perhaps fifteen or twenty feet deep and so clear that you can see the bottom as if there was nothing in the way. You may go close up to the rock by keeping out of the

3. Big Spring, a few miles south of Van Buren, Missouri

way of the whirlpools it makes. It makes a person shiver of cold to be their any time. You cannot hear one another speak it makes such a roaring.

I must tell you that fish you can see in any quantity some larger then I shall mention. Perhaps you might doubt my varacity. After being satisfied we returned down the river and go home that night. We went a gigging fish, took a torch.[4] One to stear the canoe one hold the torch and the other gigs the fish and it did not take us long before we had fish enough. We soon returned home with our loads, cleaned the fish that night and in the morning feasted on them. Take notice of this ye that are strangers to this, if you should wish to enjoy such times, be not dismayed. A little money will take you there and when you are there you want none. Now is the time to embrace the opportunity.

❦ ❦ ❦

Big Spring, Missouri

Maley's description of "the big spring" is one of the earliest written accounts of Big Spring, Missouri, located approximately four miles south of Van Buren, in Carter County. According to the National Park Service,[5] *Big Spring is the largest spring in Missouri and one of the largest in the world, with an average flow rate of 286 million gallons per day. As described by Maley, the spring's outflow boils out of the base of a bluff and creates its own tributary, which joins the Current River approximately a thousand feet downstream. While Maley may exaggerate a bit (e.g., the bluff is only three hundred feet—not five hundred—high) his description is generally accurate. The water does create something of a whirlpool on exiting the mountain, and it remains between 55 and 58°F year round. The site has continued to enchant visitors since Maley's visit; it became Missouri's first state park in 1964, and it is currently managed by the National Park Service as part of the Ozark National Scenic Riverways.*

In addition to Big Spring, it is possible to track with some precision Maley's other finds in the area. He explored a cave on a steep hillside approximately two miles above the spring. According to a local expert, his description matches that

4. "Gigging" is the art of spearing fish instead of catching them with a hook and line. Generally done at night with the help of a light, it is still a popular sport in the clear, shallow rivers of Missouri.

5. National Park Service, *Big Spring*.

of Granite Quarry Cave, east of the river opposite the existing campground.[6] *The "granite" quarry located near the cave may, in fact, be a vein of hard quartzite, possibly the vein of ore that Maley followed across the countryside before arriving at the river.*

❦ ❦ ❦

Exploring the Current River

I was not satisfied till I had seen the head of this river so I prepared myself and started up the river took our traps in order to catch beaver if they should come to hand. We went one days journey and made a halt in order to explore more of the country. In general the course of this river is nearly WNW. I took off on the north side and ranged the woods. Found the country very broken lands very poor the timber chiefly pine. Found vast mountain of iron ore and fine brisk running streams of water, some bodies of good land on the water courses. Game is very plenty. We killed a bufaloe, cut the meat off the thighs and legs and throwed the bones in the fire and cooked the marrow which is very luscious eating. Traveled on three days and then found that I was coming near the lead mines, woods that I have gone over before, so we turned back to our pirogue where we reached in three days. All here was well. We then took up the river another days journey, found great sign of beaver, set our traps that night, catcht three beaver and an otter.

I then concluded to leave my partner here to catch more beaver and I would go and explore the country south of this river, which would give me knowledge of the lands lying betwixt this and White River which was the next river. I started, found the land the same as we found the north side of the river, all a piney and broken country, only good land on the water courses. I traveled on till the water run on to White River.[7] I went no further south, but struck my course west in order to strike higher up the river. I found plenty of game. I killed a deer occasionally. I traveled on till I thought I was nearly at the head of this river. I then shifted my course down a small water course which proved to be as large as any of the branches when they came together the country

6. Dr. James E. Price, interview, October 7, 2015.

7. Maley apparently crossed over into the watershed of the Eleven Points River, possibly around Winona, Missouri, and mistakenly assumed he was on the waters of the White River.

Big Spring, Missouri.
Photograph by the editor.

one general thing on that river. Took down the river and came to an Indian encampment. They were of the Shawnee tribe.[8] They had a great many beaver skins, otter, bear and deer skins in abundance. They were very friendly to me. I told them I had some goods down the river I would trade with them if they would go down the river with me so they readily concluded, loaded their pirogue with beaver, which was the only kind of skins I would take.

We started down and the second day got to my companion. He had catcht seven beaver and four otters in my absence. We then took down the river altogether. In one day we arrived where my goods were. I made a very advantageous trade with the Indians. I had articles that suited them well, which was red striped silk handkerchiefs. They are very fond of red. They took vermilion to paint themselves, small looking glasses and I got all their beaver.

8. According to local experts, this Shawnee village was located at the mouth of McCormack Hollow on the Jacks Fork River near Alley Spring. Dr. James E. Price, email to editor, October 12, 2015.

Next day they returned up the river and I fitted myself for down the river. Started the second day went down that beautiful Current which is all alike.

The Spring River

After going down about a hundred miles, there came in another river of the same size of this. It came in from the west, a beautiful clear stream.[9] We took up it and found the lands up that were very rich in deer. We still catcht a beaver or two every night. We found game still plentiful than ever. We killed another bufaloe. We rambled often both sides of the river, the land all good, it will make a beautiful settlement on this river. It is a lime stone country, very large springs and them very plenty. The fourth day's traveling up this river, we came to the head spring of it which was nearly as large as the big spring I had seen before, but it was not such a sight to look at.[10] This spring formed the best mill seat that I ever saw, such a quantity of water falling about fifteen feet. I explored the country above the spring, got in to the piney hills of iron ore. I was then convinced that I had been near that place, so we turned again for River Currents which we supposed to be about fifty or sixty miles. This was but a short river but it was navigable for barge boats almost to the head. What a grand place this will be for iron works. Ore so plenty and easy obtained, wood so handy and navigation from their at all times and any parts of the world.

We took down the river again, and in one days journey we fell in with another small river from the left hand and our joy was over for there was no more swift current but deep still water this river coming in was by the name of Black River and it holds its name.[11] The river very crooked, it runs

9. The Spring River.

10. Maley offers a good description of Mammoth Spring, Arkansas, which lies at the head of the Spring River. At a flow rate of 216 million gallons per day, it is the largest spring in Arkansas—second only to Big Spring, Missouri, in the Ozarks. The Spring River continues for fifty-seven miles below Mammoth Spring, where it joins the Black River. "Spring River," Arkansas Department of Parks and Tourism, accessed December 2, 2015, http://www.arkansas.com/outdoors/water-activities/canoeing-rafting-kayaking/spring-river/.

11. Today the Black River joins the Current River before its union with the Spring River, and Maley's recollection may be muddled in this case. Alternatively, it is possible that in 1810 the Black River joined the Current River further south. Satellite imagery indicates that, at some point in its history, the Black River may have followed the channel of Big Running Water Creek and Coon Creek, joining the Current River near Powhatan, Arkansas, rather than turning northwest to join the Current River at Pocahontas.

in regular bends the general course about south. The banks of the river here are mostly overflowed. We could not land on account of the high water. We therefore made the best of our way down the river. We got to high ground and an Indian encampment. We made a halt but traded none as they had nothing but deer and bear skin that did not suit me. They told me that it was about fifty miles in an east course to the Mississippi and lands generally overflow in times of high water in the Mississippi. These Indians were Cherokee, emigrated from South Carolina upon the account of good hunting. They could speak some English. They were very friendly, gave me as much bear meat as I wanted. We stayed with them all night.

Maley's Travels on the Ozark Plateau

Maley explored extensively on the Ozark Plateau in the spring of 1810. Traveling from Cape Girardeau, Missouri, he arrived on the Current River a few miles south of Big Spring, Missouri. After visiting the spring, he and his companion, Cox, went two days up the river, then explored lands north of the river. Maley then explored south of the river until he thought he was on the waters of the White River, and then turned west. In reality, he was likely on the drainage of the Eleven Points River in the vicinity of present-day Winona, Missouri. His westward hike took him to the Jacks Fork River, where he met a tribe of Shawnee (Area 1 on the map).

Maley and Cox then canoed down the Current River to its junction with the Spring River and ascended that river to its primary source, at the current town of Mammoth Spring, Arkansas. Maley explored the area north of the spring (Area 2) until he thought he was on the waters of the Current (again, likely on the drainage of the Eleven Points River), and the pair returned downstream.

According to his account, the Current River joined with the Black River downstream of the Spring River, and Maley continued down the Black to its junction with the White River, near current day Newport, Arkansas. At that point, the travelers were joined by a French hunter for the trip up the White. After a "few days" travel up the stream (and before reaching the first island), they reached "higher lands" and stopped to trap beaver. This was likely a bit upstream from current-day Batesville, Arkansas (Area 3).

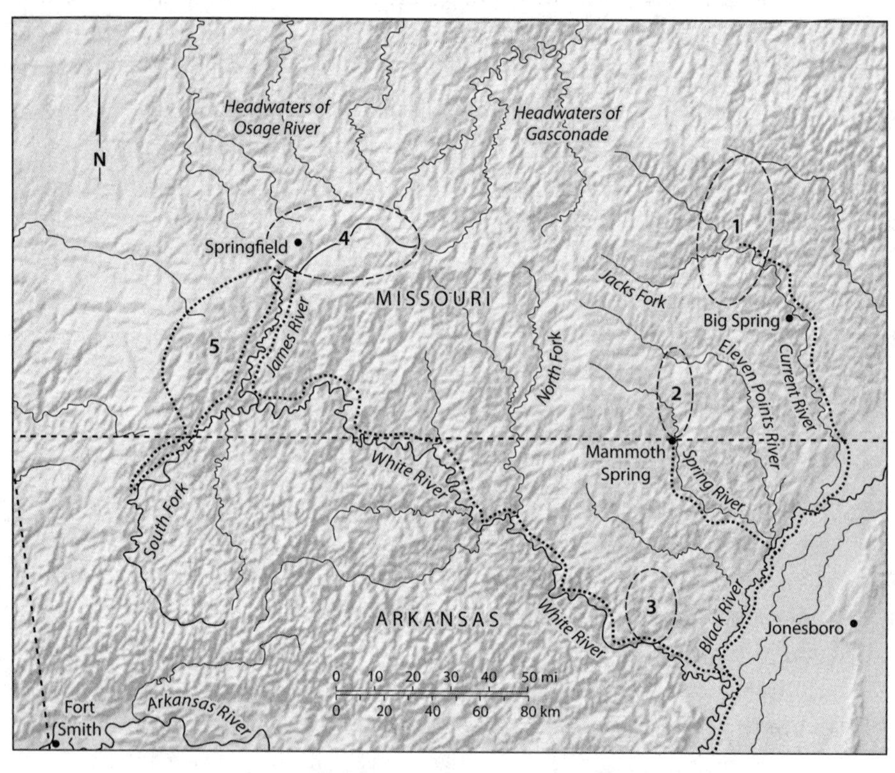

Travels on the Ozark Plateau.
See the accompanying text for a description of the numbered areas.
Map by Bill Nelson. Copyright © 2018 by the University of Oklahoma Press.

The trio then traveled to the "North Fork" of the White River, approximately three hundred miles from their starting point. This was almost certainly the James River, which today branches from the White at Table Rock Lake, and which Schoolcraft later referred to as the "principal north west fork of White River."[12] *Maley and his companions ascended the James approximately one hundred miles, to near current day Springfield, Missouri. This route is supported by Maley's observation of the prairies that begin on the west side of the James, as well as the lead deposits that Maley found there. Schoolcraft, in 1819, described a lead mine in the same area, and the town of Galena, Missouri, was later founded to exploit those deposits.*

After reaching the headwaters of the James, Maley and his companions stowed their pirogue and continued north on foot until they were convinced they were on the waters of the Gasconade (Area 4), then turned south on foot to explore the waters of the South Fork of the White. They saw great numbers of buffalo, suggesting that they traveled on the plains west of the river until following watercourses down to the South Fork of the White (Area 5). They then traveled three days up the South Fork until finding a fresh Osage encampment, which convinced the travelers to hightail it back to their pirogue and back down the river. This camp may have been in the vicinity of current-day Springdale, Arkansas.

Up the White River

Started again next morning, found again overflowed bottoms and large cane brakes. After coming about three hundred and twenty miles, we hove in sight of White River coming in from the westward and made a majestic appearance and their was an improvement on the south side. We made for that. This was a Frenchman who had a Cherokee squaw for his wife. Here was a place to deposit my beaver and this Frenchman undertook to go with us to the head of White River, as he had been most part of the way before and told us it was good hunting and trapping both. So we joined together and were to share alike in our game.

We were disturbed that night by a Cherokee Indian who was hollowing to get across the river and this man would not fetch him. He told us that

12. Schoolcraft, *Journal of a Tour into the Interior of Missouri and Arkansaw*, 54.

he had killed an Indian, one of his own tribe, that a few days before had set him over to that side of the river, and he did not know of the murder he had committed at that time until the friends of the unfortunate came there in pursuit of him in order to take his life if they can catch him, and short of that, he does not get clear by being refused by this man of fetching over the river. He, after night, shot across the river at the light of the fire. They shut the door for fear a ball might do some injury. He shot three times. One ball hit the house which made the Frenchman very angry. He wanted to go across the river and kill him at once. Another young Indian was there that night wanted to go with him. So they hollowed to him that they were a going to fetch him to that side, and started with their rifles well charged. They had not been gone long and got across till we heard the fatal shot as we thought, and so it proved to be for we immediately heard a shout and then the dying groans. They took nothing from him but his gun. They tied him up in his blanket and committed him to the deep and they returned home. This made the squaw shed tears in abundance and did not get over it that night.

Now it took us two days before we got started up the river. Where we were then was seven hundred miles from the mouth of the river. I came down to its source and about four hundred and fifty miles to where we had been with our pirogue and not much of anything to obstruct the passage—only swift current, no works to interfere.[13] The third day we started up White River it was then the middle of April. Everything looked pleasing to the eye, the rich bottoms bringing forth their timely leaves and all kinds of birds chirping their early notes. This alone was enough to enchant the traveler with the beauties of this country where trouble and care are strangers. We got about twenty miles the first day, found a great deal of overflowed bottoms.

In the mornings we killed bear. They would be up in the trees a bawling upon the account of the high water, they being catcht there, and had a great distance to go to get to dry land, and it was very difficult getting through the cane brakes, and so we could kill them up in the trees by going out in

13. This passage is not entirely clear. According to his journal, Maley was at the junction of the White and Black Rivers, near current-day Jacksonport, Arkansas, which was located 390 miles (not 700 miles) above the mouth of the White River. Maley's reference to 450 miles is the distance he subsequently traveled above this point on the river. Lloyd, *Lloyd's Steamboat Directory and Disasters on the Western Waters*, 236.

our pirogue, but some would not stand it. They would come down and swim for their life, but finally we killed a great many that way. After getting a few days journey, we got to higher lands. We then began to find some signs of beaver and soon began to catch some. Bufaloe began to get plenty. We then made a halt and took off of the river.

The land lays very handsome. It is on the north side of the river we found creeks with plenty of beaver in them. They live by making of dams. This Frenchman was well up to catch them. We caught fifteen out of one dam. There are two kinds of beaver; one they call the bank beaver and another kind that makes these dams and builds their houses in the water. They have different apartments, one above the other, still have communication through from one to the other. They have one story above the water. We ranged through till we got to the piney woods of River a Currents then retreated back to our boat. We had our loads apiece twenty six large beaver skins.

Got to our boat and found everything as we had left it and next day took up the river again. We passed the first island. The river is in general very crooked, the course about NW. The lands in general very good. The timber is shell bark hickory, piquaun, sugar tree, ash, over cup and different kinds of oak. The piquan is a fruit tree. It produces a nut much like unto a hickory nut. The meat is just like them in two pieces but much better to the taste. Their shells are very soft and they have a hull that parts from them like a hickory nut. We caught two beaver and an otter at that island. Game is still very plenty mixed with bufaloe. We never suffered for provisions. Meat was all we had to live on and that without salt. I never felt myself as hearty in my life.

In three weeks we got to the forks of the river which was supposed to be three hundred miles from where we started from.[14] We then concluded to go up the north fork as far as we could and then explore the country by land betwixt the forks. Now in a couple of days of journey, the country makes an alteration on the north side, comes in praries, very bare and barren all run out in deep gullies the soil but thin. There were dry bufaloe licks where they have eaten the earth away for several rods round, and eight or ten feet deep which was done upon the account of salt being there. It was a crust of salt on the top of the earth. We found it farther up, much one thing on that side of the river. We had to range in the forks for our game, which was very

14. This appears to be the James River.

plenty there. The land in general very good. We still continued up the river one hundred miles further. The country then began to be very broken and the river difficult to get up so we found a commodious place for our pirogue and laid her up, secured every thing in dry.

We then took it by land went on the north side first but did not travel many days before we had to return. It was too barren a country, no game to live on. We got on the dividing ridges of the northern and southern waters which we supposed to be the waters of the Gaskanade River, which empties itself into the Missouri, which was the river I was defeated on by the natives and had to turn back. Now I am at the head waters of that river. As we returned we found lead ore in several branches[15] and there was great appearance of it being in abundance by digging for, but we were not fixed for that purpose so we returned to our boat again and found everything safe.

Next day we took our route the other way to find the waters of the south fork. We proceeded with an immediate relief of hunger. Game we found plenty. We killed several bufaloe and saw great numbers but did not want to kill many. We found lands tolerable good but some broken. It took us three days before we got to the waters of the south fork. We then kept down the water courses till we got to the river thence we took up the river for three days journey. We found an Indian encampment fresh which daunted us. The Frenchman tolds us they were Ozaas [Osage],[16] that it was our best way to get away undiscovered for as sure as they saw us they would rob us. So we took this advice and returned back with sly and hasty steps, got safe to our pirogue and found all well.

Took down the river with speed, even drifted after night. We never made much of a stop until we got down where we had trapped beaver. We then made a halt in order to catch all the beaver we could, which we made out to catch a good many. So we kept down the river and trapped all the beaver we could and then took down the river. We soon got to the drowned lands of White River in two months from the time we started. We arrived at the Frenchman's house again, the distance we supposed about four hundred miles which makes the extent of navigation on White River one thousand

15. This part of Missouri is known for its lead mines. Schoolcraft in 1819 described a lead mine on the James River, approximately eighty miles above its junction with the White. Schoolcraft, *Journal of a Tour into the Interior of Missouri and Arkansaw*, 55–56.

16. Maley uses various spellings in the text.

The James River at Galena, Missouri.
Maley identified lead ore near this location. *Photograph by the editor.*

miles total length twelve hundred.[17] We had forty three beaver skins which we had caught and twelve bear.

❦ ❦ ❦

The Osage

Of all the challenges Maley faced on the frontier, the Osage Indians proved his greatest nemesis. At the time of Maley's travels, no American Indian nation was

17. Maley's distances appear to be in error. As noted earlier, the distance from the Frenchman's house, at the junction of the White and Black Rivers, to the mouth of the White was 390 miles. If Maley and his companions traveled four hundred miles further up the White, the total extent of navigation on that river would have been approximately eight hundred miles, not a thousand. Lloyd, *Lloyd's Steamboat Directory and Disasters on the Western Waters*, 236.

Tál-lee, an Osage Warrior of Distinction, by George Catlin, 1834.
Courtesy of the Smithsonian American Art Museum, Gift of Mrs. Joseph Harrison, Jr.

more powerful. As pointed out by Burns, in the 125 years prior to the Louisiana Purchase, the Osage had simultaneously halted the westward expansion of European and American settlers while significantly expanding the size of their own domain—something no other tribe had been able to achieve.[18] *The Osage were one of the more warlike tribes in North America,*[19] *and their warriors were universally described as extremely large and brave.*[20] *At the time of early contact with Europeans, they were living in three core groups in what is now southwest Missouri and northwest Arkansas. Osage hunters and war parties ranged far beyond these villages, however, and by 1750 they had driven the Wichita south from the Arkansas River, to the Red. With the adoption of the horse, the Osage expanded their dominion west onto the Great Plains, where they came into conflict with other tribes, including the Southern Cheyenne, Comanche, Kiowa, and Lipan Apache.*[21]

French traders, operating out of St. Louis, had established a fur trade with the Osage in 1764, but excursions into Osage territory by other European hunters and traders were often met with violent resistance. This was particularly true for hunters operating out of the French settlement at Arkansas Post, which was closely allied to the Quapaw, traditional enemies of the Osage. Between 1733 and 1803, there were repeated attacks by the Osage on hunters up the Arkansas River, and the Osage also committed atrocities against the French as far south as Natchitoches. French and Spanish authorities tried a number of measures to address the problem, ranging from diplomacy to force of arms, but with mixed results. At the close of the eighteenth century, the Osage remained a formidable barrier to European and American expansion west of the Mississippi.[22]

With the purchase of Louisiana, the United States inherited the challenges of dealing with the Osage, and attempted to address them in the Treaty of 1808. That treaty stipulated the establishment of a trading post at Fort Osage, about twenty miles east of current-day Kansas City, and payments of trade goods to the tribes. In return, the Osage agreed to cede all lands east of a line running south from Fort Osage to the Arkansas River.[23] *On its face, this was an enormous land cession, more than fifty-two million acres.*[24] *In reality, however, it had little impact on*

18. Burns, *A History of the Osage People*, 35.
19. Ingenthron, *Indians of the Ozark Plateau*, 60.
20. Bradbury, *Travels in the Interior of America*, 50.
21. Burns, *A History of the Osage People*, 34.
22. Arnold, *Colonial Arkansas, 1686–1804*, 112–24.
23. Kappler, *Treaty with the Osage, 1808*, 96.
24. Burns, *A History of the Osage People*, 168.

Osage activities in that region, as the treaty permitted the Osage to live and hunt on those lands until they were assigned to other tribes. Following the Treaty of 1808, more than two thousand Cherokee relocated to Arkansas, settling on the lower White and Arkansas Rivers,[25] *and a number of other eastern tribes were settled in Missouri, including the Sac, Fox, Kickapoo, Delaware, and Shawnee nations.*[26] *The movement of these emigrant tribes, many of them traditional enemies, onto former Osage lands gave rise to almost continual conflict in the first half of the nineteenth century. In 1817 the United States established Fort Smith, in current-day Arkansas, on the boundary line in an attempt to quell hostilities between the Osage and Cherokee. In his 1819 visit to that post, botanist Thomas Nuttall commented that "scarcely any nation of Indians have encountered more enemies than the Osages."*[27]

The treaty did not deter Osage attacks on white hunters and traders, either. As he noted in his journal, a year after the treaty was signed, Maley was shot at by Osage warriors on the Gasconade River, approximately 140 miles east of the boundary line, and in the following year he had to retreat from the headwaters of the White River for fear of being robbed by the tribe. Maley's experience seems to have been the norm. In his 1818–19 exploration of the Ozarks, geologist Henry R. Schoolcraft was repeatedly warned that the Osage would plunder and sometimes kidnap travelers in the region, and one of his hosts reported being robbed twice at his home at the junction of the White River and the Little North Fork, approximately ninety miles east of the boundary.[28] *While robberies were common, writer H. M. Brackenridge commented that the Osage were not known to kill their victims.*[29] *In a similar vein, Nuttall noted that when they found white hunters in their territory, the Osage would normally confiscate their possessions, but, while not killing the intruder, would leave them nearly naked in the wilderness to perish.*[30]

With an estimated population of 12,000 in 1815, the Osage remained one of the most powerful Indian nations in America long after Maley finished his travels.[31] *Like other tribes, however, it faced increasing pressure from white settlers and ceded additional lands in 1818, 1825, and 1839. Many of the ancestral lands of the Osage were assigned to other tribes after their "removal" to Indian*

25. Ibid., 191.
26. Ibid., 187, figure 27.
27. Nuttall, *A Journal of Travels into the Arkansas Territory during the Year 1819*, 193.
28. Schoolcraft, *Journal of a Tour into the Interior of Missouri and Arkansaw*, 6, 37–38.
29. Brackenridge, *Views of Louisiana*, 246.
30. Nuttall, *A Journal of Travels into the Arkansas Territory during the Year 1819*, 211.
31. Burns, *A History of the Osage People*, 242.

Territory. Ultimately, the Osage domain was diminished to a reservation, forming current-day Osage County, Oklahoma. The tribe also suffered through several epidemics: influenza in 1829–31, cholera in 1834, and smallpox in 1837,[32] *and the population had declined to an estimated 3,500 by 1860. Notwithstanding these challenges, the Osage Nation survived and ultimately prospered, as their remaining lands proved valuable for cattle ranching and oil and gas production. The estimated Osage population in 2002 was slightly over 18,000.*[33]

Down the White River

We fitted ourselves for down the river next morning. We got our plunder ashore and took our leave of the Frenchman and his lady. My aim was then for the Arkanzas River. This was now the twentieth of June, the weather very warm and the mosquitoes very troublesome, the bottoms all overflowed. We could get no dry ground to put our feet on. We drifted mostly night and day as the river is not dangerous. We ventured to lay down and sleep and to keep drifting. Along the fourth day we got to the first high ground and a settlement.[34] This man by the name of Trimble had a large improvement there and keeps goods to trade with the natives as the high grounds were now frequent on the river and thickly inhabited by Indians of the Cherokee nation. It was in an east direction from there fifty miles to the Mississippi and to follow the river three hundred. It was but fifty miles to the post of Ozarc on the Arkansas River by land and three hundred and fifty by water the way I had to go. At this place I got some bread to take on our journey. We found high ground all covered with Indian huts. The squaws cultivate the ground they raise vegetables of all kinds, such as squashes, pumpkins, beans and finally every thing almost that is eatable. The soil is generally light it being that the bottoms overflow and these bluffs they have to cultivate.

About the fourth night that we left this house, we encamped on an island.

32. Ibid., 239–40.

33. Ibid., 480.

34. This settlement was possibly at present-day Georgetown, Arkansas, on the west bank of the White River, about 125 miles below the junction of the Black River. Initially settled by whites in 1789, some historians claim it to be the oldest existing town, and the second oldest settlement (after Arkansas Post), in the state. Miller, "Georgetown (White County)."

Had about an acre of dry land to lie on. In the night we heard an uncommon noise it sounded like some distant pounding and this continued all night. We could not think what it was nor could we satisfy our curiosities till we started next morning and went about a mile where we got the sight of about fifty drunken Indians all naked, seemingly, some a dancing and others fighting and tumbling one another about. I did not want them to see me, for a drunken Indian is not to be trusted. I kept close under the off shore and slipt by undiscovered. After I got below the village I saw the squaws all hid from the men having with them all the implements of war so that they could not kill one another. This is a practice of the women and when they are sober they return home. The men will never say why did you so. These Indians get their whiskey by going down to the Mississippi and wait for boats coming down and trade with them give their furs and skins for whiskey.

The next Indian village, I made a stop and stayed until I traded away all my goods I had for furs which I found to be very advantageous. The trade here with the natives is very lucrative by being acquainted with the articles which suit their fancy. I'll give a small sketch of the articles suitable: common calicoes, red striped or any gay thing, handkerchiefs of all denominations, first and second qualities both silk and cotton only gay colors, blue striped blankets from 2½ to four pointed, red and purple striped Indian blankets, vermilion paint, small cased looking glasses and silver breast plates in shape of a half moon six inches in diameter, silver finger rings, broaches.

And after finishing my trade, I started. Had but fifty miles to go to the cut off, a communication from this river into the Arkansas which saves me a hundred miles. I got there the next day. Now this current runs into the Arkansas by this river being the fullest; if otherwise it is to the reverse so I still had the current in my favor. It is about twenty miles through here, the banks are high enough to keep the water out, soil very good, the bottoms thickly grown with cane and abundance of piquan timber. I got through in less than half a day into the Arkansas river which was in appearance much like White river. There was another long and tedious road for me to travel, but I began to get so much used to it that I made nothing of it any more. I was then thirty miles from the post of Ozark.[35]

35. The settlement Maley refers to as Post of Ozark is better known today as Arkansas Post.

CHAPTER 5 ❦ *Summer of 1810*

Up the Arkansas

I got the second day by twelve o'clock here. I found a place of business, a country well settled, good farmers raising of wheat and corn, French and natives trading. This is an ancient place of trade, this a branch of the NW company. This town is situated about two hundred and fifty miles from Natchez, about sixty miles from the Mississippi river. The soil here is not so rich altho it is suitable for wheat. It was there almost wheat harvest. They have great difficulties to encounter in order to save their crops as birds are so numerous in that country they have to watch round their fields from morning till night, otherwise they would reap none. They are our common black bird and the parriceet, a bird like the green parrot only a smaller kind. There are about one hundred and fifty inhabitants. The town is very thriving and it is about one hundred and ten miles to Prari Maronze[1] a smart settlement, all Americans, but this passage in time of high water cannot be used for several weeks at a time.

After taking all necessary observations I fitted myself for to start up the river. I left my furs here till my return. I bought some articles at the poste, altho at a very high rate at about one hundred and fifty per centum higher than I had paid for goods of the same kind at Shawnee Town, Illinois Territory, but goods I thought would be a cloke[2] to me going up the river, so I fitted myself and took my leave on the last of July with my companion still with me. The first day we still found settlements on the river, the land getting much better. We started the second day. We had hard pulling, the

1. Maley later refers to this community as "Prarie Marouze," both phonetic spellings of "Prairie Mer Rouge," a small town in northeast Louisiana now known as Mer Rouge.

2. Maley appears to imply that trade goods would be a "cloak" to cover up the true purpose of his voyage—exploration—though it is not clear why he would need to do so.

current very strong, went but a small distance that day. It also came on bad weather. We had to halt and make us a camp so as to keep dry from the violent rain. We were detained there two days. The third day, took an early start, the weather very pleasant. We found no more inhabitants, no overflowed land to be seen, game was not very plenty.

They told us so at the post that we should find no game for a great distance up the river. For that reason, we provided ourselves with a week's provisions at least. We still had the river in a strong current, travelled but slow and it was very fatiguing, only about fifteen miles a day at the most wonderful. The fatigues that a man will bring on himself only to satisfy his curiosity. What will I gain by this? These were my thoughts at this time, but resolution and fortitude always conquered so I always revived myself merely by a good resolution. We still continued on by hard pulling the oar for about ten days. It then got considerably easier, the river getting very crooked and the current not so strong. We there made a halt and took the woods for to see if we could not kill something to eat. We found game plenty. We killed two deer and a turkey which supplied us handsomely. We went to our pirogue and cured our venison, jerkt it so that we might not be hindered so much.

When we had this done, we took a fresh start and went on much better than we had done heretofore. The river bottoms were very good, fertile and level and did not overflow. We saw the first signs of beaver. We stopped to catch some, but the furs was no more in season, so we tryd no more. We then took off of the river towards White River, which we found in two days travel. The land in general good and level, went some higher up the river, found places that we were acquainted with. We turned back to our boat, game plenty. We killed a bufaloe and brought some of the meat to our pirogue, cut it up in small thin pieces and barbcued it and took it along. So went on winding up the river for it run from north to south and south to north in succession. Sometimes in going eight or ten miles, you would not gain more than a hundred yards. This was tedious traveling indeed. The timber here is the same of that of White River.

We then made a halt which was about three hundred miles from the post. We had then been coming thirty days. We laid up our pirogue in a safe place so that she might not be found only by accident. We started our route to the southerd in the direction towards the Ouatchitta [Ouachita] River. We found plenty of game, found some high ranges with some growth of pine, traveled on south till we were convinced that we were on waters of another river, so we then shifted our course to the westward which brought us higher up the river.

Ozark (Arkansas) Post

In the summer of 1810, Maley reached a community he referred to as the "Post of Ozark," now more commonly referred to as Arkansas Post.[3] *This settlement, which was established in 1686 at the behest of explorer Henri de Tonty, was the first European settlement in what would become the Louisiana Purchase.*[4] *It was originally established on the Arkansas River at Lake Dumond, but following a 1749 attack by the Chickasaw, the town was relocated to a Quapaw Indian village site called Écores Rouges, about fifteen leagues up the river from the Mississippi, for protection.*[5] *Only five years later, the French moved the post closer to the Mississippi, in part to better support French supply lines on that river during the French and Indian War. However, this site was subject to periodic flooding, and in 1779 the settlement returned to the higher ground at Écores Rouges and remained there.*

Following the French and Indian War, France surrendered its territories east of the Mississippi to Britain and ceded its territories west of the river to Spain. In 1783, as a result of Spanish support for the Americans during the Revolutionary War, Arkansas Post came under an attack by Chickasaw Indians,[6] *who were allied with the British and led by Scotsman James Colbert.*[7] *This was one of only two Revolutionary War battles that took place west of the Mississippi, but the Spanish ultimately retained control of the post. In 1804, following the Louisiana Purchase, the United States took possession of the site from Spain.*

Although Maley seemed impressed by the settlement as a place of business, Arkansas Post was a commercial backwater through much of its history.

3. A decade later, Nuttall would lament that the post was "now not very intelligibly called, Arkansas," instead of "Osark," which was its original name and one still being used by the Quapaws. Nuttall, *A Journal of Travels into the Arkansas Territory during the Year 1819*, 247.

4. Arnold, *Colonial Arkansas, 1686–1804*, 25.

5. Ibid., 32.

6. Ibid., 111–12.

7. James was the father of George and Levi Colbert, whom Maley met on his Tennessee River trip earlier that year.

Agricultural production remained modest during the colonial and early American periods, despite the post's location in what is now considered some of the more productive farmland in the country. In 1805 the American agent at the post reported that settlers had abandoned raising Indian corn due to its destruction by crows and black birds;[8] *based on Maley's account, this appeared to remain a problem five years later. A more important element, as pointed out by Arnold, was that the vast majority of the population in Arkansas was engaged in hunting and the fur trade rather than agriculture.*[9] *However, that trade was not very profitable. During the half decade that the United States maintained a fur-trading "factory" at the post (1805–10), more than 80 percent of the trade consisted of low-value deer skins.*[10] *It is possible that private fur-trading companies operating out of Arkansas Post may have handled a greater percentage of the more valuable skins, such as beaver, but the pelts of the southern beaver were considered inferior to those from colder climates in the northern and Rocky Mountain regions.*

Another factor that stymied development at Arkansas Post was a continuing conflict between Osage Indians and white hunters in the region throughout much of the eighteenth century. Repeated efforts by both French and Spanish authorities to either negotiate with the Osage or defeat them militarily came to naught. While the Osage were the most bellicose Indian tribe in the region, Osage enmity against Arkansas hunters may have been driven, in part, by a Spanish policy that would not allow development of trade with the Osage in Arkansas, reserving it instead for St. Louis merchants.[11]

Despite the lack of economic development, in 1819 Arkansas Post was still the largest town in the new Arkansas Territory, and it briefly served as its capital. Prior to the Civil War, the town became an important shipment point for cotton from the surrounding region, but much of the settlement was destroyed in an assault by Union forces during the Civil War. Arkansas Post became a state park in 1929 and a national memorial, operated by the U.S. Park Service, in 1960.[12] *No one lives at the site today.*

8. Arnold, *Colonial Arkansas, 1686–1804*, 61.
9. Ibid., 63.
10. Polechla, "Fur Trade Records from Arkansas Factory," 69–70.
11. Arnold, *Colonial Arkansas, 1686–1804*, 112–24.
12. Duval, "Arkansas Post."

Encounter with the Choctaw

The fourth day that we left our pirogue, about an hour by sun, we was surprised by yells and holloos but were not yet in view. We could not conclude what to do, whether to run and hide or stand our ground. Finally before we determined, they were in sight and discovered us. Behold, it was a company of Indians, thirty in number. They had several horses loaded with beaver and otter skins besides their own back loads of the same kind. When they approached near to us, we observed that a number of these were objects of pity. They were tied, their hands upon their back and a stick in their mouth in order to prevent them from making any noise at all, and some I saw had the blood running down their legs and they limping along as well as they could. They had cut the hamstrings of those that had made an attempt to run away. This was to prevent them from running. This was a party of Chocktaw Indians that reside on the east side of the Mississippi River which had been on a hunt and came across an incampment of the Ozases and made prisoners of them and took all their plunder. They had eleven prisoners and they meant to butcher them all in their own way when ever they thought they were out of danger.

One of those Chocktaws could talk some English and he gave us to understand that the grass before[13] they had killed fourteen of their nation, burnt them all up in a cave, so they were determined to have satisfaction. I told them that I had some goods at the river, which made them insist on my going down with them, and they would trade with me. Finally I did, but alas I had to behold that dreadful catastrophe to see them mortals all murdered and sculpt. They undertook it the second day. It was chiefly on the account of these they had hamstrung. They began to be troublesome so they concluded they would put an end to them.

They made a halt about the middle of the afternoon, gathered a large quantity of wood. They made a small fire. Now the dreadful scene was a going to commence. They had their spot of execution pickt out, a stake drove in the ground for the center, all the brush cleared away for a great distance round. The executioner painted himself in an awful appearance, then one of these mortals were led to the stake and their tied down, hands

13. It is unclear, but perhaps "grass" is referring to the previous spring.

and feet in a sitting position. They then enclosed a ring, all taking hand and hand but the executioner he placed himself inside of the circle with his tomahawk and sculping knife. Now they all set up a mournful tune. As they sung, they danct around and round. Once and a while they yelled that they made the wood echoe in this mirth. As they took it, the executioner would dance round and began to cut him in the head with the tomahawk until he expired and would take of his sculp in the same manner by dancing around him. In this way, they were all served till the whole eleven were killed and sculpt. One of them, I presume a king, they skinned his whole head and stuffed it with dry leaves and took out his jaw teeth and all and set them in the skin in a grinning manner and stuck it on a pole. When they had this completed, it raise a great laugh and yell among them. Their laid this pile of dead beings till morning.

How could a Christian heart forbear mourning in secret? Although these were the nation that wanted to take my life when going up the Gaskanade, yet my heart softened my feelings to the very heart. I could not rest that night thinking what I had brought myself too. Reflections on my self were very pierceing to me. Left my mother country and came here to see this dreadful spectacle. Wonderful indeed. How much did I feel myself rejoice when day light once more appeared.

As soon as day light, they built a large fire for this purpose. They got this pile of wood which before I did not know and after it burnt well they committed these bodies to the flames and then raised another dance with mournful singing. After this which was then almost the middle of the day they had to eat and then take a start. My appetite was very small. I wanted only to be off, which at last we accomplished. There was one that carried all the sculps strung on a pole and the head with the teeth set in was carried by one separate, stuck upon a pole, and he generally went in front. The second day we got to our pirogue and made a trade with the Indians and bartered all my goods for beaver as I had not many.

You generally trade with the Indians there in this manner. You have no particular price for your goods, but such an article as they want, they will pick it out and lay it down and then point at it that they want it. Then you go to their skins and pick out what you think you ought to have, lay them down by the side of the articles he has chosen. Then point to them both, making signs that he may take one for the other. If they are not pleased with that, they will pick out another small article and lay it by the others and make signs that will do. If you give away to this, they are sure to demand it every time. Therefore it is best not learn them the habit, but take away the last article he put there and shake your head that you will not do it and put on a frowning look and they will soon take up with your offer thinking more of their bargain than they would otherwise. They then value such an article much more. This gives a little sketch how to deal with Indians.

After these Indians had completed their trade, they fixt to take their leave of us and told us to take care of the Ozaas, making signs that they would kill us if they caught us. So we smoked a parting pipe and they started. They manner in which they show their friendship in smoking a pipe is performed in this way. Either in meeting or parting, the eldest or chief, if any present, will fill his pipe and light it, gets up and goes to the stranger and holds the pipe for him to take a few drafts. When he has gone around to all the company in that manner, he sits down and smokes his pipe himself.

Roaming the Ouachita Mountains

After these Indians were gone, we then concluded how to proceed further, which was soon determined. The conclusion was so that we would hide our pirogue and furs their and take it up the river by land. It gave us much better chance to explore the country in general. We therefore run our pirogue up a small branch and covered it with cane and made a scaffold for to put our furs in a thick cane brake and then covered it over with a bearskin so as to keep it dry then bent and broke down the cane over it and so trusted to fortune. Next day we took up on the south and meant to return on the north. The land in general we find good on the river, but off from it is but light and hilly. We found great signs of salt in that country. This is not a great distance from the river. We found a large branch that was too salt to drink. Bufaloe are very numerous in this part. We only killed them occasionally. We ranged to and from the river.

After travelling ten days from our pirogue, we were on the river bank and saw two pirogues a coming down the river filled with Indians. This gave us a fright, but we squat down and they did not see us so they passed by us and we were not sorry. We could but feel thankful that we were not on the river for we were sure that they were in pursuit of the Chocktaws that had taken them prisoners. We soon forgot our fears then we took a route off of the river and then found much higher ground with stony branches, found different kinds of ore, some that was very good and some of an inferior kind. We found dog teeth crystal and many other minerals that are symptoms of royal metal to be in the neighborhood. I could not satisfy myself that day. We struck camp and staid there until morning and then to view that range of mountains well and see whether they are of any extent.

So in the morning, took our breakfast and raised the mountain, but it was not very high. Only high ground in that country was not very frequent, so we took this to be a mountain. This was on the water of the Ouattchitta river and about seven hundred and fifty miles up the Arkansas.[14] We travelled this ridge which bore about WSW leaving the Arkansas river to the northerd. This range appeared to be very extensive; we could see a great distance. Timber was but scattering in that country, nothing to obstruct the sight, which made it a pleasing prospect to us as we had been so long confined to the dreary wilderness, nothing but low river bottoms. This seemingly revived us to breathe this pure air. We still continued on the ridge for that was our object as we had command of all the low ground from where we were. We found several curiosities on the ridge as pirites of different kinds come to hand, but they being chiefly of iron. Now there was all the appearance of rich metals being there to be found in searching in a proper manner, which is by digging, but we were not provided for that. We therefore only give an account of the superficial signs from that all mines are discovered.

By continuing in one direction on this ridge we saw the wonderful works of nature in its highest degree of beauty to see all the stone showing something magnificent. After traveling ten days on this ridge, I thought I could, if possible, see one hundred miles. I then observed a range of mountains stretching from north to south. I discovered that the ridge we were on must soon come to an end and that there must come in the waters of Red River. In two days more the ridge fell a way and got to be much lower and nothing but one continual prarie, but the soil is not so rich and also very broken, not

14. As seen elsewhere in his journal, Maley's recitation of distances here is confounding. According to his account, he and his companion originally left their pirogue 300 miles above Arkansas Post, or about 360 miles up the Arkansas River. It is simply not credible that, at this point, after an additional ten days of travel on foot, they were 750 miles up the river. Furthermore, this would have placed them on the Great Plains west of Tulsa, Oklahoma, an area that bears no resemblance to the topography he is describing.

like praries mentioned heretofore. Bufaloe were very numerous. We lived in plenty, had nothing but bufaloe meat or the marrow, which we lived on without any salt, but that did not impair our health by any means for we never knew what it was to be sick at any time since we started on our expedition.

Now as we drew nearer to this mountain, although yet a great distance off, I concluded that the foot of that mountain would be the distance of our journey in that direction, and so traveled on for two days and we accomplished our distance. We were then convinced that we were at the head of the eastern waters. We then shifted our course to the north, keep along the foot of the mountain, this representation itself in different forms of cones and pinnacles. The second day that we shifted our course, we had the view of a shining pillar, the sun being opposite the reflection on the mountain makes it appear very dazzling although at such a distance. Now I thought I could not be satisfied till I had seen what this shining mountain meant. We started to go too it, traveling in that direction two days but found traveling very tedious and lost sight of our object. We found nothing to eat. This disheartened my companion and concluded to turn back, which we did and found ourselves almost hungered out before we got relief. The third day we got again in the low grounds where we soon found something to eat.

Return to Arkansas Post

We then steered for the waters of the Arkansas. We had chiefly prairie to go through. It was difficult to cook our meat upon the account of wood. We had to eat our meat very often not half broiled. We had to burn grass and dried bufaloe dung to make a blaze to scorch our meat. We soon discovered that the waters we were on was Arkansas water. We came to one branch that was entirely salt. We found several great bufaloe licks. At these licks the earth was covered with the bones of bufaloe and many other bones that we did know what the animal might be. These animals, we suppose, must die there of old age being they resort this place and never leave it. Now we followed down the waters of the Arkansas and still found the country broken and soil very thin.

We one day found the greatest natural curiosity we had met with yet which was a large ledge of rocks in a place where rocks were not frequent and in the center of this cliff we saw a black salty looking hole. I was curious to see what it was. I got upon the cliff to examine it, put my head down to look in. I was struck with the most nauseous smell imaginable and an air strong enough to make your hair quiver and that disagreeably warm. I did not like to try the operation of getting the scent for fear it might be pernicious. I therefore shunned it all I could. It had a substance like lampblack outside of the mouth of the hole.[15] We could not ascertain the cause of this great curiosity as it was a mistery to us, so we left it and traveled on again for the river and that day we got to a different soil of land all together.

No more prairie but found a good timbered country and in the after part of the day found a smart stream which was the first water course of any note that we had found of the Arkansas so, as I found no material difference as to the situation of the country, I thought I would not leave the water any more but keep chiefly down the stream. We now found deer very plenty which was a change of diet to us. We had lived on buffaloe meat for better than 8 weeks. Here the country is very extensive with bottoms. Another branch comes in from the north which makes a navigable water not less than 60 yards wide. We kept on the north side as we had explored on the south going up so we would try to give an accurate account of the soil and face of the country which now is level and fertile. It will undoubtedly some day make a great country. Every thing seems to suit the times. On the river the lands are generally very good and more at a distance the soil is thin but the earth is impregnated with mines and minerals. Salt in that country will be nothing to obtain as there are licks and springs in great abundance; it only wants inhabitants. Surely the climate is healthy, no overflow lands nor stagnant waters, the deer and buffalo in numerous herds around in this bottom land.

We traveled for 9 or 10 days, all a fine fertile country. In two weeks it brought us safe to our pirogue which was unmolested nor was our furs injured. We soon fitted ourselves for a start; loaded our pirogue with our plunder and set sail down the river and in ten days we reached the Post of Ozark. The nighest calculations we make as to the length of this river is 1280 miles, which nearly one thousand may be navigated at any season of the year with large keel bottom boats.[16] It was the 6th of October that we arrived at the post.

15. This may have been a natural gas seep. A number of gas fields have been discovered in this part of Arkansas.

16. It is not clear what Maley is referring to with these distances. He and his companion clearly did not travel 1,280 miles upstream from Arkansas Post. In this case, he may be referring to distances on the Arkansas River plus the distance up the Mississippi to the mouth of the Arkansas.

Maley's Travels in Western Arkansas

As with other parts of his journal, it is difficult to track exactly where Maley went on his 1810 trip up the Arkansas River. He did not visit settlements or other specific sites that might be identifiable to historians, and there are internal inconsistencies in the account. For example, by adding up the days Maley spent in each segment of his trip, one would conclude that the excursion took a minimum of three months, but based on the dates he departed and returned to Arkansas Post, Maley and his companion were gone only sixty-eight days. Furthermore, Maley interjected mileage estimates into the account that cannot be reconciled with the rest of his story. Notwithstanding these challenges, one can make a reasonable guess as to his travels.

Maley noted that after thirty days of travel, he and his companion left their pirogue about three hundred miles upriver from Arkansas Post. This is a reasonable distance to cover in that time frame and would have put the explorers upriver of Little Rock, possibly in the vicinity of Maumelle or as far up as current day Conway, Arkansas.[17] *Maley stated that they first traveled in a southerly direction, across some high ranges, until they were convinced they were on the waters of a different river. This likely would have been the headwaters of the Saline River, which drains south from the Ouachita Mountains. They then returned to the Arkansas River, witnessed the execution of the Osage, and returned to their pirogue to trade with the Choctaws.*

Maley and his companion then hid their pirogue and wandered on foot 10 days on the south side of the Arkansas River before seeing two pirogues of Osage warriors bent on revenge. This convinced the travelers to strike a course away from the river. At this point, Maley stated that he was about 750 miles up the Arkansas River, a distance that clearly seems to be in error. Not only would that have required Maley to have hiked more than 40 miles a day since leaving his pirogue, but it would have also put the travelers somewhere on the plains west of Tulsa, Oklahoma, an area which bears no resemblance to the terrain he describes.

17. As noted by Nuttall a decade later, the distance from Arkansas Post to the early Cadron community, west of Conway, was estimated to be three hundred miles by water. Nuttall, *A Journal of Travels into the Arkansas Territory during the Year 1819*, 100.

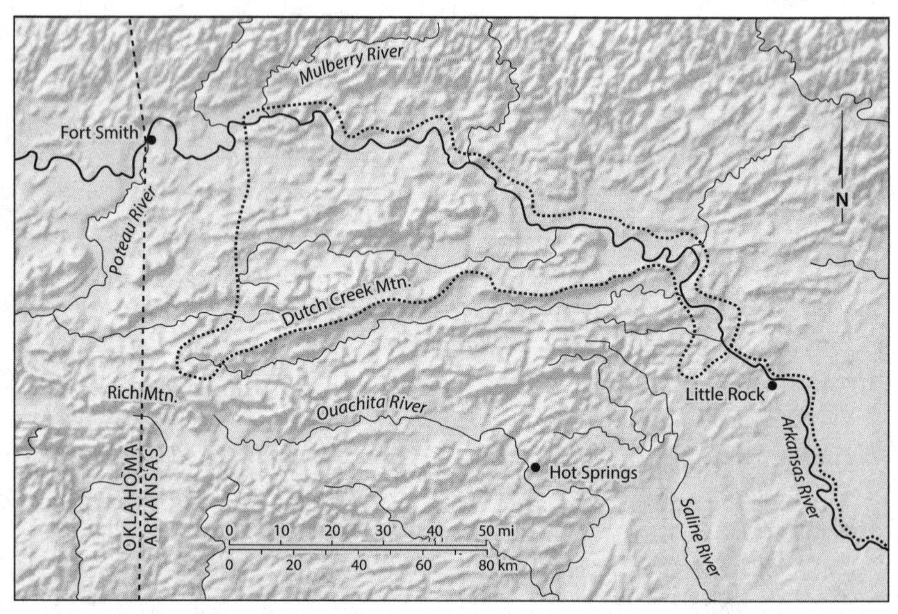

Projected travels in western Arkansas.
Map by Bill Nelson. Copyright © 2018 by the University of Oklahoma Press.

After leaving the river, Maley and his companion ascended a ridge running west-southwest and followed it for ten days, searching for minerals. Most of the ridges in the Ouachita Mountains have a west-southwest orientation, but few are as long as implied by Maley's narrative. Dutch Creek Mountain seems the most likely candidate. It is a continuous ridge, rising near Ola, Arkansas, and extending almost fifty miles to the south-southwest. The ridge top would have provided relatively easy passage in that direction.[18] *Higher than the ridges to the south, Dutch Creek Mountain also would have provided the extensive views Maley extols in his account. Whichever ridge Maley followed to the southwest, the mountain that he saw in the distance, and to which he tried to travel, was very likely Rich Mountain, northwest of Mena, Arkansas. Rich Mountain rises to more than 2,500 feet in elevation and is easily visible from Dutch Creek Mountain many miles to the east. As one descends the ridge, however, the view of Rich Mountain is blocked by intervening hills, which may explain how Maley lost sight of his objective.*

Maley and his companion ultimately abandoned their effort to reach the mountain and returned north to the Arkansas River. At this point, his narrative becomes a bit more ambiguous—it is not clear whether the "shining pillar" he subsequently tried to reach was the same mountain he saw from the top of the ridge or a new mountain. It is possible the travelers made it as far as eastern Oklahoma, skirted the western end of Poteau Mountain near Heavener, Oklahoma, and then traveled north towards the Arkansas River. In that case, Maley's shining mountain might have been a reference to either Sugar Loaf Mountain or Cavanal Mountain near Poteau, Oklahoma. However, Maley makes no mention of the Poteau River that would have been passed on this route. It seems more likely, therefore, that the pair went north past current day Waldron, Arkansas. In that case, the "smart stream" they encountered could be Doctor's Creek, near Charleston, Arkansas, and the significant branch they identified entering the north side of the Arkansas could be the Mulberry River. They then returned down the north side of the Arkansas to their pirogue.

18. A U.S. Forest Service road was built along the crest of Dutch Creek Mountain, but it is no longer fully maintained.

Lower Mississippi and Red Rivers.
The "Great Raft" was an enormous logjam
that restricted passage on the Red River at this time.
Map by Bill Nelson. Copyright © 2018 by the University of Oklahoma Press.

CHAPTER 6 ❦ *Fall of 1810*

Down the Mississippi to Natchez

We made no stay there but took all our beaver skins aboard and started for the Mississippi River, which did not take us many days. This river comes into the Mississippi only nine miles below White River. The day that we got into the Mississippi, the wind blew strong NW which rather seems dangerous for us to encounter such waves and a current so rapid and turning in whirlpools. As our ship was too small, we concluded we would land and wait until a boat should come down the river and then to board her and take a passage to Natchez. In the mean time, a pirogue with 4 Indians came down the river and landed. They also wanted a boat to come down as they wanted to trade for some whiskey. They told me they were Ozaas, that hostile nation and of whom I had seen them murdered. I was struck with dread for fear they might rob me, but they feel too much cowed when they are such a distance from home. They are always in dread that they may be discovered by some of their enemy; that is any of the Indians south of them are their enemy.

It was about the middle of the day we discovered five flat bottom boats in sight which was about 10 miles distance. When we first saw them, the Indians took immediately up the river in order to meet the boats, but we took to the middle of the river and so let them drift in upon us. We got safe aboard, put our firs and baggage aboard. These boats were all from Tennessee loaded with flour, and others with iron and castings, and others with families moving to the Natchez country. When you are on that extensive and lengthy river, then to see from shore to shore the unbounded country that is yet in a manner unknown. This now is better than 300 miles above Natchez. On the east the land belongs to the Chocktaw Indians and west the state of Louisiana.

In navigating this river with these boats is rather a difficult thing. It requires a great deal of care. Look out for a good harbor, as you have got to land every evening. By drifting after night, you might drift on those sawyers which are very dangerous. You may hear them roar in a still time the distance of half a mile, but it wants daylight to see which way to pull to clear it as the current of the Mississippi is very uncertain. It turns, foams and rolls itself in whirlpools. The body of water of the Mississippi is so unbounded that it is impossible for human nature to have the least idea. To think back the distance I have already come and down its lengthy rivers we must there stop to think, for the quantity is inconceivable. The Mississippi is always in a muddy state. You cannot drink the water unless taking it up some time and let it stand to settle. The water is exceedingly healthy and palatable. It has great medical virtures; it makes a perfect cure of the itch and scurvy. We drifted sometimes in company lashed together and were all jovial and jolly together and drink our can of cider without any interruption.

We still see no inhabitants on the Mississippi bottom. The first view of high ground we had was what is called the Walnut Hills[1] which exceeds all the beautiful sights that ever nature adorned. The width of the river and the bend it made from the bluff made it a delightful scene. The hills were covered with the greenest of grass and not less than 1000 head of cattle on it a feeding. We made a stop here and raised the hill to see the prospect which was delightful. It commands a great scape of the Mississippi. There is yet old remains of ancient forts made by the Spaniards before it was ceded to France.[2] Back of this hill is a fine fertile country chiefly settled by emigrants from Kentucky. It is out of the Indian territory; it belongs in the Mississippi territory.

Now comes on that great cotton country. Now you may see inhabitants on both sides of the river and all support themselves in bread by buying off the boats that come down the river as their land is too valuable to raise corn or wheat although they can raise either.

1. Present-day Vicksburg, Mississippi.

2. In 1791 the Spanish erected Fort Nogales on what is now referred to as Fort Hill, in Vicksburg National Military Park. The Spanish abandoned the fort in 1797, after Pinckney's Treaty created a new southern boundary of the United States. Settlers founded the town of Vicksburg at the site in 1819. "Historic Sites and Buildings," Founders and Frontiersmen, National Park Service, accessed September 17, 2015, http://www.nps.gov/parkhistory/online_books/founders/sitee11.htm.

The Jolly Flatboatmen, by George Caleb Bingham, 1846.
Courtesy National Gallery of Art, Washington, D.C.

❦ ❦ ❦

River Navigation in the Pre-Steamboat Era

Rivers held the key to transportation on the frontier, and Maley's narrative provides insights on the nature of river navigation in the early nineteenth century. For his excursions on the Missouri, Wabash, Current, Spring, White, Arkansas, and upper Red Rivers, Maley traveled in a "perogue" (pirogue) or dugout canoe. There was no standard size pirogue; the vessels varied depending on the size of the available tree, the size of the cargo they were to carry, and the art of their builder. Smaller pirogues designed for one paddler might be as small as sixteen feet in length. Geologist Henry Schoolcraft and his companion wrestled a thirty-foot pirogue through the Bull Shoals on their return down the White

River,[3] *and Daniel Boone reportedly built a sixty-foot dugout to carry his family from Kentucky to Missouri. Maley doesn't describe the various pirogues he used, but vessels for two to three paddlers would likely range from twenty to thirty feet in length.*

While pirogues were good for navigating smaller streams and rivers, Maley and his companion decided to wait for a flatboat to navigate the rougher water they encountered on the Mississippi. Flatboats were cheap, crudely built vessels that could only travel downstream with the current, with limited maneuvering provided by a steering oar and long sweeps. However, they accounted for the bulk of cargo moving down the Mississippi prior to the age of steamboats and a significant share of traffic into the middle of the nineteenth century. Typical cargoes from the Ohio River and upper Mississippi included flour and whiskey, but flatboats were also used to carry cattle, corn, molasses, and sugar from lower Louisiana to New Orleans. On reaching their destination, the boats were normally dismantled for their lumber. As noted by Maley, a number of flatboat owners operated as peddlers, selling agricultural products and manufactured goods directly to riverside plantations instead of carrying their cargoes to New Orleans. It has been estimated that from 1820 to 1830, an average of three thousand flatboats descended the Mississippi each year.[4]

Two types of boats were commonly used to move cargo upstream. For his excursion up the Tennessee River and his first trip to Natchitoches, Maley traveled on a "keelboat." Up to fifty feet long, these had a pointed bow and stern, typically had an enclosed cabin amidships, and carried between twenty and forty tons of cargo. They traveled downstream with the current but had to be poled, towed, rowed, or "bushwhacked" (hauled on the overhead branches on the banks of the stream) upstream.[5] *On his 1812 return to Natchitoches, Maley took passage on what he called a "barge," a term that, at that time, applied to a long, narrow rowing boat or galley.*[6] *For travel on the western rivers, these vessels were larger than keelboats—carrying forty to one hundred tons of cargo,*[7] *they were longer and narrower, with a flat bottom, and appear to have been more commonly propelled by oars. In their 1804 expedition up the Ouachita River, explorers*

3. Schoolcraft, *Journal of a Tour into the Interior of Missouri and Arkansaw*, 70.
4. Dixon, *A Traffic History of the Mississippi River System*, 11–14.
5. Ibid., 10.
6. Chapelle, *American Small Sailing Craft*, 9.
7. Dixon, *A Traffic History of the Mississippi River System*, 10.

William Dunbar and George Hunter hired a barge at Ouachita Post that was fifty-five feet in length, nine feet in beam, and was propelled by twelve oars.[8] *The boat that took Maley to Natchitoches had twenty oarsmen and could travel seven or eight miles per hour in slack water, suggesting a craft that was probably greater than sixty feet in length.*[9]

Maley's journal also illustrates the importance that backwaters and bayous played in navigation on the lower Mississippi before the age of steam. He used a "cutoff" to travel between the lower reaches of the White River and the Arkansas, for example, and he and his companions later tried, and failed, to move a keelboat through another cutoff between Natchez and the Red River. Similarly, in 1813 Maley and two companions avoided a long trip down the Black River and up the Mississippi by paddling their pirogue through Bayou Cocodrie and Lake Concordia to return to Natchez from Ouachita Post. Bayous could provide relatively slack water for moving larger cargoes, as well. Bayou Boeuf and Little River were important transportation links for the planters in Alexandria and Natchitoches. Bayou Bartholomew, which runs 359 miles from the Ouachita River near Monroe, Louisiana to Pine Bluff, Arkansas, was used by steamboats to transport cotton and timber until the construction of railroads in the 1890s.[10]

NATCHEZ

We at last arrived at Natchez. It was in a healthy time of the year in November; the season of the boats was just coming on. Natchez is a post town and port of entry and capital of Adams County, Mississippi Territory, situated on the east side of the river and built on a hill almost perpendicular and nearly 200 feet above the surface of the river. It is about 300 miles above Orleans and contains about 2000 inhabitants; N Lat 31–33 & Lon 91–15. Below this high bank is the landing place or levy so called there. This is stuck full of grog shops, fruit shops, gambling houses and ladies of pleasure.

Here Natchez loses its reputation as to health. In a great measure these

8. Berry et al., *The Forgotten Expedition, 1804–1805*, 48.

9. The so called "hull speed" of man-powered vessels is dependent on length; everything else being equal, the longer the vessel, the faster it can travel.

10. DeArmond-Huskey, "Bayou Bartholomew."

hands coming down from different parts of Kentucky, Tennessee and Ohio, as soon as they arrive here, they have a little money which causes them to set to drinking and gambling, whoring and carousing. As long as money lasts, they take no rest night nor day but what they get when liquor has overpowered them, they lay about anywhere and everywhere exposed to the unhealthy dews of the night. In this way he continues till his money is spent and then he must lay out, for nobody will take him in. Then goes about from boat to boat a begging for something to eat. If he lives at all, he will start after a while and trust providence, perhaps not one cent in his pocket. He then begs as he goes which does perhaps tolerable well as long as he travels among white inhabitants, but alas they have but about 100 miles of white inhabitants then 400 miles through the Indian nation—that generally wilderness.

Although the natives and half breeds croud on this road to get the travelers' penny, they don't pay any attention to these travellers that have no money. To go through this wilderness is a sight that would make any person feel for the human creation. To see them lay and die, not being able to reach a house, leave their bodies there to be pulled and hauled about by the wild vermin of the forest. Also, every Indian house you come to you see more or less laying sick with nobody to take any care of them. This is so frequent that these Indians have worn out their patience by assisting them. The Kentuckians are despised by almost every nation of Indians in hearing of them for they generally boast on their prosperity. It is generally thought by the Indians that all the people that travel through there are Kentuckians as they have always understood that they would kill an Indian as soon as a deer.

Natchez

In the fall of 1810, Maley arrived at Natchez, one of the oldest populated sites on the Mississippi River. In 1716 France built Fort Rosalie there, at the site of a Natchez Indian village. The French population was annihilated, however, in the Natchez rebellion of 1729, a conflict that resulted in the destruction of the fort and the ultimate destruction of the Natchez tribe. The French rebuilt the fort, but in 1766, following the end of the French and Indian War, relinquished control to

View looking up the Mississippi from Natchez Bluffs.
Photograph by the editor.

the British. Spain seized control of the fort during the American Revolutionary War and held it until 1798, when it came under the jurisdiction of the United States.[11] *Situated on bluffs that rise two hundred feet above the river, Natchez offered a commanding position on the river and was considered a healthier site than the often flooded lands on the opposite bank of the river.*

At the time of Maley's visit, Natchez was growing as a commercial and political center for the region. The Mississippi River was navigable by sailing ships up to that point, and the town was the southern terminus of the Natchez Trace that led to Nashville, Tennessee. On his 1808 visit, Cuming reported between eighty and a hundred houses in the town, as well as a Catholic church and a brick meeting house for Presbyterians or Anabaptists. He was particularly struck by the mixture of people, including free people of mixed race and French and Spanish creoles, which reminded him of towns in the West Indies.[12] *The respectable town on top of the bluff, however, stood in stark contrast to Natchez "Under the Hill": the community that developed along the river to serve the needs and desires of river men. Most*

11. Barnett, "The Yamasee War, the Bearded Chief, and the Founding of Fort Rosalie," 23.
12. Cuming, "Cuming's Tour to the Western Country (1807–1809)," 322.

observers shared Maley's opinion; the botanist John Bradbury, who arrived there in 1811, noted that the port contained thirty to forty houses and a few stores, and stated that "there is not, perhaps, in the world, a more dissapated place."[13]

Natchez remained an important commercial center throughout the steamboat era, and it was the home of a number of wealthy cotton planters. Not many traces of its early nineteenth-century history can be found in the city, but it survived the Civil War relatively unscathed and is today famous for its later antebellum buildings, including thirteen National Landmarks and over a thousand buildings on the National Register of Historic Places.[14] *Natchez "Under the Hill" was largely destroyed in an 1840 tornado that killed approximately three hundred boatmen and steamboat passengers. While there are no remnants of the grog shops and ladies of pleasure noted by Maley, a riverboat casino docked at the waterfront is a modern successor to the gambling houses he saw in 1810.*

Up the Lower Red River

Now we leave this and proceed on our contemplated route up the Red River which, if possible, I should wish to be well acquainted with, and to inform myself so that nothing shall escape my eye, so that I may be of service to the public, that this may all come from a source that may be relied on, as this country once more has an opening to vend its produce that is so valuable to her sister states, which is the cotton, which she wishes to be the means of establishing and reestablishing their factories, which must otherwise fall to the ground. At Natchez, I sold my beaver, otter, etc. and laid in some goods for the Red River market. Put my goods aboard a keel bottom boat that was bound for Nachitoches.[15]

Now to be particular, I must tell you this, that the mouth of the Red River is 75 miles below Natchez but there is a cut-off broke through only five miles below. That I was credibly informed that they have gone through in 15 minutes through into Red River by the Mississippi being high and Red

13. Bradbury, *Travels in the Interior of America*, 216.

14. "Natchez Celebrates Tri-Centennial in 2016." Natchez Pilgrimage Tours, accessed December 11, 2017, http://www.natchezpilgrimage.com/natchez-ms-group-tours.php.

15. Natchitoches (pronounced "Nack-a-tish"), Louisiana.

River low. We tried our skill to get through, but we could not it being so obstructed by timber that we could not get it cleared out. There we lost 100 miles by not going through the cutoff. This strikes Red River 30 miles up. Therefore we had to keep down to the mouth. Now the Mississippi is well inhabited on both sides with entire cotton plantations, the soil very fertile. The west side of the river is very often overflowed by the June fresh of the Mississippi but the east is higher ground.

The second day we got to Red River, the first of my seeing it and sure enough it merits its name for it is red indeed. Now at the confluence of this river, it is one mile wide, the banks very low and much grown up with willow, no chance seemingly for any settlement to be made there. We found the current of this river tolerable stiff to stem. The way they go up this river is chiefly by bushwhaking as the boatmen call it. They keep in shore so that they rub the willows and then they begin in the bow of the boat and each man takes hold of the willows and pulls and walks back and then to the bow and renews his hold. This way they make very good way. The first night we started on Red River we had a bad place to camp, the ground very wet and disagreeable, wood very scarce, that is such as will burn. The timber here is chiefly cottonwood and willow. The former is a general growth of this country, grows very tall and bears a ball similar to a cotton ball and opens in the fall of the year and drops its cotton which is of no use. The timber is of no use neither to burn nor any thing else. This night I spent very uncomfortable on account of our situation being so wet.

Next morning we started pretty early. After going on perhaps a mile or two we saw the first alligator that ever I had seen. They are very plenty in this river which makes me hate even to drink the water they swim in for their looks are so despisable and their size so enormous that they are a monster to look at. This day we got to the mouth of Black River which comes in from the north. At the junction of this river it is inhabited. This is 30 miles up Red River. People that live here live chiefly by hunting. They find abundance of honey and barrel it up and send it to market. Stock they can raise without any assistance at all and them always fat. We stayed at a house all night which I was not sorry for.

I got a good night's rest, in the morning started early and found the river to make a great many bends. I sported myself that day by shooting of alligators. We never could get one after shooting of him; they would always sink before we could get to him. The planters on the river lose a great many of young cattle by them. They will watch for their prey for days upon a stretch where they find out that cattle come to the river to drink. There they lay concealed; they keep their whole body sunk in the water and their eyes being right on the top of their heads they have the advantage by keeping their eyes out and their bodies sunk. When cattle come near enough they grab them and pull them right in the water and struggle till they drown them and then devour their prey. The lands in general are too low near the river. The river's common width is about 100 to 150 yards with the shores grown very thick with willow. We went from twenty to twenty five miles a day.

Cotton Country

After four days travel up the river we got to some improvements and very large planters. Appearingly, a great number of slaves were held by these planters in order to raise cotton. How can men avoid making an independency in this country when they raise from 25 to 30 hundred of seed cotton to the acre and every hand to tend five acres? From that an estimate may be made allowing 1000 wt. of ginned cotton to the acre which the five acres makes 5000 wt. of clean cotton to the hand, that is every hand that you employ and allowing cotton only at $18 per hundred amounts to 900 dollars per hand per annum. This is pretty near a true estimate.

This man that owned the boat and cargo was from Wheeling on the Ohio River in the state of Virginia. He had a brother that left his native country and came on Red River. He had then been gone 14 years in this country. He lived about 25 miles from Alexandria. He called to see his brother whom he had not seen for 14 years and did not know exactly where he lived. Only by enquiry after he was up the river, we made a stop where he heard his brother lived and found out that he lived four miles from the river. Where we made our stop was a small improvement. A man lived there that had an Indian squaw for his wife. There we got our directions how to find his brother. I went with him and the man there went with us as a pilot for we had to go chiefly by water upon account of the river being high. We went in a canoe, took right into the woods. Sometimes we had plenty of water and at other times our channels but very narrow so that we had to drag this canoe along. This man told us that in higher stages of water they would go through in that direction into the Tuckapaw[16] country and proceed on to the Gulf of Mexico.

We at last arrived at an extensive prarie, all inhabited and seemingly very ancient buildings. They were chiefly French. These planters here appeared to be all very wealthy. They seemed to hold a great number of slaves here. This man found his brother living in plenty, was married to one of those French ladies and had got a fortune by her. People here know not what want is, they live in splendor, they have peaches and figs in abundance, but apples it will not suit. We stayed two days and then went on in order to reach Rapiddes or Alexandria.

We got there the second day. Here I was surprised to see so much business going on, in as I thought this wilderness country, but here I found chiefly Americans and buildings going on very rapid. This, of course, must come to be a great place in time. They have named it Alexandria. It is a post town and capital of the Parish of Rapides. It is situated on the south side of the river about 150 miles from its confluence with the Mississippi. It contains a handsome courthouse, 40 dwelling houses and 120 inhabitants. It is the center of the western district of Louisiana and the point of intersection of all the great roads in the country. Through it passes all the merchandise for the Spanish territory and all the trade for the Indians N and W.

Alexandria is situated near the middle of the fertile valley of Rapides which extends about 30 miles above and below the town. It is about eight miles wide. The valley is enclosed by Red River on the east and by Bayou l'Boeuf on the west, which is a navigable stream up in the country that saves land carriage for the planters and it extends as far as this rich valley continues. The soil here is better than I could possibly describe. The country would charm any man only to see it. Nothing can be compared to it but a bowling green for level, and its fertility beyond description. That is to those

16. "Tuckapaw" is an obscure name, but according to one source ("Tuckapaw Media," accessed December 24, 2015, http://tuckapaw.com/about/), it is an Anglicized version of "Atakapa," the name of an Indian tribe that lived in southwest Louisiana. As noted in Stoddard (*Sketches, Historical and Descriptive, of Louisiana*, 166, 180), the "Atakapa" or "Attacappas" region included lands in southwest Louisiana west of the Atchafalaya River, ranging from the Gulf of Mexico to the Opelousas region to the north. Although flood-control structures have altered the drainage of the region significantly, at the time of Maley's visit, it seems likely that, at times of high water, one could have navigated from the lower Red to the Gulf of Mexico via Bayou Boeuf and Bayou Teche.

that have only seen the lands of any of the northern states even better than that in highest state of cultivation.

Alexandria is equally distant from Natchez, St. Francisville, Point Coupee, Opelousas, Nachitoches, and the crossing of the Sabine, about 80 miles from each and about 300 miles from New Orleans and 1499 miles SW of Washington, N Lat 31–15. They make use of the rain water chiefly to drink as it is considered healthier. Some have cisterns to gather their water that will hold a 1000 hogsheads and they supply their neighbors. The people here form a good society. When strangers come there they are much taken notice of and will receive all the information from them that they know concerning the advantages of the country. When I arrived here, it was in December 4th 1810. The weather was very agreeable, not unseasonable with cold nor rain.

After staying two days at this place we started on for Nachitoches which was called 150 miles further. From that on, we had all an inhabited country nothing but French planters, all very wealthy, their improvements very large. They generally own from 1 to 200 slaves and some more. That is in order to raise cotton. They raise very little else. Corn, they chiefly buy, which is the most the negroes lives on. Meat they get none, only some fish they catch of nights themselves, which are chiefly very large catfish and them they only boil and make a soup of them. They have no water mills in that country at all. They have to pound their corn only in hominy mortars. This they have to do after doing their day's work, which the overseer makes them do by task: so many hills of cotton to clean or so many pounds of cotton to pick according to the ableness of the negro. Clothing they give them but little. They generally wish to make a fair estimate what they can make yearly by the number of hands they employ. Some of these French planters are very hospitable and others despise the Americans since that country was purchased by the United States, which is merely on account that they are rather doubtful that all their claims of land will be allowed them that they hold under French government. I was several times denied by them even of a night's lodging, even in my own blankets, under their roof.

Now we have fine shores to walk on, stay but little in the boat. They now pull the boat along by a tow line. This way they make very good speed. The river makes a great many bends but the general course is about W by N. Every few minutes I stand in a surprise thinking that I have a town or village in sight and find myself mistaken it being only a planter with all his negroes houses and other outhouses all standing in miniature. The cotton gin is generally the largest building. Them are for cleaning the cotton from its seed. They generally go by mules. Their dwelling houses are large on the ground, but only a story and a half high, a porch all round the house. They are framed and filled in with clay and whitewashed. Thus they live in splendor.

Land not yet may be got cheap, $2 per acre only. Come Americans! Now is your time before this country is filled up with men from over the ocean. See how anxious they were to enjoy those delightful situations on the Mississippi, but that brave hero Jackson with his sharpshooters grandly disappointed them.[17] The madams even were impatient to see the day that they should be landed into the promised land, but a few years more and land in that country will not be bought for $20 an acre that may now be had for $2. If you read this you get a correct information.

I still keep on the shore mostly to make myself acquainted with the nature of the country. Dry goods here is a grand article to trade upon. They make great inquiry for all kinds of finery such as elegant shawls and handkerchiefs which they wear a great many. They spin none in that country nor make any of their wearing apparel [. . .[18]] although there is so much cotton raised it only wants men of spirit and enterprise, with means that they are not afraid to risk, in erecting factories, as this is the place to commence such works where cotton can be had upon reasonable terms and your cloth fetch a good price. Perhaps you have never considered this before. We are now five days journey from Alexandria and not an American settled on the river. The French, they populate no more here. Now lies the land waiting only for you to come and occupy it.

The 7th day we got to Little River which forms an island of 20 miles in length. The main river makes a great bend and Little River is broke through in a straight direction which makes half odds in the distance, but it being so narrow that it very often stops up by [. . .[19]]

. . . continue long so as they have a law between themselves that every planter has to keep the river open as far as his lands extend. On its banks we

17. Presumably a reference to the Battle of New Orleans, December 1814–January 1815.

18. At this point, the account switches from the journal held by the DeGolyer Library at Southern Methodist University to that held in the Silliman Papers at Yale University.

19. Apparently one or more missing pages here. The following paragraph begins with a remnant of a sentence fragment from the missing text.

found a raft within five miles of Nachitoches which we thought impossible to get away in a month, but the planter, for fear of paying his fine, came with about 200 hands and in less than a day he had the passage open for us to proceed up the river and soon got to Nachitoches. Immediately below Nachitoches, the Little River leaves the main stream. This island is very extensive, 20 miles in length and 12 miles in breadth. In some places this looks like a garden.

The Emerging Cotton Industry

In his 1810 travel from Natchez to Natchitoches, Maley was a witness to the early stages of the cotton boom, a manifestation of the industrial revolution that would transform the South. For hundreds of years, China and the Indian sub-continent had been the world's largest producers of cotton, but that began to change in the final decades of the eighteenth century, as British entrepreneurs employed new water-powered spindles and looms that provided competitive advantages in producing cotton yarn and cloth. Britain's climate was unsuitable for growing cotton, but it imported raw cotton from the Ottoman Empire, the Caribbean and other sources,[20] *and its exports of finished products increased sixteen-fold between 1780 and 1800.*[21]

Cotton had been grown in small amounts in America for domestic use, and American planters began raising long-staple Sea Island cotton for export in 1786. That variety only thrived along the coasts of Georgia and South Carolina, however, and it wasn't until Eli Whitney's 1793 invention of the cotton gin that it became profitable to grow upland varieties of cotton on a large scale. Cotton production moved rapidly into the upland regions of Georgia and South Carolina, and by 1810 Alabama, Mississippi, Louisiana, and Tennessee had become significant producers. Part of the expansion was driven by the fact that cotton readily depleted nutrients in the soil and could only be produced for several years on one plot of land before the land required fertilization or crop rotation.[22] *Lands along the floodplains of the Mississippi and its tributaries, however, were*

20. Beckert, *Empire of Cotton*, 42, 86.
21. Ibid., 67.
22. Ibid., 100–4.

an exception. Every few years, they would be inundated by floods which brought new nutrients to the soil and allowed cotton to be produced year after year.[23] *In addition to soil fertility, cotton planters in the region were also able to transport their production by water to markets in New Orleans.*

The cotton gin also boosted the profitability of slavery. Maley calculated that one slave, working five acres, might produce $900 worth of cotton per year along the Red River. His estimate is much higher than others; in 1816 Darby concluded that the average "workman" on a cotton farm might produce $180/year of cotton.[24] *Whatever the actual figure, however, a young adult male slave cost only $500 in the New Orleans slave market in 1800, and incredible profits could be realized by planters using slave labor.*[25] *Cotton production in the United States grew dramatically, from 1.5 million pounds in 1790 to 167.5 million pounds by 1820, and the slave trade grew with it, including a significant shift of slavery within the South. Following the Revolutionary War, tobacco production in the Upper South had become less profitable, and an estimated quarter million slaves were sold or relocated to work cotton fields in the Lower South.*[26]

At the time of Maley's travels, it would have been difficult to foresee the ultimate ramifications of this emerging industry. The demand for land to grow cotton was already adding pressure for the removal of Indian tribes from east of the Mississippi. However, the cotton boom in the South would continue for another fifty years, and cotton would comprise more than half of all American exports between 1815 and 1860.[27] *The industry would create fortunes among southern planters, northern financiers, and British manufacturers, but the concurrent rise of slavery would ultimately drive the nation to war and the South to financial ruin. The cotton industry ultimately recovered, and with the use of mechanical cotton-pickers, remains an important crop in the region today.*

23. Lynette Tanner, "Cotton Industry," presentation given at Frogmore Plantation, April 4, 2016.

24. Darby, *Geographical Description of Louisiana*, 162.

25. Beckert, *Empire of Cotton*, 118.

26. Ibid., 104, 108.

27. Ibid., 119.

The "Yucca House" at Melrose Plantation, near Natchitoches. Built between 1810 and 1815, at the time of Maley's travels through the region, this structure exhibits the use of wooden gutters and a cistern for collecting rainwater. (As noted in Association for the Preservation of Historic Natchitoches, "Melrose Plantation History," http://www.melroseplantation.org/history/.) *Photograph by the editor.*

CHAPTER 7 ❦ *December 1810–Spring 1812*

Natchitoches

We arrived in Nachitoches the middle of December. The weather now was getting cold and disagreeable to travel by water. I thought best to take my winter quarters at this place. I took my board for which I had to pay at the rate of $4 per week. This is a place of a great deal of trade. If there were men enough of fortitude and resolution to refrain from their vices that this town is given to, which is gambling and night strolling, they make themselves entirely unfit for the business of the day. There are so many of those ladies of pleasure who take most of their money and zest of the night, which of course was set aside for us to enjoy as such. These girls are all the copper color. Some are slaves and others their own mistresses. Some of those inhabitants that are wealthy purchase their own misses such as they fancy. They are generally captivating figures but when they think them worn out in the service, they sell them and buy others. I was credibly informed that there were but three men in all the town that had lawful wives and it contains upwards of 300 inhabitants.[1]

The town stands upon a level on the south bank of the river. It has no place of worship but a Roman chapel. They have a black priest who attends worship for them. His dress looks very reverent, wears a wig made of his own kind of hair and a large three cocked hat. His ceremonies are all in French. His performance is different from any that I have seen before of the same profession. Immediately in the rear of the town is an eminence where the American fort stands where they always keep soldiers in peaceable times for fear of an invasion by the Spaniards or Indians. There is an abundance

1. As noted by Flores, this assertion by Maley's informant is not supported by Natchitoches marriage statistics. Flores, "The John Maley Journal," 17.

of yellow ochre on this mount, this being on the south side of the river. The road goes immediately in that direction to the Sabine River. It is about 40 miles distance. This river divides the Louisiana and Spanish dominions.

Natchitoches

Natchitoches, Louisiana (pronounced "Nack-a-tish") was founded as a trading post in 1714 by Frenchman Louis Juchereau de St. Denis, making it the oldest European settlement in what would become the Louisiana Purchase. Built, at the time, at the lower end of a massive logjam (the Great Raft) on the Red River, Natchitoches served for the next fifty years as a base for projecting France's political power in Louisiana and onto the southern plains. The boundaries between French Louisiana and Spanish Texas had never been clearly established, and Spain established a post only a few miles west of Natchitoches at Los Adaes, and garrisoned a post, as well, at Nacogdoches, Texas, on the other side of the Sabine River. While there was little direct conflict, the two European powers vied for influence with the Indian tribes on the frontier, competing to establish trading relationships and collaborating, at times, to bring Catholicism to the tribes.[2] *France and Spain did find themselves on opposite sides of a battle in 1759, when French advisors supported Taovaya and Comanche Indians to repel a Spanish led assault on their fortified village on the Red River near current-day Spanish Fort, Texas.*[3]

Conflict between the two European powers ended when France ceded its territories west of the Mississippi to Spain in 1762. However, St. Denis had established strong relationships with Indian tribes along the Red River, and after his death in 1744, his son and sons-in-law, Césaire de Blanc de Neuveville and Athanase de Mézières continued to manage Indian relations out of Natchitoches even following the transfer of formal power to Spain.[4] *Forty years later, with the Louisiana Purchase, the United States inherited much of the French trading relationship with the tribes along the Red River, but the question of the boundary between Louisiana and Spanish Texas again generated conflict. Spanish forces blocked the Red River expedition of Thomas Freeman and Peter Custis in July 1806, and war*

2. Johns, *Storms Brewed in Other Men's Worlds*, 197–225.
3. Ibid., 351.
4. Ibid., 343–44.

was only averted by an agreement to establish the area between the Sabine River and the Arroyo Hondo as a de-militarized neutral ground.[5] *The military post referred to by Maley was Fort Claiborne, which was established in Natchitoches shortly after the Louisiana Purchase. It was replaced in 1822 by Fort Jesup, located several miles west of town.*[6]

Although Natchitoches had existed primarily as an Indian trading post, plantation agriculture began in earnest in the 1780s, focusing primarily on indigo and tobacco. However, by the time Maley arrived, cotton had become the preferred cash crop. Unlike other areas of the South, many of the successful planters in the Natchitoches region were "gens de couleur libre"—or "free people of color"—the offspring of French planters and enslaved Africans and American Indians.[7] *The descendants of these people in the Cane River region are known today as Cane River Creoles, many of whom still occupy the same land where their ancestors' plantations once stood. The status of the Creole population, along with public land, the role of church and state, and political representation were among the issues that had to be addressed as Natchitoches passed from Spanish rule to that of the United States.*[8]

Today, Natchitoches is a charming town of 18,000 with some of the country's best-preserved historic sites from the French colonial period. These include a number of structures in its thirty-three-block National Landmark Historic District and several historic plantations preserved in the Cane River National Heritage Area southeast of the town. Following the removal of the Great Raft, a hundred-mile long logjam on the Red River north of Natchitoches, the main channel of the river shifted east, away from Natchitoches. The town now fronts Cane River Lake, a thirty-five-mile-long oxbow lake formed from the old river channel.

Foray into Spanish Texas

After staying at this place about 2 weeks, I got tired of the place by seeing so much disapation. There were a certain number of men that were always

5. Tyson, *The Red River in Southwestern History*, 72–77.

6. "History of the Cane River Region," National Park Service, accessed April 29, 2016, https://www.nps.gov/nr/travel/caneriver/history.htm.

7. Ibid.

8. Ibid.

trying to delude strangers in order to raise a company of men that would furnish themselves with a good rifle a piece to go and join the republican party of Spaniards at Nacogdoches. This was actually an invitation by the Spaniards that 200 good riflemen could, with their assistance, subdue the royalists and take all their plunder and then go on and waylay the caravans that come from Santa Fe loaded with silver from the mines. They generally go once a year with about 500 mules loaded on to Mexico to the mint to get their silver coined. They have been plundered by the Indians of their mules and silver. Once they were taken by them and their silver left behind but they rode off the mules. This nation is called the Hyatans.[9] They are a wandering tribe; they cannot be found for more than a month at one place.

This was the prospect that was laid before any man: that in less than one 12 month, they would make an independent fortune, that there was no doubt of success. There was eight of us nearly of one opinion. We thought it most prudent to go and see how they were situated. We fitted out in order to go and buy mules, as they have very fine ones. We started on horseback, each equipped with a good rifle and dirk,[10] which is the custom of the country. The lands between Nachitoches and the Sabine are chiefly pine timber but very level and open. It looks like a meadow. There are some inhabitants that go there in order to raise cattle, as the range is so good that they have nothing to provide for their stock, neither winter nor summer. I have seen 300 young calves of one spring's increase to one grazier. Think of this product—only the trouble of marking and branding them.

The second day we crossed at the Sabine where there is an American lives that keeps a ferry.[11] The river land here is very fertile. We crossed the Sabine and then had 30 miles of a wilderness to go before we got to any inhabitants, which we rode in one day. The house that we got to was a Spaniard that called himself a republican, which we were glad to see, thinking that we would get a general information. He treated us with great hospitality, but the fare we got was nothing but some jerked beef which they have very plenty, but bread they have none. Their cattle are wonderful to look at. They have horns like our common 4-year old steers. Cowhides here are nothing thought of; they lay about spoiling. Tanners they have none among them.

9. Also spelled "Hietans," more commonly referred to today as Comanche.
10. A long dagger.
11. According to Flores, the ferryman was Michael Crow. Flores, "The John Maley Journal," 22.

This man gave us broad hints to know if the Americans would not assist them in gaining their independence, but we would not let on to pay much attention to him concerning such a thing. Still, we made inquiry which was our best route to go to find republicans and he directed us on towards Nachadosh.[12] We traveled on another day and stopped at every house we could find to engage mules if they had any. We found several but left them until our return as we would not drive them backwards and forwards. Some used us with great kindness and others treated us with great suspicion and contempt. I would rather travel among Indians for they have some corn among them, but the Spaniards have none. Therefore I promised myself that I should not undertake to come and join the party that meant to come on and fight for that that they have no right to. I said but little about it, but thought the more.

As soon as we had a prospect of mules enough, we turned back and took our mules as we had engaged them, bought and paid for them. We gathered 50 elegant mules and drove them off and got safe out of the inhabitants, but behold, before we got to the Sabine, we were overtaken by a strong party of the royalists and took our mules from us. But we had the heels of them. Our horses could outrun theirs, so by that means we kept out of their way. Otherwise, they might have killed us if not taken prisoner. They tried to fire at us but they missed in their attempts. They had not a gun, perhaps, that would fire once in ten times snapping. When they were going off with our mules, we could not but show some spirit of resentment. We divided by four on each side of the road in the woods and got as near to them as we could to make a shot at them. They made several attempts to overtake and pursue after us for some distance, and fire a number of shots at us, but to no effect. When they turned, we pursued again until night came on. We could do no more. They kept up after night and so did we, but we did not let them hear anything of us.

After the middle of the night, they made a halt and kindled some fires as it was very cold and disagreeable. As soon as they had settled themselves round the fire, we made our approach as near them as we could. It was near enough for our rifles to do execution. We discharged 8 at once or nearly so at which they jumped up all in a confusion. We then retreated a distance off to keep out of their way. They soon extinguished their fires that we should not

12. Nacogdoches, county seat of Nacogdoches County, Texas.

see them and gathered up and started on again. We still pursued them till day light. By that time we got to the inhabitants. When day came so that we could see, we gave them fire again. They turned upon us and gave us chase; got very near us and gave several shots at us and wounded one of our men slightly. We got away from them and got before them into the settlement and immediately got assistance. The republicans turned out and we met them, but they soon left the road and left us the mules. We soon gathered them; they were all tied two on two. We left some to mind the mules whilst some pursued this party, but they cleared themselves.

Our mules now wanted some rest and they were hungered out as they had not eaten any for 24 hours. We then let them take some refreshment and then started again on our route to the Sabine which was nearly 40 miles. Twenty of the republicans accompanied us to the Sabine. It was about the middle of the day when we started and we never made a halt until we got to the river and crossed over our mules and there we stayed till next morning and rested our weary limbs. These Spaniards concluded to stay there till we could go on to Nachitoches and return again with a reinforcement of about 200 men, well armed. With this force, we could subdue them and should be entitled to an equal share with them of all the plunder that we could get. Some of these men took resolution that they would come and assist, but it was the prospect of obtaining silver that I was determined not [to] join in. The second day we arrived safe at Nachitoches and rumor spread abroad and preparations made to go and join that party at the Sabine. So I declined going and also my companion, who I got at the River Currents. He still remained with me and was determined so to do until we had seen the source of Red River, which was a wrong time of year then to start.

New Orleans

As I had 20 mules for my share, I thought best to take a trip to New Orleans by land. I sold my goods that I had bought to take up the river to good advantage in order to purchase more at Orleans. We started the 4th of January, 1811, steered our course for Bayou Boeuf. We found a great deal of pine plains, chiefly the longleaf pine and the long moss very plenty. It is all a grazing country, grass very tall, woods without any underbrush. We went along very well with our mules, when they wanted to eat, stopped and let them feed. There was no want of food for them. We also found houses that we could get accommodation. The land continues near one thing till we get to Bayou Boeuf, then it changes to the most beautiful country that ever eye beheld, as level as a house floor and very fertile. They raise some Indian corn and wheat here. There are several Americans settled at the place. They appear to live very sumptuously. They used me with great hospitality. We again arrived at Alexandria and encamped outside of the town with our mules. I got a man to keep them that night and I slept in town, for I felt myself indisposed. Had a good dish of coffee and slept well, took breakfast in the morning and started for New Orleans.

We had a great many difficulties to encounter such as water courses very bad crossing, especially that time of year. We found a great deal of poor land and also fine praries for grazing of cattle. We at last got in the Apalouse[13] country, which is very fine for raising of stock, not to be exceeded by any. They have a great many horses which are very serviceable, cattle in abundance. Same breed of the Spaniards beef may be bought cheap in that country. If men were only there that were acquainted with barreling of beef and smoking the rounds, they undoubtedly would make a fortune in a few years. This will be found out after a while. We drove on our mules till we got them on the coast of the Mississippi. We immediately found good sale for them among the sugar planters. We sold some at $70 such as we gave but $20 for. It was not many days before we had sold all our mules.

Maley's Filibuster into Texas

John Maley's foray into Texas to buy mules came at a volatile time on the Texas/Louisiana frontier. As mentioned previously, the location of the boundary between French Louisiana and Spanish Texas had never been resolved, but the question became moot with the French transfer of Louisiana to Spain in 1763. The U.S.

13. Maley is referring to the Opelousas area, which, according to maps at the time, was centered southeast of Natchitoches, west of Bayou Boeuf and Bayou Teche. See, for example, Lafon, "Carte Generale du Territoire D'Orleans," New Orleans, Louisiana, 1806, U.S. Archives. accessed December 15, 2015, http://www.usgwarchives.net/maps/louisiana/statemap/lafla1806.jpg.

purchase of Louisiana, however, resurrected the issue and in 1806, in order to avert hostilities, U.S. general James Wilkinson and Spanish lieutenant colonel Simón de Herrera agreed to establish a neutral ground between the Arroyo Hondo and the Sabine River.[14] *The area, which fell outside the control of either government, quickly attracted American squatters, bandits, runaway slaves, and military deserters. In 1810 American and Spanish officers coordinated in a joint effort to remove the miscreants, destroying a dozen buildings and forcing thirty-four people to leave the zone.*[15]

In addition to uncertainty along the border, Spanish officials had reason to fear American schemes to detach Texas itself. Even before the U.S. purchase of Louisiana, the supply of wild horses on the Texas plains had attracted the attention of American "mustangers" such as Philip Nolan.[16] *Nolan, who was a protégé of U.S. general James Wilkinson, carried out four expeditions into Texas to obtain horses between 1791 and 1801. Spanish authorities were suspicious of his motives and opposed to efforts to undercut their own influence with the tribes. Nolan was killed in 1801 on the Brazos River by Spanish troops sent to arrest him, and his men were imprisoned.*[17]

Spanish concerns could only have grown with the 1803 Louisiana Purchase, when it found its previously well-defined boundary with the United States—located at the Mississippi River—replaced by ambiguous and conflicting claims to lands much further west, all of which was further complicated by increased American emigration to Louisiana. The Aaron Burr conspiracy of 1806–7 to seize Spanish land and form a new republic also did little to allay Spanish concerns over American intentions. Finally, Spanish control over Nueva Espana received a fatal blow on September 16, 1810, when Father Miguel Hidalgo y Costilla issued his "Grito de Dolores" [cry of Dolores], which initiated the decade-long Mexican revolution.[18] *Maley arrived in Natchitoches only three months later, but, as noted in his journal, schemes to profit from the revolution were already being widely discussed there.*

14. Haggard, "Neutral Ground," accessed May 19, 2016, https://tshaonline.org/handbook/online/articles/nbn02.

15. Townes, "The Neutral Strip," 3.

16. There were an estimated two million wild horses on the Great Plains in 1800. Flores, *Journal of an Indian Trader*, 8.

17. Jackson, "Nolan, Philip."

18. Warren, *The Sword Was Their Passport*, 4.

It was against this backdrop that Maley and seven well-armed companions crossed the Neutral Ground and ventured well into Spanish Texas to buy mules. Unsurprisingly, they only achieved their objective after a shootout with Spanish forces and assistance by Mexican revolutionaries. Despite the scuffle, it appears to have been a profitable venture for Maley. He apparently bought twenty of the fifty mules purchased on the trip, and he may have made close to a thousand dollars in profit selling them to the sugar planters on the Mississippi—enough to spend the rest of 1811 in New Orleans.

WE WAITED FOR A BOAT to come for us to get aboard and take passage to Orleans. We viewed their sugar works and plantations, which if I was to tell you the product of some of these plantations, you would think that I exaggerate, but one man told me that he at least cleared fifty thousand dollars yearly. They make a great deal by making taffy,[19] a kind of rum they make from their sugar cane after the best is taken out. They live in the greatest style imaginable. Their houses are large and commodious, but not high although they are built on high blocks and open below to let the air circulate underneath the building. I left here and took passage to New Orleans for the first time I was there. I shall give a small description of this place here as I was at this place afterwards but I was then engaged in matters of more importance than making remarks on the situation of the town.

New Orleans, the capital of the state of Louisiana, founded in 1717. It is situated on the east bank of the Mississippi River in a county of the same name. The town is regularly laid out and the houses are partly built of brick and partly of wood. It extends upwards of a mile along the river and in the center stands the town house and cathedral. It contains a convent, two theaters, and contains about 24,000 inhabitants in 1811, of whom 10,000 were blacks. An embankment extends along the river directly in front of the town called the levee. It commences at Fort Placquemine, 43 miles below the city, and it extends to the Iberville, 115 above.

19. According to Flores, Maley is referring to "tafia," a rum made from distilled sugar cane juice. Flores, "The John Maley Journal," 30.

This town was attempted to be taken possession of by the British forces in December 1814. On the 23rd day of that month, the van of their army was landed within eight miles of the city, who were immediately attacked by a party of Americans under Gen. Jackson and compelled to retire. A second attempt was made on the 28th and met a similar fate. Both armies now entrenched but so near were they to each other that an almost continuous skirmishing was kept up until the 8th of January when the enemy determined on a grand assault, their army consisting of 10,000 chosen troops. They advanced by the dawn of day against the American lines but the contest was short and decisive, ending in the complete victory and discomfiture of the British army with the loss of their commander in chief killed, two major generals wounded, one of them mortally, and about 3000 men killed, wounded and prisoners.[20]

New Orleans is 1231 miles SW of Washington, W longitude from the same 14.13, N latitude 30.4. It commands a vast trade which now will increase very rapid. The steam boats running on the Mississippi certainly must give great encouragement to eastern traders. They now can export their goods all by the way of New Orleans and up the Mississippi ten percent lower than formerly.[21] The steam boats undoubtedly must be a public good. No doubt but steam boats will soon become a general thing, even to run up Red River, which I call the garden of the world, and also higher up the Mississippi and the Missouri which at this time is populating very rapid. The manner of exporting goods by the way of Pittsburg and down the Ohio River certainly took a land carriage of at least 300 miles. They then had to go down to the mouth of the river thence turn up the Mississippi entirely in a backward course for St. Louis and the Missouri. The country above the confluence of the Ohio and Mississippi gives vent for large quantities of goods. Consider the vast Indian trade up those several rivers which are at the present chiefly occupied by the British traders. Is it not a shame and disgrace to our country after fighting for our rights and privileges and so honorably obtained it that we don't enjoy them? What an assistance would it be to our revenue if we

20. Maley's account of the Battle of New Orleans took place well after his 1811 visit to that city: an example of including later events into his contemporaneous account.

21. Maley's discussion of steamboat travel on the Mississippi is also a reference to events that occurred after this visit to New Orleans. The first regular steamboat traffic on the river dates to 1817, which indicates Maley's book was written after that date. Lloyd, *Lloyd's Steamboat Directory and Disasters on the Western Waters*, 45.

could deprive the British of our just rights. This perhaps may open your eyes. If you believe not this, it puts you in the way of making more inquiry as to the situation of the country. I leave the readers to judge for themselves.

Return to Nachitoches

After this you shall have an account of Red River as I am at New Orleans at present. I purchase my goods such as answer that river trade both for the inhabitants and natives. After making my purchase, which is at a high rate, I put them on board of a barge bound for Nachitoches. Myself and companion took passage in the same. In going up the Mississippi, I had the view of all the planters on the coast, their situations, and beheld the most delightful country that ever nature or art has formed. These barges are manned with 20 hands, all very dexterous with their oars, 10 of a side they strike as one. They are as particular with an oar man as you'd be to have a good seaman. Every man there must do his part, otherwise inevitably fall back to stem a current that runs at the rate of five miles an hour. They will go from 2 1/2 to 3 miles an hour, which on slack water would average at the rate of 7 and 8.

They make a halt at or before sunset. They have their general stages, they then cook their provisions to serve the ensuing day. That is for the hands. In case of passengers, they cook on board. These hands are generally French, very nasty and any cookery suits them. They are very biddable to their employers. They undergo a vast deal of fatigue; they bear it with great fortitude. They keep regular hours in reviving themselves with a dram which is every four hours. They get their measure and wind 15 minutes and so on. It took 3 weeks, all but two days to Nachitoches, where we arrived on the 24th of February 1812.

Now I had to fit myself for to start up the river and enquired for all the information I could get. There are a great number of hunters here that go up a great distance in order to kill buffalo and hunt bees. They only bring down the beeswax, buffalo tallow and their tongues dried. The carcass and skin is thrown to the vermin. What a vast destruction here is only for the benefit of a few stragglers who in such a country as this might be a public good and also a good to themselves where they now are an entire nuisance. When they come to market with their produce, they never return until they have spent all they made in the season before it is necessity that compels them to retire to the woods, there to live like Indians and also commit depredations on the natives. If they come across their encampment, will plunder them of all their products which causes those friendly nations to become hostile and have reason to suspect every honest trader that should wish to venture among them and also get a general information of the country which from such men we cannot get with any accuracy.

They should wish it never to be known in their time there might be a stop put to so great a prodigality. They are compelled to bring their booty down the river. If there was agents appointed at the different ports where they have to land, they there might be brought to an account. I wish for the welfare of the country that some may read this and also see cause to feel himself interested so much as to enter complaint to some of the executive of the United States that they might make laws that would bring these now dissapated characters to be men fitting for useful societies which otherwise they will never become.

Now I will give an account of this party that started to assist in subduing the Spaniards. They crossed the Sabine River and raised all the force they could and undertook to overrun the country, but to their great mistake found themselves overpowered. The Spaniards soon fled and left them to fight their own way through.[22] There was several of the Americans killed, some taken prisoner and the remainder, rather than to return home so completely disappointed, they would go in quest of silver if they should obtain it in being highway men. They started for St. Antonio and undoubtedly on the coast of the mines they kept it as much a secret as possible. They still keep making attempts to raise a sufficient force and would have accomplished another expedition but the President issued a proclamation against it which has put a final stop to it.[23]

Continuing American Schemes in Texas

In retrospect, Maley's decision not to pursue further filibusters into Texas was a wise one. When he returned to Natchitoches in February 1812, he found that

22. This is an apparent reference to the José Menchaca filibuster that took place in October 1811. Warren, *The Sword Was Their Passport*, 5.

23. Apparently a reference to a proclamation by President Madison on September 1, 1815. Ibid., 125.

the men he had left at the Sabine had failed in their effort to return to Texas, apparently as part of what is now known as the Menchaca filibuster. In August 1811 two Mexican revolutionaries, José Bernardo Gutiérrez de Lara and Captain José Menchaca, fled Texas and found refuge in Natchitoches.[24] *While Gutiérrez traveled to Washington to seek assistance from the U.S. government, Menchaca remained in Natchitoches to organize an invasion force. In October 1811 Menchaca led three hundred American volunteers against Nacogdoches, but after encountering Spanish troops, he defected to the Royalists, and the American invasion was thwarted.*[25] *Maley's interlocutors were apparently referring to this when they told him that after crossing the Sabine, the Americans found themselves outgunned and were abandoned by their republican allies.*

The Menchaca filibuster was not the last effort to undermine Spanish control of Texas. In April 1812 Gutiérrez returned from Washington, and began organizing an invasion of Texas.[26] *The invasion, known as the Gutiérrez-Magee filibuster, began in August 1812.*[27] *By November, the invaders had swept south to capture La Bahia (current day Goliad),*[28] *and in March 1813 the filibusters captured San Antonio and established the Republic of Texas. However, their success was short-lived. In August 1813 the filibusters were routed by Royalist forces at the Battle of Medina River, and refugees from the invasion force fled back to Natchitoches.*[29]

Maley's journal mentions a proclamation banning further filibusters by U.S. citizens. Like several other references in his manuscript, this apparently refers to events that occurred after his travels, in this case a September 1, 1815, proclamation by President James Madison warning American citizens not to participate in unlawful enterprises against Spain.[30] *Madison's action came in response to Spanish protests over preparations taking place in New Orleans for another expedition against Mexico. The schemers in this case included prominent businessmen such as Edward Livingston, Abner Duncan, John K. West, and Auguste de Castera Davezac, as well as smugglers like the Lafitte brothers.*[31] *The venture openly recruited a number of disbanded soldiers who had participated in the earlier Battle of New*

24. Ibid., 5.
25. Jackson, "Menchaca, Jose."
26. Warren, *The Sword Was Their Passport*, 22–26.
27. Ibid., 34.
28. Ibid., 42.
29. Ibid., 52–68.
30. Ibid., 125.
31. Ibid., 119, 124.

Orleans.[32] *Contrary to Maley's assertion, Madison's proclamation did little to stop these efforts. However, the scheme fell short of its objectives after one of the key participants, José Álvarez de Toledo, betrayed the other filibusters in 1816.*[33]

Although Maley's account ends with his 1813 return to Nashville, he alludes to being in New Orleans at a later date, "engaged in matters of more importance than making remarks on the situation of the town." We will likely never know, but his references to the Battle of New Orleans and Madison's proclamation suggest he might have been in the city at the time.

The Texas Iron

Now as I was making preparations to ascend the river and also made known my business that it was in quest of mines and minerals and also that I had some knowledge of making assays on ores of different kinds, I found that there was a company of men that had been up the river as far as the Pawnees and had obtained a piece of pure metal which they did not know the value of. The weight of the lump was 2300 pounds weighed at Nachitoches. The way that it was found was hunters coming across it. It was in an open prarie, no sign of it ever growing in this place. It laid on top of the earth and no appearance of stone near it. We know that metals are not engendered in level fertile plains but generally on mountains and stony cliffs. It certainly has been dropt there by the Spaniards.

This metal is worthy of remarks. A solid mass of ductile metal, to snap your fingers against it, it would ring like unto a church bell. The Pawnee Indians had found it and by touching of it they heard the ring of it. They thought it to be some great spirit and afterwards worshipped it as such and made an offering to it of stone, that every one that passed that way had to provide himself with a peculiar stone and throw it on the heap which they made very near it. There had been several attempts made by the Spaniards to take it away but got defeated by the Indians. There was a company of hunters that undertook to go and fetch it down the river. They were 14 in number, went up prepared for a 12 month voyage. They had 70 miles land carriage

32. Ibid., 120.
33. Ibid., 137.

before they got it to the river. They got to it but soon found out that the Indians would not let them take it without paying such a quantity of goods for it. Their demands were a certain number of rifles and ammunition and also a quantity of blankets which the whole of these men could not furnish as they had there all with them which was their rifle so they had to return without it but they made out to obtain a good sample of the metal to show.

They got back to Nachitoches and showed what they had. It was immediately pronounced to be iron, which it favors very much in color but not otherwise. Blacksmiths tried to work it but in vain. The greatest blast would not operate on it. They could not flux it by any means. They could plate it to any degree of things. When a certain Doctor Sibley came to see this metal, he judged it to be the platinum which this answers all the descriptions; a metal that has been obtained in small and also has been found in its virgin state in South America, although in small lumps. This Sibley is very wealthy. He made an offer to this company if they would ascend the river again for this piece of metal that he would furnish the articles to purchase it from the natives and then to share alike if they were successful. They soon took up with the offer and the articles provided and they again started on horseback well provided with every necessary they stood in need of. Got up safe to the Pawnees and paid them for the metal.

The Indians went with them to assist them in getting it to the river. They had to make a truck wagon to haul it on, which they accomplished in a few days. They got started with the metal but found it very tedious. The Indians left them to do for themselves. The third day they were pursued by a company of Spaniards but they were too well equipped. The Spaniards did not dare to attack them but they watched their opportunity and took all their horses when they were asleep for they had to let them run out in the range. Behold, next morning they were in a bad fix, not a horse to be found. They immediately mistrusted the Spaniards which for them proved to be true. What to do now they did not know till they thought of the Indians having plenty horses and mules both. They soon dispatched a party for to go and try the Indians for horses and also their assistance which they got, giving them two more of their rifles.

They, after several days fatigue and trouble, got their prize to the river then they built them a pirogue and launched her and started down the river but they were soon compelled to make a halt and wait for the river to rise.

There was not water enough to swim their boat. It took several months to get it to Nachitoches. It was a great sight. The people crowded in from all quarters to see this wonder, such a solid mass as this to sound like a church bell. It was surprising who would not be curious enough to go 100 miles to see, especially it formed by nature. There was great prices offered these men for their shares but they refused selling at any price.

All the art of that town was displayed, but nothing could ascertain what the metal was, no more than iron which it most looked like in color. Dr. Sibley then sent it on to New Orleans to have it tried there and received an answer that nothing could be done with it but that the artists pronounced it to be white iron. Where was there ever iron known but what a blast would operate on it, but this it would not. It was consigned to a merchant in Philadelphia by Dr. Sibley and in a few months Sibley told the company concerned that it was taken to the mint and the returns was nothing but iron. He would not give them the satisfaction of showing the answer in writing.

The time whilst these men were in town waiting in great suspense, I happened to be in there and soon found these men that had been up the river. I made inquiries of them and told them my business and what was my object in view that I was acquainted with making small assays on ores of different kinds. They then told me the circumstance, how Dr. Sibley had served them and also described the metal which my author gave an account to be the platinum. They told me that Sibley had some of the metal, that he would show me some of it if I would spend my opinion or make an assay of it, that they would give me all the information laid in their power and also told me that the Indians had two pieces more which might be purchased from them. This made me very willing to render my services. They took me to Sibley's and acquainted him with the circumstances, but he soon replied "damn the luck; I have none of it nor would any man make anything of it but iron if he was the greatest artist in the world.["] They then told me they thought they could find some in town as there were several men had cut small pieces of it if they could find it.

Dr. Sibley sent a messenger to my lodging to call and see him. I waited on him. He was very pleasant and conversant. I got a great deal of information from him. He, at last, introduced the story about the metal and told me it was not worth my attention to give those men any satisfaction concerning this metal; that I would receive no thanks for it after telling them, that he

Dr. John Sibley, Indian agent in Natchitoches. *Courtesy of Lindenwood University.*

was the Indian agent for that state and without his assistance, I could not trade with the Indians. Therefore, if I promised to shun them, he would grant me my license free, otherwise, none at all. I was then bound so to do. I kept myself out of their way.

❦ ❦ ❦

Meteorites on the North Texas Plains

Had it not been for Maley's discussion of these meteorites on the Texas prairies, it is not clear what would have happened to his journal. Maley apparently wrote the work in 1817 or later and sold it to Philadelphia publisher Isaac Riley. Riley never published the journal, but he did furnish it to Yale's Benjamin Silliman, a prominent early American scientist who was interested in Maley's account only as it related to his studies of meteorites.[34] *The latter half of Maley's journal, as well as a copy of the journal of Anthony Glass, which also described meteorites on the Texas plains,*[35] *ended up in Silliman's papers at Yale, where it has been available to scholars for the last fifty years. The first half of his journal, presumably*

34. Taibi, "The Early Years of Meteor Observations in the USA."
35. Flores, *Journal of an Indian Trader,* 94–99.

retained by Riley, was only uncovered in 2012. In 1824 Silliman published an article on the "Malleable Iron of Louisiana," which summarized the retrieval of the meteorite in 1810 and Maley's subsequent efforts to retrieve two other stones in 1812–13. In addition to furthering the science of meteorites, the article also provides several of the very few details we know about Maley.[36]

Much of the interest in Maley's account relates to the location of smaller meteorites that he saw in his 1812 trip up the Red River. In his 1808 travel with the Pawnees, Indian trader Anthony Glass was shown the Texas Iron,[37] *and was told of two smaller meteorites, thirty and fifty miles distant, respectively.*[38] *Maley learned of the additional meteorites while in Natchitoches and on his exploration up the Red River persuaded the Pawnee to show him where one or both lay.*[39] *Unfortunately, in his journal, Maley simply noted that the piece (or pieces) lay across the river, three days travel southwest of the village, and a few miles from the mountains dividing American and Spanish territory. It is not clear where the village, itself, was located, but from Maley's description, the meteorite was presumably north of the Brazos River.*

Following Maley's venture onto the north Texas plains, several meteorites have been found in the region. In 1856 Indian agent Robert Neighbors retrieved the "Wichita County" meteorite from a location about eight miles northwest of current day Graham, Texas. This mass, weighing 320 pounds and similar to the Texas Iron in composition, had been an object of veneration by the Comanche. The Wichita County meteorite may have been the stone visited by Maley, as it was located north of the Brazos and about sixty miles south of the Red. According to the Comanche, however, the Spanish had attempted to remove the meteorite, and it is not clear if it had been in a different location in 1812.[40] *In 1940 the forty-five pound "Comanche County" meteorite was discovered approximately 6 miles east of Comanche, Texas.*[41] *While this might have been the second stone mentioned to Glass, it was well south of the Brazos, 150 miles south of the Red River, and therefore unlikely to have been visited by Maley.*

36. Silliman, "Notice of the Malleable Iron of Louisiana," 221–23.

37. In his reconstruction of Glass's travel, Flores places the location of the Texas Iron near current day Breckenridge, Texas, approximately ninety-five miles south of the Red River. Flores, *Journal of an Indian Trader,* map of Glass's Travels, 62.

38. Ibid., 69.

39. It is not clear from his journal whether Maley saw more than one meteorite.

40. Wilson, *Oklahoma Treasures and Treasure Tales,* 87.

41. Flores, *Journal of an Indian Trader,* 137.

CHAPTER 8 ❧ *Spring of 1812*

Up the Red River to the Great Raft

Dr. Sibley also put me in the way of getting up the river, as there was then a number of Kashotoo Indians down that had been trading and were a going to start up the river in a couple of days. As they had five pirogues with them, that they would take me up the river as they went up the distance of five hundred miles and then to purchase one of their pirogues and proceed by myself. He went with me to these Indians and told them the circumstances and they were friendly, accepted of me and told me they were a going to start next morning, for me to be ready and get my goods up to where they were encamped, which was about half a mile above the town.

I then prepared myself for a long journey. I got another man whom I engaged to give an equal share of all the furs that we should catch, as I was well provided with steel traps. Our company now was three white men and 12 Indians. I bought provisions enough to take us out of the inhabitants, as game was not to be found so near the settlements. I got some bacon and some hard bread such as they make use of aboard of the boats. I did not see that these Indians had anything to live on. They were all equipped with a good rifle, knife and tomahawk and so were we. I had a quantity of knives and also cooking utensils. I was provided with a small laboratory with a good set of crucibles to make assays on ore if they should come to hand.

We divided ourselves in five pirogues, three in each, and so took our departure on the 5th day of March, 1812, about ten o'clock. I keep myself a time piece. It was a fine morning and everything appeared to enchant my feelings with regret, every tree putting forth its timely leaves and planters putting in their cotton, the country very level and fertile, the songsters of the grove warbling their melodious notes. The current we had to stem was strong, the river now very flush. After going a few miles, they left the main river, took into a brushy bayou, sometimes in lakes in appearance and at other times in large cypress swamps through brush, and none but well acquainted characters could navigate here. We had the advantage of the current not being so strong against us. About an hour by sun, we came into the main river and no appearance of any settlements, but the banks were very thick grown with cane.

We went a mile further and came to an Indian camp. There was but one man and his wife there. We made a halt and took up for the night as this was a good place. The cane was cut down for half an acre and the squaw was then at work planting her corn. Those Indians with me could not understand this one we came to; they told me that he was a Cherokee. They could make out to understand one another by signs, which Indians go by a great deal in their discourse. They treated us very friendly, making all the sport they could to please us and took pains to teach us their language. As soon as we were first on shore, some gathered wood and others went to cooking. They had bags made out of skins of different kinds of animals such as I was not acquainted with. They had them filled with dried buffalo meat and some with parched corn. They made a kind of soup they called tompulla. We also made our cookery; boiled some bacon and made some broth by putting in some hard bread.

When they had their broth made, they took it up in an earthen bowl and put their buffalo horn spoons [in] it, set it down on the ground and placed themselves round it. They invited us to sit down and partake with them, as our soup was not ready. We sat down, the other Indian man sat down also. We were now 16 at the table and but one spoon to eat with. The first one took the spoon and took but one sup and passed it down in the dish again, so on every one took but one sup. I observed their custom. I took but one sup. In the meantime, they have to wait with patience till it comes to their turn again. While the spoon goes round, you eat some dried meat which they have laying on the ground. So many of us there, what they had did not half satisfy my appetite. I then took up my broth and invited them all. They took it very friendly and arranged our supping in the same style. They appeared to be very fond of the bacon. When the second table was cleared off, the third one was furnished with dainties, some kind of broth and a bowl full of dried peaches which they had got among the inhabitants, I presume. So we had our three suppers and I felt as if I could have taken the fourth.

After supper, the oldest in appearance among them got his pipe, filled it, lit it, then came to me turning the stem of the pipe for me to smoke, which I, at that time, did not know the meaning of but I took the pipe and smoked a few whiffs and he then took the pipe and went round till he had served the whole company. This, I found, was a token of friendship among them. After this, their youngsters began to make some music on a flute, sounded similar to our German flute. They blowed in the end and played with their fingers on holes. It was made of a large sized cane. Their music is in some part very melodious, but not many variety of tunes. After a while in which another pipe was introduced and then each one took his bed where he chose to lay and rested very well that night as it was not a new thing to me to lodge in that manner. In the morning, I awoke and was saluted by the songsters of the valley whom were so numerous that you could scarcely hear one or other speak. The parakeets are very numerous and noisy. They are a small green parrot.

We made some breakfast before we started. I had some whiskey with me and gave each of them about half a gill that pleased them much. We started for our second day's journey, proceeded up the river about three miles, the lands apparently very fertile and covered with cane. We then reached another settlement, both sides of the river. The planters there were still French. Their buildings appeared very majestic. Everything seemed to fill my mind with agreeable sensations. Nothing can be more inviting that those delightful plains in such a state of cultivation. Americans fail not to come and be eye witnesses of my story! Thousands of you stand in need of such a country; why will you not come and enjoy it? The river is not over 200 yards wide. It makes various windings a few miles only and we leave the inhabitants. We then had several miles without a house. About the middle of the day, we came to a mill near the river and several buildings in a cluster. We made a stop and smoked our pipe.

I walked up to these houses to make some inquiries. They were Americans, a company of men that were there only to tend their saw mill and so raft their stuff down the river. Mill seats in this country are not frequent. They informed me that the country back from the river was chiefly piney woods and cypress swamps. Nature seemingly formed everything right among those rich and fertile valleys for such a beautiful mill and stream of water must certainly induce the settler to think that there never was such a country as this. It was 35 miles from Nachitoches then no more inhabitants to come to but one or two. We took up the river again and at about half an hour by sun we hastened to fix our lodging. We proceeded the same way as we did the night back, eat our soup together and every man made his own bed. Slept unmolested and awoke to another fine morning.

Prepared ourselves for our third day's journey; found the river land still very good. The growth of timber is chiefly cottonwood, poplar and black walnut. The underbrush spice wood which makes an excellent tea; we make use of it very often. We proceeded on till about 10 o'clock when we came to our last inhabitants and were then only five miles from an Indian village of the Pascagoula tribe. When we arrived there, we made a stop. They all seemed to congratulate us with a hearty welcome. Here everything appeared uncommon to me. Their town laid in miniature very good log houses with very good clapboard roofs and hung doors, peach trees in great abundance, no fencing, all land in common. They cultivate a good deal of land which is very fertile. They raise Indian corn, squashes, pumpkins, cucumbers, water and muss melons, sweet potatoes in abundance.

The Unknown Red River

When Maley ascended the Red River in 1812, little was known about the upper reaches of the stream, and it would remain largely "terra incognita" for another forty years. The route from Natchitoches to the Wichita/Taovaya settlement near present-day Spanish Fort, Texas, had been well-traveled by French and Spanish officials,[1] *and the village had also received several visits by American traders.*[2] *Much less was known, however, about the river above the Taovaya/Wichita settlement. A list of distances on the river, gathered from hunters by Peter Custis in 1806, contained thirty-eight landmarks between Natchitoches and the Taovaya/Wichita village. Above the village, however, it became quite vague, citing only one additional landmark and suggesting that the source of the river*

1. Wilson, *Oklahoma Treasures and Treasure Tales*, 103, includes a map of eighteenth-century Spanish exploration of Oklahoma and Texas from the Oklahoma Historical Society.

2. These included those of John House in 1805, John S. Lewis and William C. Alexander in 1806, and Anthony Glass in 1808. Flores, *Journal of an Indian Trader*, 20–30.

might lie an additional three hundred miles upstream after dividing "into many branches."[3]

Maley would not have gleaned much useful information from the maps of the time, either. Early French maps showed the Red River continuing north-northwest from Natchitoches into what would be present-day Nebraska, and this error was plagiarized by other map makers through much of the eighteenth century. By the beginning of the nineteenth century, cartographers had begun showing the great bend of the river, but they continued to depict the river running too far north. The 1809 map by Alexander von Humboldt was one of the better efforts, but he mistakenly assumed that the Mora and Vermejo Rivers in northeast New Mexico were the headwaters of the Red River, rather than the Canadian. The 1810 map by Zebulon Pike, which may have been copied from Humboldt,[4] *repeated that mistake, as did the 1810 map by Aaron Arrowsmith. So did John Melish's 1818 map of North America, which was formally referenced in the Adams-Onís Treaty, which established the Red River as the boundary between Spain and the United States. The Melish map also added a number of details of the rivers crossing the plains of current Oklahoma, but most, unfortunately, were fanciful, at best.*

Ignorance about the geography of the Red River was not due to a lack of effort. Shortly after the Louisiana Purchase, President Thomas Jefferson authorized an expedition up the Red River led by Thomas Freeman and Peter Custis, but it was intercepted and turned back by Spanish forces in 1806 about twenty miles west of present-day Texarkana, Texas. In his 1820 return from an expedition to the Rocky Mountains, Major Stephen H. Long intended to explore the Red River, but (presumably influenced by the maps of the time) he descended the Canadian River instead. It was not until the 1852 expedition of Captain Randolph Marcy that the upper reaches of the Red River were mapped, and it was discovered that the headwaters of the river were located on the Llano Estacado of the Texas Panhandle, rather than in the Rocky Mountains.

Compounding the problem was the question of nomenclature. On its upper reaches, the Red River splits into several branches, but at the time of Maley's travels, there appeared to be no agreement as to what these streams were called. Maley noted that the stream that he called the Salt Fork was referred to as the North Fork by the Coushatta Indians. The confusion over names persisted for

3. Flores, *Southern Counterpart to Lewis and Clark*, 327–32.
4. Martin and Martin, *Maps of Texas and Southwest, 1513–1900*, 111.

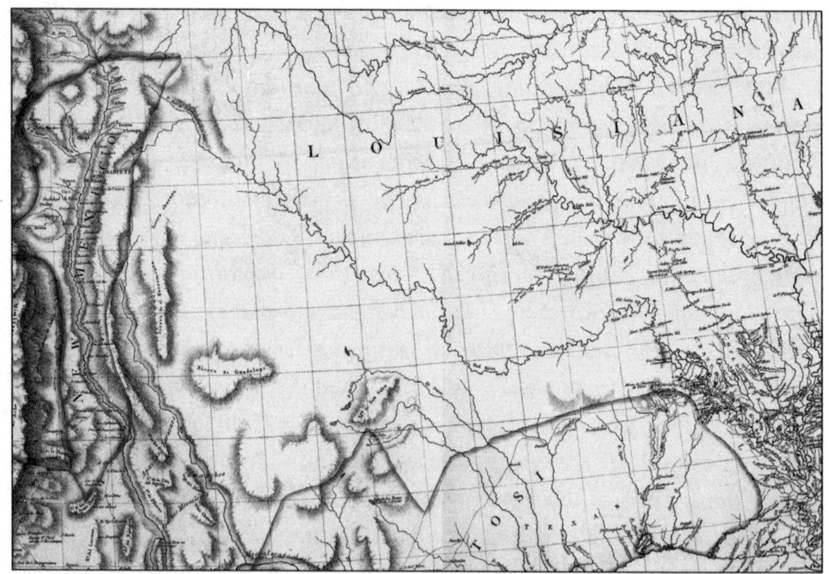

Portion of 1810 Arrowsmith map of Mexico and adjacent provinces. Like the earlier maps of Humboldt and Pike, Arrowsmith showed no major branches of the Red River, and mistakenly assumed that it extended to the northwest, with its headwaters near Santa Fe. (As noted in Martin and Martin, *Maps of Texas and Southwest, 1513–1900*, 109–13.) *Map courtesy of the David Rumsey Map Collection, www.davidrumsey.com.*

some time: the stream that Captain Marcy mapped as the Salt Fork in 1852 is today known as the Elm Fork, a tributary of the North Fork. There was also longstanding disagreement as to which branch, the Prairie Dog Town Fork or the North Fork, comprised the main channel of the Red, an issue that ultimately had to be addressed by the Supreme Court to resolve the boundary between Oklahoma and Texas.[5]

The lack of geographic knowledge extended to other streams as well. At one point while exploring North Texas, Maley believed he could see "the dividing ridges between Red River and Little Missouri, a branch of the Ouachitta." There is a river called the Little Missouri, which is a tributary of the Ouachita River, but it lies far to the east of Maley's location at the time. Maley possibly believed that the Little Missouri extended much further west, or he may have been referring to

5. Tyson, *The Red River in Southwestern History*, 158–76.

a branch of the Washita River, in Oklahoma. That stream had apparently been mistaken for the Ouachita by early explorers (both are pronounced the same), and was commonly referred to as the "False Ouachita." Flores notes that some hunters also referred to it as the "Missouri Branch of the Red River."[6]

From today's perspective, it seems remarkable how little was known about the Red River and how long that ignorance persisted. Maley's journal was one of the few written records of exploration of the upper Red River until the Marcy expedition, which took place forty years later. Had his journal been published in 1819 (and had he provided a clearer account of where he went), Maley might have accelerated by several decades our understanding of the geography of this part of the country.

The Pascagoula Village

When we entered the town, they took us to a house where they were gambling, which was, as I perceived, for handkerchiefs, shawls and ribbons. My company soon joined in with them as they had many goods with them that they had bought in Nachitoches. I stood and looked on, but could not find out the sense of the game. They played in this manner: They had a bear skin spread on the floor with the hair side up, then had three moccasins not made up, laid them down on the skin in an angle, then one would pretend to hide a rifle ball under one of those moccasins. The whole company at the mean time singing and he making a great many motions to hide the ball would then lift one and then the other. He did not wish to let them see which one he hid it under. Whenever he had the ball hid, he opened his hand and showed that he had not the ball any more. Then another, with as many motions as he had would try to find the ball. If he touched one of those moccasins, I perceived, was the rules of the game that he had to lift it. If he found not the ball under the first one he had to try again until he found and so on. They played partners, so many of a side as would play and make it even number they keep their game. When they commenced, one of them had 40 small splits about 4 inches long. Every time the ball was hid and found by the other, they handed over some of those splits, sometimes more and sometimes less.

6. Flores, *Southern Counterpart to Lewis and Clark*, 331n17.

They had to hand them backwards and forwards according as the game run, but they had to continue till one or the other had all. That ended the game.

So they continued playing all day. They would sit as content as men do at the card table. Their young women stood all gazing around them. They live as unconcerned as if they had nothing to do or think of whilst the married ones are all employed about something. The women are elegant. They dress in petticoats and shifts made of some gay kind of calico and large calico shawls round their shoulders hanging full size to the ground. The young women are very fond of presents such as handkerchiefs or beads, which is a great apparel among them. Whilst I was looking round, my men cooked us some dinner. I invited the party in company with us to dinner. Those that were not playing came, but the others did not. We had our camp on the river bank and several spectators came to see us. The Indians with me invited them all; none refused to eat. At this rate, they left but little for us as it was scanty enough as it was for our own men. We concluded we would eat no more till after night. After dinner, I walked round to see the curiosities of the town, went into several of the cabins, found none at home but the married women and some appeared to be as old as the hills. Every house I went in, immediately they offered me something to eat, which I accepted freely. My appetite was very ravenous. So it had needs be to eat with them, to see them standing by whilst you are eating, cracking their lice and even biting their heads off. Hominy soup is a very great dish among them.

I went up the river. I perceived there were some homes rather off from the others as much as half a mile. When I came in sight of these buildings, I discovered one building much different than the others. I directly made for that, thinking that to be a curiosity, but behold, when I came within 20 yards of it, there was an old man came walking towards me very friendly, took me by the hand and led me round the back part of the house, pointing towards the house and shaking his head as much as to say not allowed to go there. This house, or cave more like, is covered with earth, about 20 feet the base and running almost to a true taper all round to the top. I could not find use or meaning of it so I returned to the upper part of the town again.

When I came there, I found that one of the Indians that came with me had lost all his plunder that he had bought at Nachitoches, which I dare say, at the rate he had paid for it, was not less than 400 dollars. He never seemed to mind it, but then was at me for some whiskey. I was foolish enough to treat the whole party which pleased them well. A party still were gambling; this was about sunset. They then made preparations for supper. I got plenty to eat among them. They quit play and fell to smoking and handed their pipes round. As I have hinted before, it is a token of friendship among them and also had to eat with one spoon and that made of a buffalo horn.

Whilst we were at supper, there was five Indians belonging to that tribe came there. They had been to Nachitoches, they fetched a few quarts of whiskey with them and they soon drank it among them which put the devil in some of them. They got to singing and dancing and came to me for whiskey as they knew that I had some aboard. I denied them. They threatened to go and get it out of the pirogue. That was some of my own company, but some of them were still sober. They kept them from going to the boat. When an opportunity offered, one of the sober ones took me by the hand and led me to the river and told me and my companions cross over to the opposite side with all my plunder and stay till morning and then they would be sober.

We soon took this advice and started. It was very dark and we, not acquainted on the opposite shore, made it very difficult for us to find a landing place, which we made out after long struggling. It was a warm evening. We did not build a fire for fear they might discover us and come over in pursuit of us so we had to lay on very wet ground that night. They had the most dreadful yelling that ever I was acquainted with before. I heard them at the river in search of me. What they would have done if I had not cleared out, God only knows. We rested but little that night on account of the noise and the place being so disagreeable but we had one consolation: we were out of danger of being injured by them. They got settled the after part of the night. We took a little sleep and in the morning some of them came over to us and took us over with them. They appeared to be very sorry for what they had been guilty of. We took some breakfast and repaired to our boats. Several spectators came down to the river to see us off and smoked a farewell pipe. I gave them all a half gill whiskey apiece, which they seem to take as a great favor. We shook hands and parted.

Through the Raft

We have but three miles to go and then leave the bed of the river on account of a raft in the river that has stopped it up for 40 miles distance and still increasing yearly. All the timber has to lodge back, none can come down, the river being too narrow caused it at first and also the trees such a length. We came to the place where we had to turn out. We took out on the north side into a quite narrow bayou, which took us direct from the river but we had not much of a current to stem. We could make more headway. There was vast quantities of overflow lands, the timber very lofty. We found bee trees, as many as we wanted, seemingly no end to honey but it is very bitter to the taste. Only by sivering it over the fire and skimming of it; I could not eat it at all, but this makes it as good as any honey. How Indians know the way, I am not able to tell. They turn so many different courses and that all through the wilderness in a manner winding through trees and sometimes very narrow passages. Still, they are at no loss to find the course to steer, go on as if it was one plain stream.

The Great Raft

In his 1812 passage up the Red River, Maley passed through the "Great Raft," an enormous series of logjams that blocked the main river channel. While there are several theories as to how the raft initially formed, the logjam, once created, became self-perpetuating. Acting like a giant sieve, the upstream end of the raft would collect new logs with each new flood of the river, while the downstream margin would disintegrate as the logs making up the raft eventually rotted. In that fashion, the raft had moved progressively up the river for hundreds of years prior to the arrival of the French at Natchitoches. One study postulates that when it occupied the floodplain near Alexandria in the latter part of the fifteenth century, the raft had diverted the Red River from its ancient channel down Bayou Boeuf and Bayou Teche to its current channel connecting it to the Mississippi.[7] *The raft was also the source of the numerous lakes in the Red River valley. At the time Maley traversed the logjam, it held back the waters of Lake Bistineau and Lake Bodcaw on the eastern side of the river and Soda Lake and Caddo Lake west of the river.*

In part because of its movement up the river, descriptions of the raft and its location vary considerably. Natchitoches was founded in 1714, immediately below

7. Veatch, *Geology and Underground Water Resources*, 60–62.

Great Raft of the Red River, by R. B. Talfor, Photographer, 1873.
Courtesy of Northwest Louisiana Archives at LSU Shreveport.

the raft, at the head of navigation of the Red River.[8] *In 1806 the expedition of Thomas Freeman and Peter Custis encountered its first small raft approximately thirty miles above Natchitoches, below the settlement at Campti. In 1812 Maley encountered the raft at least twenty miles further up the river, in the vicinity of current day Coushatta, Louisiana. In 1833, when U.S. government engineers surveyed it, the foot of the raft was at Loggy Bayou, one hundred miles above Natchitoches, and it was estimated to be 130 miles long, with its head fifty miles above present-day Shreveport.*[9]

Wherever travelers encountered the raft, however, it proved a considerable barrier to travel. Because its main channel was blocked, water from the river

8. An early map of Natchitoches by J. F. Broutin in 1722 shows an "embaras d'arbres" immediately above the town. See Thomassy, *Geologie Pratique de la Louisiane*, plate opposite 227.
9. Caldwell, "The Red River Raft," 254.

backed up into shallow lakes and swamps and would ultimately find its way downstream through a series of smaller streams and bayous. Travelers could bypass the raft through these bodies of water, but only with smaller vessels. Maley's party, traveling in pirogues, apparently traversed the raft in three to four days. However, the Freeman and Custis expedition, which was using larger boats ("two barges and a pirogue") spent "fourteen days of incessant fatigue, toil and danger, doubt and uncertainty"[10] *to pass through the obstruction. While there were a number of factors that delayed exploration and settlement of the upper Red River, the difficulty of transporting goods by water through the raft played a significant role.*

Eventually, the United States government undertook a project to clear the raft. Beginning in 1832, Captain Henry Shreve of the Army Corps of Engineers was able to clear more than seventy miles of the raft in three months using steam-powered "snag-boats." Keeping the river free from new logjams proved to be a challenge, however, and the project wasn't completed until 1872. The removal of the raft led to the development of the town of Shreveport, but by that time, steamboats were being replaced by railroads, and the Red River never witnessed the volume of traffic experienced on other streams. The raft's removal also had unintended consequences. While the raft existed, it backed up water into Big Cyprus Creek and permitted steamboat traffic as far as Jefferson, Texas, which had a population of five thousand in 1850. Removal of the raft, however, lowered water levels and ended the town's days as a transit hub.[11] *The removal of the raft also changed river flows downstream, and apparently contributed to the creation of a new river channel, east of Natchitoches, that bypassed the town.*[12]

WE MADE A STOP before night when we came to a place of dry ground and some of the hunters went out and in an hour came back with a deer which was a welcome sight to me, as I could not eat much of my bacon, but the venison and bacon together was very luscious. We then made an excellent supper, enjoyed ourselves like nabobs. Who was happier than we when we had plenty to eat? We smoked our pipes in mirth and friendship, had some

10. Flores, *Southern Counterpart to Lewis and Clark*, 143.
11. Tyson, *The Red River in Southwestern History*, 94–101.
12. "History of the Cane River Region."

music, and then laid down and took our repose. Next morning it was cloudy and very like for rain. We made some breakfast, and before we finished, it began to rain. We had immediately to build us a camp, a shelter to keep our things dry, which we soon accomplished by peeling of barks which this time of year runs very well and the Indians very dextrous in building such cabins. We had it all completed before our things received any injury by the rain, got them all in our cabin and then made a large fire in front of it and there enjoyed ourselves that day. It rained steady and sometimes very fast, but our shelter kept us very dry. It rained all the ensuing night and until the middle of the next day. It then cleared off.

By this time we were out of provisions. We concluded it best to spend the remainder part of the day there and hunt as an opportunity might not offer where we could find game on account of water. Therefore, we made choice of six of our company to hunt that afternoon whilst the others should take care of our property. We went two by two. I went and also took my companion, but we separated ourselves, each took one of the Indians in company as they were better acquainted with the woods. We started and each party took a different course. My companion and myself did not go a great distance till we seen three raccoons climbing up a tree. The Indian very anxious to fire at them let fly pretty soon. I took it very deliberately, leveled my rifle at him and soon fetched him to the ground. By the time my companion had his piece charged again, he shot and missed the second time, which he did not like. These two raccoons by this time were as high up the tree as they could get, it being very lofty. I tried the other and dropped him. The Indian thought then he would not be outdone by me, tried for a fair chance at the third one which he had. He missed again. He then took my gun, thinking mine better than his own but missed him again for that time he had but a poor chance; his body was most part hid. I charged my rifle again and leveled at his head as that was all I could see, but I brought him down. This made the Indian wonder much thinking I shot so much superior to him. He tapped me on the shoulder and said Chicamaw, Chicamaw, Chicamaw feenee, which is to say, good, good, very good. We skinned our racoons and hung up the meat. If we did not kill any thing else we would return that way and take them to our camp.

We then traveled on through an open woods, no underbrush. We could see for a mile distance. We saw several deer but could not get a shot at them on account of the woods being so open. We continued on for some distance and found the most delightful country that ever eyes beheld. The new grass then springing up, it appeared like unto a bowling green, the timber chiefly post oak and hickory but very scattering. Going on a piece farther, we discovered a drove of wild cattle which are very plenty in that country. I first thought they belonged to some planters or Indians, but the Indian made signs to me that they did not. He, very anxious of killing one of them told me to go try to kill one as he thought I could out shoot him. He showed which way to go so that they should not get the wind of me and to keep myself hid as much as possible behind trees. In creeping up to them, they were all very busy feeding.

I started to try my luck but I was still doubtful thinking I was going to commit a crime, that these cattle had an owner and that I might be brought to justice for them. However, I ventured. I took the Indian's advice and got within 60 yards of them. I picked out a young heifer for my mark to fire at. There was an old bull much nigher to me, but thought his meat would not be so good. I took aim at this heifer and pulled trigger. She did not fall but could see that she was wounded. They ran off with great speed, as it happened, right towards our camp. We went to the spot where she stood when I fired at her. We saw plenty of blood and followed on for a mile or more till we found her lying dead. We were not a great distance from our camp. The Indian set up a hollow till he made them hear at the camp and four of them soon came to our assistance. We skinned our beef and the Indians lugged it to the camp. They were greatly rejoiced, they would not let me carry any of it. There was no mark on the heifer so she was free, nobody could prove her. She was very fat and about three years old. These woods are full of those kind of cattle. They at first strayed away from the Spaniards and increased till they have become very numerous for the range is inexhaustible either winter or summer.

When my companion told of the raccoons and that the meat was left behind, a couple of them started with all speed after it and fetched it in. They did not like to lose any meat. An Indian, when he has plenty, can eat as much as a hog and they can also fast a long while. They now hardly ever quit eating. They have constantly a piece sticking before the fire on a stick. We really live well at present. Our other hunters brought in a deer and a turkey. They almost worshipped me because I had done such exploits. This beef I was so fond of. It was so fat and tender. I thought I never tasted anything better although we made use of no salt; some foreigners perhaps would not have agreed with me. We rested comfortable that night. Next morning was fine weather. We took our breakfast and got our things aboard and started for our 5th day's journey.

We soon got into a watery world. I found out that we should have been in a bad situation had we not provided for provisions at the place we lay at before. We got into a large lake. The alligators were very numerous here and also water fowl of different kinds. The swan in particular was very plenty. The swan is white, much resembling the goose but three times as large. Another kind of birds in very large flocks all white, they sit chiefly in trees. They are about as large as our common duck. In about five miles we got out of this lake into an extensive cypress swamp. Here the alligators roared like great bulls. You might hear them in every direction answering one another. I cannot see how they find the way to go where they have to navigate through the trees. Bees are here in great abundance but they cannot be got; all the trees stand in the water.

"Touline" François Grappe

About sundown, we got to Dolins[13] Vacherie, which is the meaning of a graziery; a man that only lived out there to raise cattle. There he stayed, had no wife. I saw two Indians for his companions. They help him to take care of his cattle. All they have to do is to keep them in separate droves about in the woods and there to salt them. They cut down a number of trees at a place and cut small boxes the whole length of the tree. There they will salt them every week, putting the salt in those boxes in the trees. There they will frequent every day. He has several of these places not to use them all together for the drove would be too large. As soon as they see any calves, they cut and brand them. He lives on meat altogether, don't pretend to raise anything. Although he has not less than 20–30,000 dollars in specia, he lives worse than any Indian I have yet seen as to dirt and nastiness. He has not less than 1500 head of cattle, drives not less than 500 down the river yearly, some as far as the Mississippi and some he sells on Red River. He takes nothing but specia.[14]

13. Maley is referring to François Grappe, who was called "Touline." Flores, "The John Maley Journal," 76.

14. Presumably Maley means "specie," or coined money.

We stayed there that night and next morning we took a walk out to see one of his licks as he calls them. It was about three miles; it gave me an opportunity of seeing some of the country which I found to be delightful, indeed fine groves of timber and intersected with small praries. Oh the beauties of nature—how elegant to see those level plains bringing forth such grass in abundance. When we came to the licking logs, there were but few cattle there, but he blew his horn which they are trained to. They came in from every direction, running and skipping enough to break their legs. In less than 15 minutes, there was three hundred head, the most elegantest cattle that ever your eyes beheld.

I was astonished to see what little trouble to accumulate wealth were we but there altogether, our wives and children who are now very often crying for bread. Let us be industrious and earn a little money to get to this fine country! I know that I can make as much in one twelve month as will take me there, not only make as much but save as much. I will dispense with bitters in the morning and also spending at other times of the day. I will put that into a bag that I will not open for a whole twelve month. That will take me there. Take the resolution like this man and a great many might get to this fine country; you might even help your friends and relatives there.

After seeing the country a little farther, we returned to our boats. This man gave us as much dried beef as we would take. It is very good to travel and we could eat it without cooking. We started nearly the middle of the day. Now no more white inhabitants to pass by. This man told me that when we were at his house we were 40 miles from the main river, that it would take us two days before we would get into it again. We saw nothing material that day but the same as we had seen the day before. At night at a good camping ground, we landed our pirogues. That night we were wonderfully disturbed by the vermin, wolves and panthers hollowing and the owls intermixed with. It prevented me from sleeping that night but thanks be to providence, I was not alone as I have been and in the same predicament.

Next morning, we again had to build our shelter. We had more rain now, two days weather bound. In the meantime, I killed five raccoons, one deer, two turkeys and shot at a panther, but did not get him, I wounded him. None of the others hunted any, they fetched in the meat. They cleared me of that; they thought I could kill when I had a mind to. We had then more meat than we stood in need of. The turkeys I made soup of. Our water that we had was very bad, therefore I made soup to drink. It was only swamp water and that very muddy of a reddish color. The third day of our being there, we had fine sunshine, weather very pleasant and warm. Everything seemed pleasant to the eye, birds giving us delightful music as they were hovering round us.

We started on our 7th day's journey the 12th day of March, the leaves almost their full growth. In going about two hours our course altered. I saw that we were laying our course more towards the river and got where the water was more contracted and also considerable of a current. We could not make but slow headway. The further we go, the stronger the current. The water takes off in different directions. To our left hand it has here formed considerable of a stream, it has almost the whole river for its channel. The bottoms are very fertile. On the right hand the banks are high and grown up with cane.

François Grappe dit Touline

As he was making his way past the Great Raft, Maley and his colleagues stopped at a location that Maley referred to as "Dolins Vacherie." The individual he met there was François Grappe, commonly called "Touline," who was one of the most colorful and respected figures on the southwestern frontier. "Vacherie" is a French term that, in this case, described a cattle ranch.

Touline was born in 1748 at Fort St. Louis, a French trading post established at a Natchitoches (Caddo) village several hundred miles above Natchitoches. His father was a sergeant commanding the small French detachment there, and his mother was half-Indian, of the Caddo tribe. During the Revolutionary War, Touline served in the Natchitoches cavalry that was part of Bernardo de Gálvez's campaign against the British in the lower Mississippi Valley.[15] *Following the Louisiana Purchase, Touline proved to be an important liaison between the Caddo and American authorities. Having played a key role in escorting the 1806 Freeman and Custis expedition up the Red River, he was referred to as a "worthy and respectable old French gentleman" by Custis.*[16]

Maley had a low opinion of Touline's lifestyle but apparently didn't realize that Touline only stayed part time at his vacherie. His principal residence was a

15. Mills, "Mézières, Trichel, Grappe," 28–29.
16. Flores, *Southern Counterpart to Lewis and Clark*, 146–48.

few miles above Campti, at a site known as Grappe's Bluff, where he lived with his common-law wife, Marie Louise, who had been born a slave. In 1796 Touline was able to buy the freedom of Marie Louise, their twelve living children, and five grandchildren. On his death in 1825, Touline left approximately eighty children and grandchildren. In addition to his vacherie, which covered approximately 5700 acres along the shore of Lake Bistineau, Touline's descendants also claimed he had received a grant of almost 35,000 acres along the Red River, containing part of present-day Shreveport, from the Caddo nation.[17]

William Darby's 1816 map of Louisiana shows "Tulin's Vaucherie" to be located on the road north from Natchitoches, on the east side of what was then Lake Bistineau.[18] *There appears to be no evidence of the site today, about twenty-five miles southeast of Shreveport.*

Above the Raft

About the middle of the day, we reached the main river once more immediately above the raft. It was a sight to look at to see such piles of timber rolled on top of each other. How shall it ever be made navigable again? The Indians made signs to me that we would leave the river no more. The current here is very gentle, the river between 2 and 300 yards wide turning in various bends. The timber still a growth of cottonwood, poplar, hackberry, very plenty black ash and sugar maple in great abundance. I saw a few piquan. We took up camp a little before night, it being an old camping ground where Indian frequently stop as they pass that way. There was the best water I drank since I came on Red River. The land high and timber, chiefly Spanish oak and Hickory. Game was very plenty, but provisions we did not stand in need of. Therefore we did not hunt any. The evening was clear and cool. We made us a comfortable fire and laid down by it and slept well that night. Fair in the morning, took breakfast and started the eighth day's journey.

This day we have the finest situations on the river that I have yet seen,

17. Mills, "Mézières, Trichel, Grappe," 29–32.

18. The original Lake Bistineau was drained with the clearing of the Great Raft. Current Lake Bistineau, formed by a man-made dam, appears to occupy the upper reaches of the original lake.

the banks high and land very rich. Water comes in from every side with delightful silver streams. The timber here is all highland growth, different kinds of oak and hickory. The middle of the day we made a halt and cooked us some dinner. Whilst they were making dinner, I took my rifle and walked off to see how the country was situated. A little off from the river, I soon found a raccoon and killed him. They were very plenty in that part of the country and it being running[19] time made them more out in the day time. The lands are all good and arable fine range. The pea vine is coming here in great abundance. I had to return back; I did not go far. I took my raccoon with me; game very plenty. I saw several deer but did not get a shot at any. By the time I got back they had dinner ready to eat and set sail again. Found no alteration that day. Camped at night at a fine stream of water which pleased me well as our water had heretofore been very bad. The Indians had a fine feast of the raccoon. I did not care much about it if I had venison and turkey aplenty. They were all very jolly that night. They struck up a dance and also made us join in with them, which we did. I exerted myself and tried to outdo them. It pleased them well to see us dance with them. After dancing, we smoked a pipe in friendship and had some music on their flute then retired to bed. Nothing but the owls to disturb us, rested very well that night.

Next morning, we started before breakfast, went about five miles and stopped to cook something to eat, which we did by every man roasting his own piece of venison. We soon dispatched business and started, this being the 10th day since we left Nachitoches and the 15th day of March. This day the river runs very crooked; it makes such bends that in going 12 miles we don't make more than 3 by land. We came to a large creek on the south[20] and an island a little above here. We saw a great many fresh signs of beaver. We made a stop in order to catch some of them. The ensuing night, we saw numbers of otter slides on the island. The Indians were anxious of seeing the operation of catching beaver with the steel trap. We had a dozen with us. We landed and made us a camp and myself and one of the Indians started into the woods, as I was not the trapper, but one of my companions was good at it. We rambled up the creek till we came to high ground and found signs of buffalo for the first on that river and all kinds of game very plenty. These

19. As noted by Flores, Maley presumably means "rutting," or breeding time. Flores, "The John Maley Journal," 82.

20. Probably the Sulfur River.

high ridges are chiefly timbered with pitch pine with a mixture of oak. After traveling a mile or two, my companion saw a deer and got nigh enough to kill it. We took the skin off and hung up the meat, and walked on further.

From one ridge to another I began to discover great signs of ores in the branches. There were many of them. I found pieces of the latacana, so called by the Spaniards, a black silver ore, a sign of the richest of ore not being far. Distant from that, I found the dog teeth crystals and imperial stone of different kinds. It had all the appearance of rich mines being there. This some day or other may come to be an immense worth to the United States. It is only bordering on the Spaniards, where they make such mints of silver. These places cannot be worked by one man alone, otherwise I should not leave it for there is an abundance of riches here. I took several piece of ore and stone with me to make an assay at a more leisure time.

We killed nothing more that day, but took our venison home. By this time, it was nearly night when we came to our camp. My companion had all his traps set for catching of beaver and otter. We barbacued some of our fresh venison for supper and after took our repose. In the morning, we had six beavers and two otters. Skinned them and braced the skins on bows and pursued our journey. The 16th, after going about 3 miles, we got to vast bottoms on both sides of the river with some cane brakes. The timber very lofty, I saw numbers of piquan[21] trees, sugar maples very plenty. The middle of the day, we made a halt to make us some dinner. I took a little walk off from the river. I found the cane very thick.

As I was scrambling along through the cane, I discovered a she bear within ten steps from me, laying under the root of a tree that was blown down. I immediately leveled my rifle at her head in which she received the contents of the charge. She made out to struggle from under the tree, but soon yielded to the conqueror. I retired to my company and got assistance to help me in with my prize. This pleased the Indians better than any deed I had done yet, as they were so fond of bear meat. When we came to the place, I had to show them where she laid when I shot her. When I came to see the place, behold there laid two quite young cubs that yet had no spirit

21. At this point in the text, Maley's spelling of the word "piquan" is stricken, and someone, in a different hand, has written "pecan (Juglans Olivaefermis)." The author of the correction is unknown, but as noted by Flores, this is not the correct Latin name for the tree. Flores, "The John Maley Journal," 86.

of resentment. The Indians very much taken with them took them aboard. We skinned the bear, but they would not let me touch my hand to her to do anything. They took the meat to the boat and they soon had some of it before the fire to roast. I then did not care much about it as long as I have venison plenty. They took their young cubs along but they did not live for the want of milk; they were too young to raise without.

We went about 12 miles further that day and camped where there were signs of beaver, which we now had all along. The traps were set for them. We had a very warm evening. The mosquitoes for the first were very troublesome. We had to keep a brisk smoke to keep them away. In the morning, we had three beaver. Skinned them, roasted our meat and started the 17th, the weather very pleasant and growing [warm?]. The river makes a great bend NW, the land exceeding fertile, timber the same as heretofore. That day we saw very little alteration. At night, or rather before night we camped for to catch beaver. Signs were very plenty all day. No sooner we landed but I took into the woods. I walked two miles or more but killed nothing. The river bottom was thick grown up with spice wood and other brush. I could see nothing although game appeared to be plenty so I had to return without anything for the first time but we, as it happened, did not stand in need of any meat. They told me they had a great prospect of beaver that night. This evening same clear and warm. Our companions mosquitoes visited us severely that night. I rested but very indifferent on account of them. In the morning, had five beaver and one otter and one beaver eat out of the trap by some vermin or alligator.

Fixed ourselves and started the 18th. Cloudy this morning and like for rain. The river makes a great cove about two miles across but it does not go far before it gets its natural width again. The land exceeding fertile. After passing this bay the river runs about west. Going on about two miles, we saw a craft coming down the river. When they came near to us, we landed and hailed them to come to us, which they did and to my surprise, it was only a man and his wife who had been up the river 15 months. They had a valuable cargo. It consisted of beaver, muskrat, otter, raccoon, beeswax and buffalo tallow, bears oil, etc. This man, by the name of Hardy, he told me this was his third trip up that river; that the trip before he made 1000 dollars which he had deposited at the post of Ouattchitta[22] and he thought he would

22. Ouachita Post, located at current Monroe, Louisiana.

Fur Traders Descending the Missouri, by George Caleb Bingham, 1845. *Courtesy the Metropolitan Museum of Art, Morris K. Jesup Fund, 1933.*

make nearly double this time as his wife had been a great assistance to him as to rendering tallow and beeswax. This was the first time she had been with him and expected to return with him again. See what a resolution can do. She appeared rugged as a bear and full as greasy when skinned. We dined together. This man had some dried buffalo meat, very good. After dinner, we parted.

We went on till nearly sunset and camped still set for beaver. We had a very comfortable place to lodge, the winds being very high from the southerd and we surrounded in such a thicket that it could not touch us. Next morning it commenced raining. We fixed to keep our things dry which never took us long. I could always sit and look on—they termed me their hunter. It rained so much and steady that day that I could not walk out to see the country but it appears to be very good land, sugar tree plenty and blue ash, a timber not frequent in any country, the shell bark hickory is very plenty and grows very tall. Next morning, the 20th, very fine weather, birds of all descriptions here, more than I can name at present but make delightful music. We caught two beaver. Now the weather fair and wind high from the NW.

We had to keep close under the windward shore. The river about 300 yards wide, a large creek comes in on the N side.[23] The banks now began to alter, the land not so good. When we stopped the middle of the day, I took a route out from the river where I found the land poor but well timbered with a good deal of pine and considerable broken. Here I saw some buffalo but could not get a shot at them. My time was too short to go far therefore I soon had to turn back. In going to the river, I shot a turkey which was the largest I ever saw before. I took it to the boat and dressed it thinking that for my supper. After taking some refreshments, we started on. About one mile and another creek comes in from the south. Land still poor but well timbered. We found considerable of a bluff that came to the river. There we made our camp for that night. These Indians had camped there when coming down the river. There they would stop although it was not night, it was an hour by sun.

After landing we had time to take a hunt. Myself and one of the Indians went together and several of the others went also. This was on the south side of the river. We walked off from the river for a mile or two, saw deer plenty but got no shot at them. We saw fresh signs of buffalo. We followed on their tracks till we got them in sight. My companion crept close enough and fired and wounded him and we pursued him with all speed. He led us away from our camp, which I did not like, but I did not like to leave the Indian. The buffalo bled so much made him [easy?] to follow and so rapid we got in sight of him, but he did not appear to be much hurt. Although he was separated from the others, he seemed to run fast as ever. The Indian still pursued and I followed. When almost night, he gave up. Then we had not less then five or six miles to our camp and very broken, bushy country. When I got to the camp, I was worried out that I could hardly set one foot before the other and I was all crawling alive with ticks that I had no rest that night. I was rejoiced to see day light that I could extricate myself of these loving companions that hug so close that a man must pull very hard to make them let go. When I came to see myself, I was surprised to think

23. Probably Little River, which enters the Red at present-day Fulton, Arkansas.

how I rested any. They stuck on me so tight that I could hardly get them all of without half skinning myself. All the others that had been out were in the same predicament. The other parties brought in two deer.

After cleaning off ticks and eating our breakfast, we started. The weather delightful. We had but poor land all that day, saw nothing new. Went a fine day's journey that day, had a good place to camp. I rested well that night for I had a poor chance the night before. In the morning, we started early. These men then thought to get home in one day more. They went on very rapid and steady and also went on without eating the middle of the day. At night, I had a good appetite. I saw no good land today, all very thin. When we made our stop, there came 3 pirogues of Indians down the river and made a halt and struck up camp together.

There were 8 of them that came down. We were then a merry company. These were of the Caddo tribe that lives about 40 miles above the Cashotoos village. They showed all the friendship imaginable. They also had the custom of handing round their pipe to smoke in friendship. They were heavy laden with furs and skins of different kinds. They entertained us that night in music and dancing. These Indians with me made it known to the others that we had danced with them which made them laugh. They soon took me by the hand and made me dance again. I did not refuse but kicked about with all my might. They thought it a great miracle to see us dance. I soon learned to sing their tunes. This still pleased them more. By this time, I could understand a great number of their words. After dancing, we sat down and smoked our pipe. These new Indians had some pounded corn and they made some tompulla which I got a few spoons full of. Corn was a new thing to me. They sat talking till almost day. We laid down and slept some but daylight appeared very soon.

We ate our breakfast and started. My party wanted to get home that day. The land now made a great alteration. It is as good as any on Red River. We came to an island and very large most beautiful situation on it. Its banks do not overflow. Another large creek comes in on the left. They never stopped till they got within a few miles of their village. There they dressed themselves in their new apparel that they had got made at Nachitoches. Their dress consisted of a red-striped calico shirt, scarlet leggings trimmed with blue ribbands, ornamented with silver bands round their arms, a breast plate in shape of the half moon, a band round their head an inch and a half wide, their hair grease very thick and their faces painted in different colors. They took some refreshment and started. After going a mile or two, we met more strange Indians in two pirogues all loaded with furs and peltry. My companions did not know them, nor could they converse with each other, so they passed by without detaining us long.

Coushatta and Caddo Villages

About two hours by sun, we arrived safe at the Cashotoo village on the 29th of March, 24 days coming from Nachitoches.[24] There were but few men in the village but old men that were not fit for hunting. The young ones were all out, the women were all engaged in their corn fields but when we came in they ran to us and seemed to be rejoiced at our arrival. I was conducted to the chief or king's house. He had the stateliest building in town. His manners are very familiar, he seemed very conversant and intelligent. He could speak some words in English. He learned it at Nachitoches, being there upon business for the nation. There was great preparations made for us something to eat. They brought Indian dumpling to us, they were boiled and wrapped round with corn shucks and a string tied around. We had hominy soup which they made very good. I found we had to eat according to custom out of one spoon and that by turns. They have plenty of dried buffalo meat among them which they set down with some bear's oil to dip it in to moisten it. This you employ yourself in whilst the big spoon goes round. Some times it is a good while; they don't send it round as fast as they might. Some will eat their buffalo meat and not think of their spoon and nobody touches it unless he quits altogether.

Now we concluded to stay there some time to fix ourselves for a long and tedious journey. We had some deerskins and dressed them to make our wearing apparel altogether out of leather such as hunting shirt and leggings and moccasins. I had about two quarts of whiskey left which I distributed among them. I gained great favors by that. I also gave a few presents to their young women such as beads and some particular ones a handkerchief. This pleased them so that I lost nothing by it. I got several pair of moccasins and

24. As elsewhere in his journal, it is difficult to reconcile Maley's date with the rest of his account. Based on the chronology of events, one would expect him to have arrived at the village six days earlier, on March 23.

leggings very neatly made, plenty to last me my journey. My men also fixed themselves with everything they stood in need of for the voyage. Now I had to purchase one of their pirogues for us to go on with. They were willing enough to let me have one but that I must let them have a couple of my steel traps. I did not like to spare them although I did not refuse. I got one of their best and biggest pirogues they had. In the morning, the 6th of April, we took our leave. Before we started, they came from all quarters of the town with something for us such as parched corn that pounded fine and sifted, quantities of hominy and white beans, some dried buffalo meat. They told us it would be six days before we could find any game as it is so near their town all killed up and only 40 miles to another village which are the Caddos.

These Cashotoos inhabit a choice tract of land. It is on the south side of the river and in the forks of a large creek they call Queshuck. The river here is about 250 yards wide. In going a few miles below the town, we came to an extensive island, the length was about 10 miles. We passed that but a little ways that night and took up camp. We felt ourselves more independent by great odds. Although they were very friendly, nobody knows the treachery of an Indian. We spent the evening very agreeable and rested very comfortable, we had more room around our fire. Next morning we took our breakfast and pursued our journey. The land today is all very good.

Nothing happened to us but arrived before sunset at the Caddo village.[25] Here we were not met by any men, but the squaws they came down in flocks to see us. We camped a little above the town. There they brought provisions, the same as the Cashotoos. I found that their language differed very little if any. I walked up to their town where I saw the fruits of industry—corn fields in fine state of cultivation all done by the women. The men were all

25. One can only speculate as to the location of the Coushatta and Caddo villages. Flores examines a number of possibilities, and suggests that "Queshuck" Creek might be McKinney Creek, near the Roseborough Lake archaeological site on Red River, approximately 13 miles northwest of Texarkana. (See Flores, "The John Maley Journal," 98–102.) This, however, is almost 130 miles below the Kiamichi. If Maley's mileage estimates are reasonably correct (an admittedly big assumption), the Coushatta village would have been located approximately 90 miles below the Kiamichi, and the best match for "Queshuck" would be Mud Creek, about 10 miles north-northwest of New Boston, Texas. In that case, the large creek Maley passed earlier in the day before arriving at the village would likely have been Red Bayou, approximately 7 miles northeast of New Boston, and the Caddo village, some 40 miles above the Coushatta village, would have been located near Pecan Bayou, approximately 12 miles south-southeast of Idabel, Oklahoma.

out a hunting. They go a great distance up the river where game is plenty. They have very commodious cabins to live in. This tribe is very numerous, about 3500 souls. The Cashotoos only about 1000. We got more corn here as they have yet plenty of old corn.

Indian Tribes on the Red River

On his 1812 exploration up the Red River, Maley and his companions saw, or interacted with Indians from seven or possibly eight separate tribes. While the Red River was relatively unknown to white explorers, it appears to have been a regular hunting ground and thoroughfare for various Indian groups. Furthermore, many of these tribes were far from their original homes, underscoring the dramatic transitions taking place among indigenous communities on the American frontier at the time.

The "Kashotoo" Indians that Maley accompanied up the river are today referred to as Koasati or Coushatta (with various spellings). They were an Upper Creek tribe, closely affiliated with the Alabama, and in the latter part of the eighteenth century, they lived on the Alabama River at current day Coosada, Alabama. In 1799 a portion of the tribe moved west of the Mississippi; by the time of Maley's trip, the Coushatta were occupying villages south of Natchitoches, in East Texas, and along the Red River.[26] *In their 1806 ascent of the Red River, Freeman and Custis found a small "Coashatta" village about nineteen miles above the Great Raft.*[27] *The Indians Maley accompanied, however, lived considerably further upriver, beyond the great bend of the Red.*

Before reaching the Coushatta village, Maley and his companions met several groups of Indians, including a small settlement of Cherokees, and then they came upon a Pascagoula village somewhere near current day Campti, Louisiana.[28] *This tribe was first encountered on the Pascagoula River in southern Mississippi but moved to the Red River sometime before 1791.*[29] *Maley's colleague Cox was visited by Pascagoulas ("Passacolas") on the "Salt Branch" of the Red later that year, indicating that their hunting parties ranged hundreds of miles west*

26. Hodge, *Handbook of American Indians North of Mexico, Part 1*, 719–20.
27. Flores, *Southern Counterpart to Lewis and Clark*, 145, 150.
28. Flores, "The John Maley Journal," 62n29.
29. Hodge, *Handbook of American Indians North of Mexico, Part 2*, 205.

onto the great plains. Before reaching the Coushatta village, Maley also noted meeting two pirogues of "strange Indians." It is not clear to what tribe these individuals belonged, but the fact that they spoke a language the Coushattas did not understand implies they were neither Caddoan nor Muscogean.

Beyond the Coushatta village, Maley encountered the Caddo, a name derived from "Kaddohodacho" a leading tribe in the Caddo confederacy, and applied to all members of the confederacy by the French and their American successors. At the time of contact with French explorer René-Robert Cavelier, Sieur de La Salle, in 1687, the Caddo were scattered in villages along the Red River in what is now Louisiana and Arkansas, as well as on several rivers in East Texas.[30] *One of the largest and most influential tribes in the region, they were friendly to both the French and their American successors.*[31] *The Caddo lived in grass-thatched huts and, although they relied on agriculture, were also famous for their skill in use of the bow to hunt buffalo on the Blackland Prairies of East Texas.*[32]

Above the "Salt Branch" of the river, Maley encountered a group of "Hyatan" Indians. The name "Ietan" has been applied to several tribes,[33] *but the group that Maley met were almost certainly Comanche. Considered a branch of the Shoshoni of Wyoming, the Comanche were pushed south by the Sioux, and at the time of Maley's expedition up the Red River, they roamed the prairies of Texas, Oklahoma, Colorado, and Kansas. Considered the finest horsemen on the plains, the Comanche were true nomads, living in tipis and moving every few days to accommodate the grazing needs for the hundreds of horses that were attached to each band.*[34]

Maley finally reached a village of "Pawnees" somewhere up the Red River. This group was part of a confederacy of Caddoan tribes, now generally referred to as "Wichita," that had migrated from south-central Kansas to northern Texas in the centuries preceding Maley's excursion. In 1541 the Wichita were encountered by Spanish explorer Francisco Vázquez de Coronado in present-day Kansas, and also were found on the Arkansas River in current Oklahoma by French traders in the early 1700s. By the mid-1700s, however, several sub-tribes had been forced by

30. Hodge, *Handbook of American Indians, Part 1*, 179.
31. Meredith, "Caddo (Kadohadacho)," accessed June 9, 2016, www.okhistory.org.
32. Flores, *Southern Counterpart to Lewis and Clark*, 169–70.
33. Hodge, *Handbook of American Indians, Part 1*, 594.
34. Ibid., 327.

the Osage to relocate to the Red River.[35] *The permanent villages of the Wichita were characterized by beehive-shaped grass lodges, but the tribe also lived in tipis during the winter hunt for buffalo. Until 1811 a prominent Wichita village complex had been located on the Red River near Spanish Fort, Texas, but it is not clear where Maley encountered the tribe in his 1812 exploration of the river.*

Although several of these tribes had little in common from a cultural perspective, Maley's journal reveals little apparent conflict between them. It is possible that they reserved their animus for the Osage, who appeared to be the common enemy of most of the tribes along the Red.

Exploring the Kiamichi

We started early next morning as we were in a hurry to get up as high as the Keyademish [Kiamichi], a branch of Red River, as I was informed, famous for beaver. This was about 50 miles higher. It took us two days to get there. We passed altogether good land. We took up the Keyademish, which comes in on the north side. We found the land excellent on this river. We took up it two days journey and found plenty of beaver signs. We then searched for a good camping ground as we were determined to stay there till the trapping season was over and also I wanted to see the country on to the north bordering on the waters of the Little Missouri, which is a branch of the Ouattchitta River.[36] We found a commodious place. There we built us a tight cabin to keep our things dry if bad weather should come on us. We set our traps the first night and were successful, caught five beaver.

Next morning, I then thought that it would be best for me to take a route by myself and leave my companions to catch beaver. I started with my rifle, tomahawk and side knife, plenty of ammunition. Took my leave early in the morning the 12th of April. I laid my course north, travelled on the first day in low bottom land, very fertile with some cane breaks which was very

35. Pool, "Wichita," accessed June 9, 2016, http://www.okhistory.org/publications/enc/entry.php?entry=WI001.

36. Although he doesn't mention it, part of Maley's interest in exploring the land upstream may have been reports of a silver mine approximately sixty miles up the Kiamichi, which caused the French to call the stream "La Riviere la Mine." John Sibley to Henry Dearborn, April 10, 1805, in *Annals of Congress*, 1100–1.

difficult traveling. I had a disagreeable place to camp on account of the ground being so wet to lie upon but I made out to pass the night, and that unmolested. I killed nothing the first day. I started early and by 10 o'clock, I got on higher ground, fine open woods, very grassy and no underbrush. I saw a flock of turkeys which flew and some lit in trees which I got a shot at and killed one. This answered for my dinner and supper that day. The first water I came to, I struck fire and cleaned my turkey and roasted half of him which made me a good dinner and then pursued my journey. The country here is delightful to travel through, very open and level. I saw numbers of deer but the woods being so open, they could see me at a great distance. The timber is different kinds of oak, hickory and dogwood.

Had much better place to camp that night. I made me a good fire, roasted the remainder of my turkey and nobody to divide with. All that I could comfort myself with was to lie down and rest my weary limbs. Had no one to crowd me from my fire. Slept well that night. Had nothing to eat in the morning until I killed it, therefore I had to start without my breakfast. Traveled on in woods nearly like the day before, very open. Got no chance to kill anything nor did not the day through. At night, I wanted my supper, but I had to lay down without it. I was very full of ticks which I picked off of me before dark, but they still troubled me all night. I was rejoiced to see day light. I started as soon as I could see to travel for breakfast I had none to get. This was a quick way of doing business. After travelling a few miles, I saw a large herd of buffalo. They did not discover me. I took all the caution imaginable to get nigh enough of them, which I effected. I shot and dropped one after his running a few hundred yards. This supplied my want. I skinned only part of him, struck a fire, and made my breakfast. Cut as much off as I could handily carry, then felt myself much revived. I pursued my route, saw game plenty that day, but did not want to kill anything more as I had plenty with me. I got in a more broken country, a good many piney ridges, underbrush now very thick and the ticks very numerous. I made a halt before sunset in order to clean myself of the ticks, otherwise I could not rest. Made a good fire, had plenty of pine knots to make a light to sleep by.

In the night, it began to rain, which discommoded one very much as I had no shelter. I had to stand up before the fire and turn like a basted goose, then one side, then the other. This I did not like but could not help myself. Thus I spent the night. It still rained in the morning, but I had to go on.

There was no chance for me to make a shelter, there bark could not be had. I traveled on through the rain till the middle of the day. It then abated. I then made me a fire and dried myself and ate my dinner and started and I still kept on that direction for four days longer. Had no alteration as to the face of the country, timber chiefly pine. I saw a place where there was a high bank on a branch. In it stone coal in any quantity and large quantities of sulfur in the shape of kidney form pyrites.

I thought then by appearance that I was on the waters of Little Missouri by the course of the water running.[37] I then took to the westward with an intent to strike the waters of the Keyademesh, the river that my companions were on thinking to follow that down till I got to them. In two days travelling through a broken poor country, I reached my object. I got to a stream that I thought to be the one I was in pursuit of, but it was not large. It there ran very rapid the water very clear and the bottom rocky. I crossed over on the west side and went down stream. Game now was very plenty.

One day as I was a traveling near the bank of the creek, I saw an animal on the opposite side that I was not acquainted with. When I first discovered it, it was on the ground but as soon as it saw me, it got up in a tree. It went by leaps. It seemed to take much notice of me as I took down the creek, it pursued very often, sprung from one tree to another. He still was at too great a distance to shoot at him and the creek too deep to ford so that I could not get at him nor could I exactly see the make of the animal. As it being out of my power to do anything with him, I kept down stream, he still keeping me company on the opposite shore. I saw him till nearly night when I was thinking of taking up camp. I then thought it prudent to leave the river as I could not get nigh enough to get a shot at him. I left the river for half a mile, saw some turkeys going out and killed one.

Found me a good camping ground, land still very poor here, timber but scrubby. I made me a fire and gathered my wood and pine knots, as I always liked to be well provided when alone. I plucked my turkey and had

37. As illustrated at several points in his journal, Maley believed that the Little Missouri River extended much further west than it in fact does. At its closest point, at its source in the Ouachita Mountains, the Little Missouri would have been between seventy and eighty miles east of Maley's likely position north of the Kiamichi. The streams that he believed were part of the Little Missouri watershed were possibly tributaries of the Black Fork of the Little River in present-day Pushmataha County, Oklahoma.

part of him for my supper. Now it was dark and I laid down before the fire, being weary and nobody to discourse with. I soon fell asleep. I had part of my turkey and a piece of venison hanging up in a bush within a few steps from where I lay. Sometime in the night I was alarmed by a noise I did not know. What, to my great surprise, as I awoke, looked around in amaze. I saw something jumping up to my meat hanging in the bush. By his making several attempts at the meat gave me time to get my rifle and shot him. He never moved from the spot. Now I could get a full peep at him but after all I was deceived, it was a he panther. What would have become of me if my meat had not been hanging there for a bait? In this hungry state must have made a prey on me, but who can do anything against an all seeing and watchful Providence. I could rest no more that night thinking of my great deliverance and the eminent danger I had been in. When I came to see my meat, he had it all torn into ribbands so that I could not eat it. Now I had nothing for breakfast. I cut off one of his ears to show my companions what I had done.

I started on towards the river again and in going about one quarter of a mile, I found a deer lick and saw some deer but they seeing me too soon. I saw that this lick was much used by them. I thought it best to sit and watch for them a while. I fixed myself so that if any should come that they should not see me. By sitting about half an hour, I saw five coming and made no stop till they were nigh enough for me to take my choice. I fired and killed one. I was then again provided for. I soon made me a fire and took my breakfast and carried some of my venison with me. I soon came to the river again. I kept down it all day, found no alteration in land or country that way. I took up camp near the bank of the creek that night, provided myself with wood, but pine knots I could not get any. I slept unmolested that night.

In the morning, after traveling a few miles down the stream, I found that it was a great disadvantage to keep near the river, that it took so many different windings and also the bottoms now began to get thicker timbered and land richer. I sheared off from the river a mile or two till I got in open woods then laid my course, the country all very near alike. I travelled on two days south until I got in a rich soil of land. I then shifted my course for the Keyademish. It took the best part of a day to get to it and when I got there, I discovered that I was below our camp. I had to sleep once more by myself.

Next morning, I laid my course up the river and about the middle of the day, I found my companions. They were much rejoiced to see me, they had almost given me out for lost. They had caught 35 beaver and 7 otter. They had been up and down the river for several miles. They told me they had seen a number of Indians that steered their course for higher up. They appeared to be Chocktaws. They did not discover themselves to them but let them pass on. I showed my panther's ear and told them of the dangers I had encountered. I had been out 12 days which brought us now to the 22nd day of April.

Red River near Spanish Fort, Texas.
At this point, the river lies within the cross timbers ecoregion.
Photograph by the editor.

CHAPTER 9 ❦ *Summer and Fall of 1812*

FINDING "NEW POTOSI"

We got our baggage aboard and took down the Keyademish and got safe into Red River. Took up it and in one day's travel we got to high bluffs on the south side of the river, the timber chiefly cedar and that very elegant for use, very thrifty and straight. Several cliffs of rocks made their appearance which was a new scene on Red River. It appeared to be a bastard limestone. This bluff shifted from side to side of the river according to the meander of the river, one side rich bottom and the other a rocky cliff so it changed alternatively. So it continued for two days. We then found the bottoms to give out entirely. We found a convenient place for a camping ground as I wish to see the country off from the river we then made a halt. On that intent, we fixed our pirogue so that she was not exposed to view by any person coming down the river.

We made a good shelter to put our baggage under and next morning Cox and myself started for a cruise to the SW. We left our other man Bradley to keep camp till our return. Game appeared to [be] plenty. We traveled over hills and dales the timber a very scrubby growth. It consisted chiefly of black jack and black gum. Water here was very indifferent, it all tasted sulphery. We found an extensive ridge of iron ore. Traveling on, we found the country to alter much. We got on a high ridge which had little or no timber on it. We could see the distance of 30 miles or more which brought to our view a range of mountains to a vast height. There was a peak that appeared to be as high again as the main mountain. It had the appearance of a sugar loaf. It seemed not to be connected with any high ground. There seemed to be an entire division betwixt it at the range of mountains that I mentioned before. Now I could not be satisfied till I had seen this magnificent cone. It laid from me in a WSW course. I then had to lose the view of my object by descending the ridge.

After this, I got into low ground. It appeared as if we were near some water course which proved to be the case. These low grounds were by no means rich land. The growth of timber was sweet gum, holly and ivy bushes very thick and matted together with the green briar vines, which made it very disagreeable traveling. After traveling about a mile, we came to a large creek that ran very rapid, the bottom very rocky and uneven. Its course about NE. We crossed over on the west side and took an offset west to get rid of this bottom. In about two miles we got on high lands. I then struck my course again for my place intended. I found the country very broken and bad traveling. We killed a buffalo that day which was a welcome thing to us. We feasted on his marrow bone which is very luscious eating. We camped there for that night.

Next morning raised another high ridge which gave us a view of the pinnacle that I was steering for. I saw then that I was not steering a right course. By crossing the creek I got out of my latitude, but this gave me an opportunity of taking a straight direction. On this ridge, we found several places where there was appearances of convulsions, rocks and stones of different forms and colors tinged with green blue and red some black and heavy cemented together as if it once had been a running lava.[1] A small distance from this was iron ore in abundance. Now in our travelling, we found but little alteration as to the face of the country nor curiosities but the travel very bad. We got the sight of our mountain very often as the country is very open and barren. We still found game plenty. The antelope were here in any quantities. We wanted for no provisions.

In one days travel more we reached the foot of our mountain that we were in pursuit of, which was five days from the time that we first seen it. When we came to the foot of it we could scarcely discover that there was a mountain there; its ascent was gradually till we traveled up it about half a mile. I then (saw) that it took a great rise. After ascending further up, we began to find stone that were tumbled on heaps and of a light substance burnt as it were like unto a honey comb. After going further, we found more and more curiosities, stone of different hue, some very heavy and all in fibres

1. There is no known lava in this part of Texas. However, scientists with Marcy's 1854 expedition made a similar mistake in claiming that the copper ore they found west of Cache Creek, Oklahoma, was mixed with volcanic scoria. Marcy and McClellan, *Exploration of the Red River of Louisiana in the Year 1852*, 9.

running to a center. As we ascended, we still found greater masses of these stone and mica impregnated with sulfur. I found stone crusted over with virgin copper and also copper ore verdigrease in abundance and the red iron ore in vast bodies. We continued on till we got to the top.

This mountain makes a perfect point, not more that half an acre of a level on the top where I saw a great curiosity. On the top there was a shaft sunk that I could not see the bottom of and a vast pile of dirt and stone round the hole which was an oblong square of about 6 by 10 feet. I did not know where to look first to satisfy my curiosity. To look at the extensive prospect, I had this range of mountains which I mentioned before lay in a SW direction from me there, but this pinnacle gave me a view of the country beyond it. This main mountain lays its course parallel with Red River as far as I could see, which is about WNW. When we came to the top of the mountain, it was nearly sunset, we could not satisfy ourselves that day but concluded as there was no water there to descend the mountain and return in the morning.

We took down opposite to where we came up. Going down, we found the earth covered with ores of different colors, all very soft so that I could cut it with my knife. None would make fire but the white spar. I saw several pieces of virgin copper which was almost as maleable and soft as lead. We did not go half way down the mountain till we got to a level and a spring that run very flush. The water tasted of a sweetish taste to me, but it being night, we took our lodging there. There is a good growth of timber here, different kinds of oak and hickory mixed with some pine. We rested comfortable that night and next morning. I took a view of the branch that run from the spring and descending it, I found in its bed earths of all denominations, Fuller's Earth[2] especially very plenty, paints of all colors. This will be of use some day. This shows the riches that may be obtained in the bounds of the United States.

After taking something to eat, we started to ascend the mountain again but took a different direction, took a little round the mountain. There we discovered an old works, apparently a furnace built of a different kind of stone such as would stand the fire, but it was so much decayed and tumbled down that I could not see the form of it. The stone seemed to be a soapstone. I could cut them with my knife without receiving any damage. I made some elegant pipes out of them. When we came on the top of the mountain again,

2. Fullers earth is a type of clay that was historically used for cleaning wool.

I was then particular in viewing this shaft. In looking down by laying on my belly, I discovered the bottom and also a drift out from the main shaft not more than half the way down. I supposed the shaft to be about 60 feet. I was curious enough to contrive a way to get down. I cut an Indian ladder long enough to reach down to the drift, which after putting it down, I descended it without much difficulty. Got safe into the drift. It was dark in there. Did not venture in any distance, it had a bad odor, so much like burnt sulpher. I was not satisfied.

I returned out of the shaft and got me some fat pine and split it fine. Made a torch and descended in that manner. This gave me an opportunity of making a full discovery of these works. I saw a vein of white flint that commenced at the top of the ground where it appeared to be about 18 inches wide, went down pitching about 45 degrees. This vein of flint was intermixed with ores of different colors and immediately above this vein, a strata of white kind of earth as I thought but by putting some of it to my tongue, it drawed my mouth like alum and the taste similar to it. When I came to the drift, I perceived that they had followed the pitch of the vein in that direction, which by this appeared to be about four feet inside. The flint or spar was chiefly run out and the vein now was a solid ore of a red color and very heavy, not hard. I made out to cut off some pieces with my tomahawk. The drift was not more than ten feet under. After satisfying myself and knocking off several bits of ore, I ascended safe out of the shaft. Then I examined the dirt and stone and found that all the dirt had a strong taste of alum. I discovered that they had broken all the white flint to get the ore that was mixed in it. The colors were rich, the luster of some of the stone was equal to any crystal.

After spending a half a day, I then began to think of a return. I took a full view of the country around me. The sight was delightful. I could see as far as my eyes would let me. I could discover mountains towards the NW. It must be the dividing ridges between Red River and Little Missouri, a branch of the Ouachitta. I could see extensive plains on towards St. Antonio or in that direction. We now concluded to return for Red River. Took down the mountain, which I regretted much. To change the scene in such a short space of time instead of looking over a rough country, I have to encounter the difficulties of traveling through them. We got safe down the mountain an hour before sunset. We then set out for a hunt as we were in need of something to eat. Happily, we killed a deer which supplied our wants. We took up camp and had a good supper, laid down and took our rest. Next morning, laid our course for Red River. Travelled through an exceeding rough country, found nothing new but arrived safe the 5th day where we found Bradley and everything as we left it.

Up the River to the Salt Fork

Bradley had caught 10 beaver and one otter, had been down the river where we had seen some signs of beaver as we came up. He had killed a buffalo not far distant from the camp. He had all the meat handsomely dried which was a convenient thing for us to travel on. This would last a week without killing anything more. We had been gone 12 days on our route to this mountain I call New Potosi. I believe it to be almost a solid mass of ore which was the case of that imperial mountain of Potosi in Peru. In the morning, on the 14th of May, we got our baggage aboard and started on our voyage once more. Had high grounds on both sides of the river. Cedar timber was the chief growth on the banks that we passed that day.

The next day, we came to this creek that we had crossed on our route to the mountain. Above this, the lands get much better timber, much of it ash, hackberry and sugar tree, some growth of cane. The river very crooked where we camped the second night. We were much disturbed by wild vermin that came near us and made tremendous yells which we were convinced was a panther, an animal very frequent in that country. But he did not venture near enough to us so that we could get a shot at him, but he kept us upon our watch all night. Next morning, we took an early start and in about a mile, we came to an island grown up with cane chiefly. After passing the island we fell on with another creek about 30 yards across and the soil very good on both sides of the river. A little after the middle of the day, we saw 3 pirogues with Indians coming down the river which were of the Cashotoos. They stopped a little above us and when we came to them we landed also. They knew that our pirogue belonged to some of their tribe by the build. They pointed at their pirogue and then at mine. I gave them to understand that I had bought it from their nation. I could speak a good many words of their tongue which seemed to please them very much. They then seemed to have a good deal of confidence in us, more than they had at first. One of them light his pipe and handed in round to us to smoke. This was in actual friendship.

They were loaded down with furs and skins, such as deer and buffalo, dried buffalo meat which they have for their own consumption. They told us they had been up the north fork of Red River, which we call the salt branch. They told us we were about 8 suns from said fork, every sun in their meaning is one day. We stopped about two hours and parted so we passed on for several days without any material alterations in the make of the country, soil of land or timber, which was generally good. After that, another high bluff came in on the south side of the river and immediately above came in a large creek.

We run our pirogue up in order to tarry a day or two to see the country a little distance on towards the south. We again left Bradley to keep camp but promised to return the third day. We stayed there that night and started early next morning. We raised the bluff and followed it on, but found it to incline much to the westward. We came bordering on the creek that our pirogue lay in. The bottomlands in appearance once had been very thick timbered, but for the space of two miles wide, it was swept down that there was not a single tree standing. They were either blown up by the roots or broken down in the middle. This hurricane had been from the SW by the fall of the timber. My course that I wanted to steer was crossing this wind fall but I made several attempts but I had to retreat. It was impossible to cross it. I tried in different places but in vain. I had to return to the pirogue. On the second day, we killed a bear. In the time, they were very plenty in this fallen timber. It was a great place of refuge for them. There they could lay unmolested. We got safe to our boat and found Bradley enjoying himself in cooking of marrow bones. He had killed a very fat buffalo.

Exploring North of the Salt Fork

We took up the river again, then the second day of June, the weather very warm. We then concluded not to make another halt till we came to the salt branch thence up that fork for two days journey. There we made a camp in order to stay until we explored that part of the country lying betwixt this river and the dividing mountains of Little Missouri. After having our camp built, we put in our baggage and prepared for a start in the morning, but Bradley was determined that Cox should stay and keep camp at that time as he had not been on any expedition with me as yet. Cox did so, but with great reluctance.

Salt Fork of the Red River near Elmer, Oklahoma.
The landscape here is typical of the central great plains ecoregion west of the cross timbers. *Photograph by the editor.*

We started for a week's trip at least. The bottom land of this river was very good, the course of it about NNW. We lay our course about NE which took us from the river lands and got into an open timbered country, some small praries. We found many salt licks. These licks were on dry ground. The buffalo had eaten away the clay in great gullies and the salt was perceivable on the ground like a white frost. The ground adjoining these licks was covered over with dry bones of different kinds of animals, chiefly buffalo, seeming by acres. The cause of this must be that these animals using these licks so much that they there die of old age. We found it a general thing this river deserves its name of salt fork for it is salt sure enough. We traveled two days in such open country, timber altogether post oak.

We then got the mountain in view that we had seen when on New Potosi. We thought by appearance that we could reach it in one day's travel, but we missed our guess, it took us two faithful days travel before we got to the foot of the mountain. We had some very bad traveling but not much timber, altogether scraggy underbrush. Stone here were very plenty and that of a very curious kind such as I was not acquainted with, It seemed as if the mountain had shook them all out of its bowels and thrown them on piles below. This mountain had little or no timber on it, but rocks it did not lack, and them in appearance half ore of some kind which undoubtedly must only be a base metal as royal metal is seldom or ever found on the surface but by digging. Here may be something found of value. We now traced the mountain on to the westward. Its general course about NNW. We got on a high part of the mountain where we had the full view of our pinnacle on the opposite side of the river, which from there, made a very majestic appearance.

We also saw extensive praries to the westward and also towards the SE. I perceived that this mountain did not extend far to the north west. It got to be an entire prarie although a broken one. I could satisfy myself that I saw the water of Little Missouri. I turned my course back again by examining the ores of the mountain a little closer in my return. There was no game on this mountain. That made us make more haste to get off of it. I found a great many curiosities and also vast beds of iron ore. I took some stones with metal, thinking at my return to make an assay of some of my ores. I had some from New Potosi which I got out of the shaft. We got below the mountain and traveling through the thickets, we killed an antelope which was an excellent sweet meat. The first water we came to, we struck camp for that night.

Next morning, we started early and laid our straightest course for our pirogue. The third day we arrived there, where we found Cox and everything as we had left them but he told us he had been in much dread for a number of Indians had been with him that came down the river. Some stayed with him all night. He was a little dubious that they might rob him. They seemed to be very inquisitive to know what we had aboard. They wanted the steel traps. One also wanted to change rifles with me; mine was worth three of his. All this Cox refused to do. He then mistrusted them that they might kill him and take all there was but it was not the case. They acted very friendly and took their leave in the morning without disturbing anything. They told Cox they were Passacolas.

Now then I fixed for making a trial of my different ores which could not be a correct one for I had no weights. I took two kinds of ore and calcined it, pulverized and washed it and put the mercury or quicksilver to it to both parcels alike. This that I got on Potosi and what I got on this last mountain served them both alike in passing the quicksilver through them, but I soon found out this last one had nothing in it but iron. It cut the quicksilver all into lis[?] as fine as pin heads, which caused a good deal of trouble to get it united again but the ore that I got at the first mountain was very valuable. I soon found the silver to take hold of the quicksilver. It appeared as white as snow, sticking to it. It wanted no more than common salt to be put in to work to perfection. I left it standing for three days then I squeezed it through a piece of buckskin which I had for that purpose and had a handsome sample of amalgam of silver. The ore undoubtedly is rich silver ore. The Spaniards must have occupied this place previous to the purchase of the United States and afterwards evacuated. In doing this, I lost no time.

The Search for "New Potosi"

Few parts of Maley's journal are more mysterious than his description of "New Potosi," a cone-shaped mountain south of the Red River, topped by an abandoned silver mine. According to his journal, at some point in their journey up the Red River, above its intersection with the Kiamichi, the crew stopped and Maley and his companion Cox took a "cruise" on foot to the southwest. On this excursion, they spied a peak in the shape of a sugar loaf in a west-southwest direction and walked for five days to reach it. On arrival, Maley noted that it wasn't much of a mountain, but a gradual rise for half a mile followed by a steep slope. The peak formed a perfect point, and on the top, which covered not more than half an acre of level ground, Maley found and explored an abandoned mine shaft. Later in his account, Maley and his other colleague, Bradley, climbed a mountain northeast of the "Salt Branch" of the Red River, and he noted that he could see New Potosi from that vantage point.

On first reading Maley's account, a reader might assume that this feature was located not far upstream from the Kiamichi, perhaps on the northern outskirts of what is now the Dallas–Fort Worth metropolitan area. However, there is no mountain even vaguely fitting Maley's description in this part of Texas, a fact that undoubtedly has contributed to skepticism as to whether Maley actually travelled there. After an extensive review of maps and traveling in the region, the editor has concluded that Maley's New Potosi does, in fact, exist, but that it is located much further west than his journal implies.

The geography of the watersheds of north Texas supports this conclusion. Although he was south of the Red River, Maley asserted that New Potosi was located "in the bounds of the United States." All lands south of the river would ultimately be ceded to Spain in boundary negotiations, but at the time of his travels, Maley apparently assumed that the Louisiana Purchase incorporated all lands drained by the Mississippi, including the tributaries of the Red River in north Texas.[3] *Indeed, on both of his excursions south of the river, Maley traveled in areas where the creeks flowed north into the Red. However, most of north-central Texas, including the Dallas–Fort Worth area, does not lie in the Red River watershed, but is drained by the south-flowing Trinity and Brazos Rivers. This leaves only a few areas in north Texas arguably "within the bounds of the United States" that could have contained Maley's mysterious mountain. One is the drainage of Bois d'Arc Creek, northeast of Dallas–Fort Worth, but it seems much too small a watershed to contain Maley's excursion and the area contains no peaks matching his description. It seems more likely, therefore, that Maley's New Potosi was located further west in the watersheds of the Little Wichita, Wichita, or Pease Rivers.*

The flora and fauna described by Maley also support a conclusion that New Potosi is further west. He wrote that the countryside was "very open and barren," which indicates that he was west of the western cross timbers, a forest ecosystem dominated by short post oak trees that extended as far west as Spanish Fort[4] *(on the Red River about fifty miles east of Wichita Falls). Maley's observation of pronghorn antelope "in any quantities" also indicates that he was on the rolling plains of northwest Texas. Captain Randolph B. Marcy, who explored the Red River in 1852, concluded that they were only found upriver (west) of the cross timbers,*[5] *and his 1854 expedition didn't encounter its first pronghorn until it was west of the Little Wichita River.*[6]

The most compelling evidence supporting a western location for Maley's New Potosi is provided by the geology of North Texas. Maley described finding pieces

3. This was not an unreasonable assumption, tying Louisiana to the French claim to the Mississippi and its tributaries. The United States and Spain finally agreed to use the southern and western bank of the Red River, itself, as the boundary in the Adams-Onís Treaty of 1819. Tyson, *The Red River in Southwestern History*, 79–87.

4. There are several sources of maps of the cross-timbers. A modern one is "Map of the Ancient Cross Timbers," The Ancient Cross Timbers Consortium, accessed February 26, 2016, www.uark.edu/misc/xtimber/map/index.html.

5. Marcy and McClellan, *Exploration of the Red River of Louisiana in the Year 1852*, 186.

6. Parker, *Notes Taken during the Expedition Commanded by Capt. R. B. Marcy*, 127.

of virgin copper and abundant "verdigrease"[7] *while climbing the mountain. Copper deposits are not found everywhere in north Texas—they only occur in Permian-aged "red beds," which extend from western Kansas, across Oklahoma, and into Texas.*[8] *There have also been instances of small quantities of silver found in these formations.*[9] *An explorer traveling up the Red River might encounter Permian copper-bearing rocks as far east as the western boundary of the cross timbers, but the more significant copper deposits lie roughly fifty miles west of Wichita Falls.*[10] *These copper-bearing rocks were later encountered by the 1852 Marcy expedition, which found copper on Cache Creek, north of Wichita Falls.*[11] *In addition to identifying copper, Maley's description of "fibrous" rocks and white "spar" are apparent references to the beds of gypsum that occur in these formations, and his finding of "red iron ore" refers to the red, iron-rich shales that characterize these formations. In short, Maley's description of the rocks he found leaves little doubt that he was on the plains of North Texas, west of the cross timbers.*

In this part of North Texas, there are only a few topographic features that resemble Maley's description of New Potosi. Robert O. Fay, writing for the Oklahoma Geological Survey, included a brief reference to Maley's journal in his bibliography of copper resources and suggested that Maley's New Potosi was actually Kiowa Peak, in the key copper-bearing formations approximately one hundred miles southwest of Wichita Falls.[12] *Kiowa Peak is a distinctive cone-shaped feature, and there have been reports of copper mines in the region. There are several problems, however, with assuming that it is Maley's mountain. Kiowa Peak is not in the Red River drainage basin, but instead lies next to the Brazos River; it is a long distance from the Red River, a difficult hike to cover in five days, even by a hardy frontiersman; and it is too far south to be seen from a vantage*

7. Verdigris is a characteristic green oxide of copper.

8. A map showing the extent of these formations is presented in Stroud, *Production Potential of Copper Deposits*, 16.

9. Silver has been produced from these formations at a mine at Paoli, Oklahoma. U.S. Geological Survey, "National Mineral Assessment Tract GP03."

10. The richest copper ores have generally be found in the San Angelo and Blaine formations. Stroud, *Production Potential of Copper Deposits*, 16.

11. Anderson and Kleiner, "Copper Production." George B. McClellan, who was Marcy's second in command, returned to Texas decades later to promote a copper mine along the Pease River. McClellan was better known as a Union general during the Civil War, as a presidential candidate in 1864, and as the governor of New Jersey.

12. Fay, *Bibliography of Copper Occurrences*, 9.

Big Mound viewed from Cedar Mound.
Photograph by the editor.

point on the north side of the Red River. Finally, it is a sharp peak, without enough level ground on top to contain the silver mine Maley claimed to find.

The editor believes instead that Maley's New Potosi is Big Mound, in Hardeman County, about twenty miles west of Vernon, Texas. The largest of four hills that are referred to as the Medicine Mounds, Big Mound is a cone-shaped butte that rises approximately two hundred feet above the surrounding plains. It has a flat crest that the Comanche Indians believed to be inhabited by a powerful and benevolent spirit.[13] *Copper ores have been found throughout the region, and a small copper mine was worked on the flanks of the Medicine Mounds in the early part of the twentieth century.*[14] *One challenge in accepting Big Mound as New Potosi is that it lies west-northwest, not west-southwest, of most logical points of departure from the Red River, which is inconsistent with Maley's account. Another is that while Big Mound is the largest of the features, there are three*

13. Maury Darst, "Medicine Mounds."
14. Stroud, *Production Potential of Copper Deposits*, 37.

other cone-shaped mounds in the immediate vicinity which were not mentioned by Maley.

The editor visited the region in 2015. The mounds are a dominant feature on the plains of north Texas and can be seen from the slopes of Navajo Mountain, approximately forty-five miles to the north. The buttes exhibit beds of red shale, gypsum, and gray sandstone with abundant traces of green staining indicative of copper. The crest of Big Mound is relatively flat and covers approximately one-third of an acre. There are no obvious signs of a mine shaft on Big Mound, but the editor did find a curious depression in the ground, hidden within a cluster of juniper shrubs. The feature, which measures roughly six feet by ten feet, appears to be an excavation cut through the caprock that covers the crest of the butte. The editor could not determine the original depth of this hole; currently only about a foot deep, it was filled with juniper needles and soft humus as far as could be probed with a rock hammer. It is not clear whether this is the remnant of an old mine shaft. Significantly, there was no pile of mine tailings surrounding it. However, it does not appear to be a natural feature; no similar depression is found elsewhere on the crest of the butte.

If Big Mound is, in fact, Maley's New Potosi, there remains a fundamental problem in reconciling how he could have gotten there in the short amount of time he reported traveling. Maley's recollection of the details of his travels can often be treated as an approximation, at best, but in reconstructing his travel up the Red River, he cited three specific dates, presumably from his notes, that need to be taken into account. On April 22 Maley returned to the camp on the Kiamichi, and the team returned to their voyage up the river the next day; on May 14 the group resumed travel up the Red River following Maley and Cox's excursion to New Potosi; and on June 2 they resumed travel up the river following Maley and Cox's 2–3 day excursion into tornado-ravaged country. If the first two dates are correct, and Maley's hike to and from New Potosi took twelve days, as stated, the group would have had only nine days, April 23 to May 1, to travel from their camp on the Kiamichi and paddle up the Red to the point where Maley and Cox began walking. Then Maley and Cox would have had to reach the mountain in a five-day hike. There is no plausible way that Maley could have traveled from the Kiamichi to the Medicine Mounds in this short time frame. Furthermore, it is difficult to reconcile this schedule with other details of his voyage.

In trying to reconstruct his travels, the editor has concluded that Maley probably conflated the two excursions he took south of the river with his companion

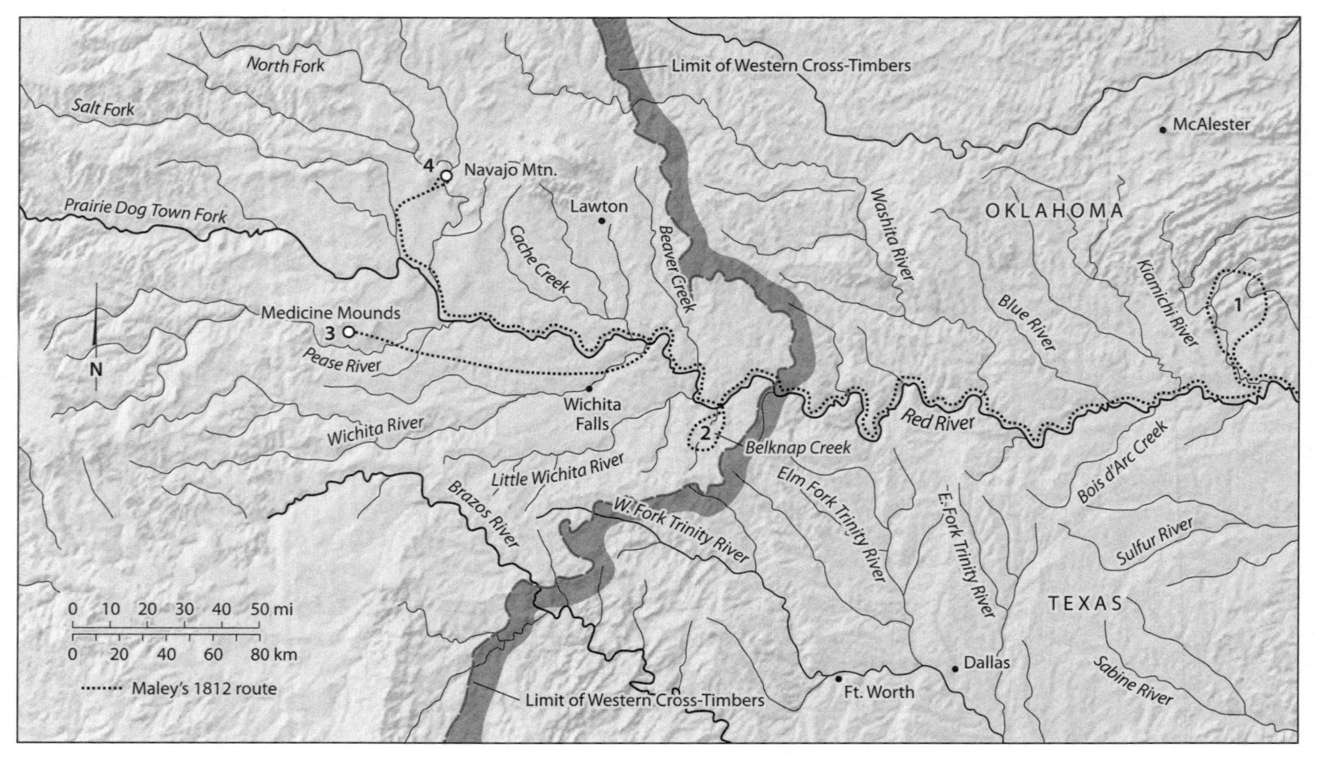

Maley's projected travel to "New Potosi."
See the accompanying text for a description of the numbered areas.
Map by Bill Nelson. Copyright © 2018 by the University of Oklahoma Press.

Cox. In other words, contrary to what is written in his journal, their twelve-day jaunt to New Potosi was not their first excursion south of the river, but their second, the first being their three-day excursion into the land of timber downed by the tornado. This conjecture assumes that Maley kept only the most perfunctory of notes, but it seems clear that he made a similar error in recounting his 1813 travel to Ouachita Post. Furthermore, it does resolve a number of inconsistencies in the distances traveled.

Under this scenario, after wandering in the Ouachita Mountains (Area 1 on the map), Maley returned to his colleagues, and they departed their camp on the Kiamichi on the 23rd of April. They returned to the Red River and continued upstream for approximately seventeen days. There they stopped and Maley and Cox departed on a 2–3 day excursion into downed timber. There are several streams where may have stowed their pirogue, but likely candidates include Belknap Creek or the Little Wichita River (Area 2). These are the first streams Maley would have seen since Bois d'Arc Creek that entered on the south side of the Red. They are 270 and 280 miles above the Kiamichi, respectively, which could have been covered by paddling a reasonable 16–17 miles/day.

On May 14 they resumed travel up the Red and two days later passed an island, followed by a stream entering the Red River that was thirty yards wide. This is a good match for Beaver Creek, which enters the Red from the north, on the north side of an island. That same day, Maley and his companions met three pirogues of Coushatta Indians, who informed them that they were eight days from the "north fork" of the Red.[15] *This also is a reasonable fit, as the North Fork of the Red River is 117 miles above Beaver Creek, a bit less than fifteen miles of paddling a day. The next feature Maley mentioned was a high bluff that came in on the south side of the river with a large creek immediately above it. This is a good description of the Wichita River, which enters the Red River from the south, immediately above a bluff that is almost a hundred feet in height.*

At that point, Maley and his companions beached the pirogue, and Maley and Cox departed for their excursion to New Potosi. From the mouth of the Wichita River to the Medicine Mounds (Area 3) is a distance of eighty-five miles, which would require Maley and Cox to cover seventeen miles per day on foot, a reasonable pace across open plains. The large creek running northeast that Maley and Cox crossed was probably the Pease River, and it is bounded on the

15. Which Maley notes, rather confusingly, is called the "Salt Branch."

west by another gentle ridge which would obscure the view of the mounds until the travelers ascended it.

Following their return from New Potosi, Maley and his companions paddled back up the Red, then two days up the "Salt Branch." There they stopped and Maley and Bradley hiked two days to the northeast to a mountain that they had seen from New Potosi. From his description of the mountain, covered with stone as if the "mountain had shook them all out of its bowels and thrown them on piles below," it seems clear that Maley is describing one of the peaks in the Wichita Mountains.[16] *If the "Salt Branch" of the river that they ascended is today's Salt Fork, the peak he and Bradley climbed is likely one of two in the Navajo Mountains, east of current day Altus, Oklahoma (Area 4). These peaks, which rise approximately six hundred feet above the surrounding countryside, would be a prominent feature to anyone traveling from the southwest, and Medicine Mounds, forty-five miles south across the Red River, can be seen from them.*

There is no way to confirm, of course, whether this proposed reconstruction of Maley's travel was the actual route he took. It seems a plausible explanation, however, for the inconsistencies that plague this part of his journal.

The Red River above the Salt Fork

We proceeded down the salt fork into the main river and ascended up that again. The river now makes a great number of short bends. The bottom lands are excellent grown up with cane, timber honey locust and black walnut, sugar tree, etc. The first day that we left the salt branch was on the 24th of June. Weather now very warm and at night mosquitoes very troublesome. We now only make a stop occasionally to kill something to eat which we generally find very handily for game is very plenty.

The does have their fawns. Cox made himself a blait[17] to blow upon that imitates a fawn. He being an experienced hunter knows the kind of woods

16. The granite exposed in the Wichita Mountains commonly appears as a pile of rounded boulders due to a process of "spheroidal weathering." Gilbert, "Tors on the Southwestern Side of Elk Mountain," 202.

17. Maley is referring to a deer "bleat." Parker recounts similar use of the instrument, including one occasion when it attracted a panther to Captain Marcy. Parker, *Notes Taken during the Expedition Commanded by R. B. Marcy*, 103–4.

Navajo Mountains viewed from the south.
Photograph by the editor.

the doe is apt to hide her young while she goes to feed. When he goes out to hunt, he tries to find such places as deer is wont to be and there blows on his blaite and, if a deer is in hearing, they will immediately run with all speed to rescue her young one, thinking its fell a prey to some vermin. They will run right up to you with their hair all standing on end in rage. We killed several bears by the same intrigue. They think when the fawn blaites that they are lost and they run to catch them to devour, but behold they miss it when they come to this fawn. They soon get a salute with a rifle ball through their head. This is the manner in which we chiefly procure our meat at this season of the year.

The 4th day after leaving the Salt Fork, we saw a great number of Indians riding on mules. They had no arms but bows and arrows. They all rode up to the shore and seemed anxious for us to come too, but I did not like to see them but as they had no arms, I thought we might drive them if they proved to be hostile but when we landed they all came running in friendship, shaking hands and slapping on their breasts crying out Hyatan. That is their names as a nation. There were about 50 men and women and children. They are well ornamented with silver. It is only silver beat out on stones with one stone on the other. It looks very rough. They make bands round their arms and head and plates on their breast. They have more silver than they know what to do with, which they have taken from the Spaniards by way laying them in the wilderness when they come from Santa Fe with their caravans, 6 or 700 mules loaded down with silver ingots going on to Mexico to the mint to get it coined. The Spaniards not being very well equipped, at them times, before they were aware of the danger. They took mules, silver and all. This way they have served them as much as three times. They now go better armed. The Hyatans dare not attempt them of late.

They all have ropes for to catch their game that they wound. They shoot altogether with bows and arrows. They don't kill their game with the entering of one arrow but after wounding any animal, either buffalo or deer, they then pursue them (that is in open) and their mules being long-winded, they tire them down till they get nigh enough to throw the rope over their head in the manner the Spaniards catch their wild horses and cattle. This is the way they war with the Osages. They take them in the open praries where their mules can out wind their horses. When they get near enough they loop them or their horses. If they take them it is sure death to them. They make no prisoners on either side. Now we stayed in company with those Indians about two hours and then started on. They proved very friendly in parting, shook hands and rode off. They told us that we were two moons from the Pawnees which is two months travel allowing 20 miles a day.

We are now going at the rate of 25 miles a day so that at that rate it will not take us as long as I am not a going to explore any more of the country in going up the river, as I will take a more convenient time for it coming down the river. So we kept on day by day, stopped only when we wanted something to eat. Game we still found very plenty, the river lands generally very good, timber is chiefly sugar maples, black walnut, hackberry and blue ash. From the time that we left these Hyatan Indians that we met as we were coming up, 6 weeks travel after that, the waters began to get very low and shallow in the river so that in places we had to pull our pirogue. The water also running very rapid. We still continued on for several days till we found it useless to pretend to go any farther with our craft.

So we found a convenient place to lay up our pirogue, hid our steel traps, and deposited our furs on a scaffold about ten feet high and covered it so that the weather could not damage it. We packed ourselves down with the remainder of our plunder and started on by land for the Pawnees. We took off from the river and left the low grounds and soon got into most beautiful open woods. The face of the country very level, the timber chiefly shell bark hickory. Buffalo were very plenty. Here we saw a new kind of squirrel and very numerous. They were a size larger than our northern gray squirrel but they were of various colors, spotted black and white. We killed several of them. Their skin must be valuable; the fur is as fine as our marten fur. We found these squirrels only where the hickory nuts were plenty.

The Pawnees

After traveling about five days, we then got into open praries that seemed to be boundless on the northerd and easterd. The range we took was just on the outskirts of the prarie, then a grove of timber and then a prarie and so in succession till we got in sight of a company of Indians all on horseback and them elegant fat horses. They soon discovered us but seemed to be struck with amaze as white people was an uncommon sight to them. Perhaps some of them had never seen any. They at first stood and every man braced his bow. They all dismounted and run in a hurl, holding some counsel. We stood fast to see what might be their design. In a few minutes, after talking together, they all faced towards us and advanced a few steps. Then one of them beckoned with his hand saying something withal for us to come to them, they looking very inoffensive. We then approached towards them. They all stood fast. When we got near enough, they put out their hands, made signs to shake hands, which we freely accepted. Shook hands and showed all the friendship imaginable.

I soon gave them to understand that we wanted to go to their town to trade with them. I showed some of the goods that I had with me. This seemed to please them very much. Made preparation immediately to escort us to their village which they gave us to understand was two days travel, which we supposed then to be about 300 miles above where we left our pirogue and from our pirogue down to Nachitoches 900, which makes the distance from the confluence with the Mississippi to the Pawnee nation 1500 miles. The whole may be gone in a stage of a spring fresh with large craft drawing 8 or 9 feet water.

Wee-tá-ra-shá-ro, Head Chief of the Wichita Tribe, by George Catlin, 1834. This chief met with Colonel Henry Dodge, of the First Dragoon Expedition of 1834, at a Wichita village located at Devil's Canyon on the North Fork of the Red River. Over ninety years old at the time, he might have been the "king or chief" Maley met twenty-two years earlier. *Courtesy of Smithsonian American Art Museum, Gift of Mrs. Joseph Harrison, Jr.*

After being fixed, (as they took our goods on their horses) we started. They made us ride most part of the way and they walked. These Indians had come out there in pursuit of their horses, who sometimes stray away for a great distance and the Osages very often stray that way and steal them, so they have to be very watchful. They took us a straight course through a beautiful open dry country handsomely timbered with different kinds of oak and hickory. Wild turkeys were very numerous. We shot them whenever we had a chance, which seemed to surprise them very much. Before night, I killed a buffalo. They were very dextrous in skinning the buffalo with their stone knives. They have but few knives yet among them, and them they are very careful of. They also have a few rifles, but will not make use of them, only in case of war with the Osage Indians as they have formerly been very troublesome to them but they don't venture so near since the Hyatans has undertaken war with them.

We feasted that night on our fresh buffalo and next morning we started after taking some breakfast. All a beautiful level country. About two hours sun, we got in sight of their village, which we could see before we got within five miles of it. They live right on the bank of Red River, which has a very rich fertile bottom of about one mile, that handsomely timbered. Then back of their village comes in an extensive prarie which to the northerd is boundless to the eye. It affords grass in the greatest abundance. When we arrived at the village, we were saluted with all the friendship imaginable. They came flocking to us from all parts of the town. We were conducted to their chief or king who lived near the center of the town, his house having three apartments, one room large enough to lodge 20 men with the fire right in the center on an earthen floor, but the smaller apartments were furnished with berths on every side to lay in. Not more than one might lay in it comfortable, which I soon found out was the case that they all sleep separate. He does not sleep with his wife although their beds are joining. The young women sleep in the other apartment. Young men, I saw none.

We were that evening entertained with music which consisted of a flute and a drum made of small hollow log and a raw deerskin stretch over one end. This only served to keep time. After a whiles music, they invited us to supper which consisted of tompulla, some fresh buffalo meat stewed, and good corn bread baked in the ashes. Their manner of eating was similar to all the other tribes that I had passed through, that is with one spoon which seemingly is a general thing. There was a great concourse of company there that evening to see us. They stayed very late. They at last retired then we were invited to lie down in the same apartment where the chief laid himself. We were furnished with plenty of buffalo rugs very neatly dressed. I found these berths very comfortable to lie in. The bottom was very springy. It was a mat of cane very curiously interwoven together. We rested well that night. This was the 10th of August. Everything appeared like industry. The squaws were in their fields hoeing potatoes, corn was laid by almost in roasting ears.

Now in the morning, I opened my goods and presented the chief with a wampum and some vermilion paint and a small looking glass. The young women I gave some beads, which seem to please them very highly. After having some conversation which was all by signs, the chief escorted us through the town. I found that they had both horses and mules in great quantities and they seem to take a great deal of care of them. They have plenty of old corn to feed them with. They ride altogether. These Indians are generally very nasty. Their wigwams are not so commodious as the other nations that we passed through, although their mode of lodging is much better and also their cookery. They make a great use of bread. They have good regulations among them. They are not a very numerous nation, only about 1500 souls, but they gave us to understand that part of their tribe were separated from them, that they had gone towards the Missouri. The warriors, about 700, were divided in classes of ten each class. One class goes out to hunt and fetch in the meat for the ensuing day and so every class takes it in rotation. They kill no more than they consume; they don't wish to destroy their game useless.

We took our lodging again at the chief's next night. I then undertook to inform myself of mines and minerals in that country, it was only by signs. I had to do it, but I got great satisfaction from the chief. He gave me to understand that there had been more there on that business and made signs that they had two pieces of metal that they would dispose of, but the goods that I then had with me was not suitable for them to take in exchange for the metal. Five of the Indians went with us to show where the metal laid. It took us three days to go to it. We crossed the river at the town and took a SW course through an open, broken country. We found in going through praries large ledges of limestone but no signs of mineral. They took us safe to this metal. It laid a few miles from the mountain that appeared to be the same that I have already spoken of. This mountain divides the Americans and Spaniards. When I took particular notice of where this metal lay, I was convinced that it never grew at the place it lay. I wanted to go on the mountains but the Indians made signs that there was nothing there but higher up Red River was plenty silver. So after looking about a little, we started back again for their town and arrived there the 7th day from the time we left it.

Finding Gold

Then I wanted to take a trip higher up the river, but I could not prevail on any of the Indians to go with me. They were afraid of the Osage nation if they go too far that way. So we took it by ourselves as I was determined to satisfy myself in my journey. Since I was that far, I would go farther & it might be as it would. I deposited my goods with the chief and started for the headwaters of Red River. We kept on the north side. The way we went was mostly prarie. Off from the river we saw buffalo very plenty. After travelling three days, we got to a very broken country, lands very poor and timber scrubby, chiefly post oak. I saw some high knobs at a distance. I steered my course that way and the next day got on to the highest ground there was. Here I had a fair view of that shining mountain that I once made an attempt to get to when I was up the Arkansas. I then had a perfect knowledge of where I was. I could see the waters of Arkansas River. I then shifted my course due west and struck the waters of Red River, which I crossed over in several small branches.

Now came in this mountain that I mentioned before. It crowded the waters of Red River much to the north. This mountain was very productive of springs issuing out of it, although the water not very palatable. I discovered a greenish slate stone in this mountain. The little rivulets that came down the mountain had the most curious kinds of gravel, in the bottom they appeared to be every color that nature ever formed. After tracing along the mountain for two days and examining every curiosity, I found some workings that I was not acquainted with. It was on a small creek that came out of the mountain although it formed a deep hollow with a flat of 100 yards here. I found piles of gravel and sand as if it had been washed. These gravel seemingly had been dug out of the bed of the creek, but the signification I did not know till I found it out by a mere accident. I found a small flat dish made out of wood and also a shovel that they had made use of for digging up the gravel. I took this bowl or dish and made an experiment. I dug up some of the gravel where I discovered that they had dug and I washed it by shaking it about in the water. After the mud was washed off, I then took off the top gravel and examined it very closely but found nothing. I kept washing and shaking of it till I had all the sand washed away. Behold, then in the bottom I discovered several particles of pure gold. Then I thought my fortune made.

We then went to work knowing then what it was for. We found several pennyweight. We searched there that day and all next and we accumulated 50 dwt of pure gold, one piece of 7 dwt and the remainder in small grains.[18] Then we were for seeing the country more extensively. We took our apparatus for washing with us and every branch or run of water we tried for gold and found more or less in every place. We took on the mountain. It abounds in minerals beyond any thing I had seen yet. After tracing on the top of the mountain, we found old diggings in abundance where the Spaniards had dug silver ore but they now have evacuated and gone on their own boundaries. We then concluded, as we were not prepared for doing much at the mining or digging of gold, to return then as soon as possible and come prepared for business next season and get more assistance with us.

❦ ❦ ❦

Maley's Confusing Journey to the Pawnee

While it is possible to reconcile much of his journal, Maley's account of his journey above the "Salt Branch" of the Red River remains a bewildering exception. The principal source of confusion is Maley's recollection of the time and distances traveled. For example, after leaving the "Salt Branch," Maley claimed that he traveled upstream more than six weeks, at twenty-five miles a day, until the water became too shallow for his pirogue. Simple math would put this location more than a thousand miles upstream of the Salt Fork, somewhere in Arizona or Utah! Only a few sentences later, he contradicts himself, indicating that the pirogue had been left nine hundred miles above Natchitoches. This is more plausible, but his assertion that the Pawnee village lay another three hundred miles upstream

18. The abbreviation "dwt" is commonly used for "pennyweight," equal to one-twentieth of a troy ounce.

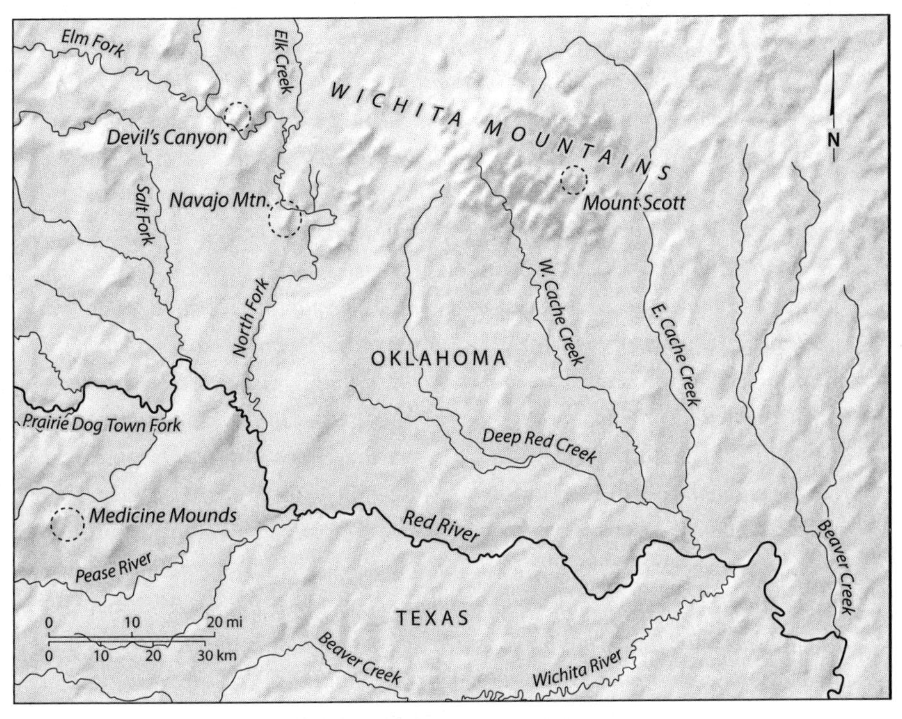

Wichita Mountains and upper Red River.

Map by Bill Nelson. Copyright © 2018 by the University of Oklahoma Press.

would still place it west of the "Staked Plains" (Llano Estacado) and outside the Red River watershed.

If Maley had ascended the river in previous years, his account might have been clearer. He would have undoubtedly encountered the Pawnee (Taovaya/Wichita) village complex near current-day Spanish Fort, Texas, prior to reaching the Salt Fork of the river.[19] *These villages, straddling the Red River, had been the most important trading center on the river since the mid 1750s.*[20] *However, they were abandoned in 1811 after the death of the Pawnee chief, Awahakei, and therefore could not have been the site Maley visited in 1812.*[21] *In fact, the tribe that Maley visited seemed to have had little contact with white traders. As he noted, they seemed to be struck with amazement on first encountering Maley's group. They also relied primarily on stone knives, another possible indication of limited contact.*

While it is impossible to identify the location of the Pawnee village based on the distances recited by Maley, there are several hints that it was located on the North Fork of the Red River. The Pawnees, for example, refused to join Maley in traveling further up the river due to fear of attacks by the Osage. This only makes sense if the village were on the North Fork, as traveling upstream on the Prairie Dog Town Fork would take the villagers west, further from any Osage threat. Another indication is that when Maley attempted to return on horseback in 1813, he decided to take a "nigher cut," a straight course to the village, which carried him well north of the river, and into the hands of the Osage. A village location on the North Fork also makes more sense from a historical perspective. With the exception of a location the Pawnees occupied temporarily in the 1770s, the tribes settled in locations where there was sufficient timber and grass to construct their lodges, and later known village sites were located either on the North Fork or the Washita River.[22]

19. Some earlier researchers, in fact, assumed that this was the site visited by Maley. See Flores, "The John Maley Journal," 138n30, and Wilson, *Oklahoma Treasures and Treasure Tales*, 82.

20. Flores, *Journal of an Indian Trader*, 92.

21. Garrett, "Dr. John Sibley and the Louisiana-Texas Frontier, 1803–1814," 403.

22. In 1772, in response to Osage threats, the Taovaya were forced to retreat further up the Red River to a "dismal site on a treeless plain, too poor and arid for their agriculture, and so bare of timber that they had to live in wretched sod huts instead of their customary grass lodges." Johns, *Storms Brewed in Other Men's Worlds*, 411. According to distances collected by Peter Custis in 1806, these "old Panis Towns" were located at a site known as "White Rock" 120 miles above the village complex near current day Spanish Fort, Texas. Flores, *Southern Counterpart to Lewis and Clark*, 331. If this distance is reasonably correct, it would place the location somewhere between the Wichita and Pease Rivers, in the vicinity of current day Burkburnett, Texas. The "white rock" may refer to a gypsum outcrop along the river.

Maley's discovery of gold, upstream of the village, was almost certainly in the Wichita Mountains, and very likely at Devil's Canyon.[23] *The Wichita Mountains, which rise from the plains of southwestern Oklahoma, are the only geologic feature in the region where gold has been discovered and were the site of the last great gold rush east of the Rocky Mountains, with perhaps as many as five thousand prospectors staking claims in the early twentieth century.*[24] *While there have been discoveries throughout the mountains, most accounts of earlier mining in the region center on Devil's Canyon, located in the western part of the range, immediately north of the North Fork of the Red River. Wilson provides evidence of Spanish mining at the site dating as far back as the late seventeenth century, and numerous accounts corroborate Mexican gold-mining activities there in the first half of the nineteenth century.*[25] *The canyon is also a good fit for Maley's description of the site: the mountain "crowded the river much to the north," and the placer site was found on a small creek coming out of the mountain.*

If the Pawnee village was on the North Fork, and Maley's gold discovery was in Devil's Canyon, his account of traveling from the village to the canyon is plausible. Initially, the group traveled on a prairie, probably between the North Fork and Deep Red Creek, before encountering post oak timber, further north. The "high knob" that Maley ascended was likely one of the cluster of peaks northwest of current day Mountain Park, Oklahoma, or, alternatively, Granite Mountain, twelve miles further east. From there, Maley believed he saw the Arkansas River and the "shining mountain" that he had tried to ascend while up the Arkansas River (which the editor believes was Rich Mountain on the Arkansas-Oklahoma border). In fact, he was much too far southwest to have seen either. What he likely saw, instead, was either the Washita or Canadian Rivers to the north and possibly Mount Scott at the eastern end of the Wichita Range. Maley then returned due west, crossing "several small branches" of the Red River, which could have been Elk Creek, or branches of Owl Creek, in addition to the North Fork, itself. He would then be only a few miles from Devil's Canyon.

Maley's account of his return to Natchitoches, though brief, also provides some clues as to his location. In his 1808 journey, it took Anthony Glass thirty-five

23. Fay, in his brief bibliographic note for the Oklahoma Geological Survey, assumes that Devil's Canyon was the site of Maley's gold discovery. Fay, *Bibliography of Copper Occurrences*, 5.

24. Wilson, *Oklahoma Treasures and Treasure Tales*, 149.

25. Wilson dedicates an entire chapter to mining in and around Devil's Canyon. Ibid., 111–28.

days to travel by horseback from Natchitoches to the Pawnee village at Spanish Fort, with the group usually averaging between ten and twenty miles on the days they travelled.[26] *According to Maley's account, it took approximately twice as long, riding mules, to return from the village to Touline's Vacherie north of Natchitoches. Maley apparently took a longer route than Glass, staying north of the river, and we don't know at what pace he traveled. The time required to return to Natchitoches, however, supports a conclusion that he began the journey much further west than the old Pawnee village site at Spanish Fort.*

Return to Natchitoches

So we got in about two weeks safe to the Pawnees. We then traded our goods that we had with us for some of their best mules and started on our route the nighest course we could go. Only had to go to our pirogue on the river to get our beaver. We tied the mules two by two and rode each one. We made a particular agreement with the Indians for these two pieces of metal and what kind of goods suited them. They went with us for one day's journey, at least a number of them. We got to our pirogue and found everything safe. Our beaver was not damaged. We left our steel traps there till our return next season. Now we had to take off from the river for the best traveling and then lay our course nearly east. We found the land a good deal broken and piney timber mixed with ridges of oaks and hickory. We found game generally plenty. We had not much trouble with our mules. They went along very gentle. They cost us nothing for feed at night. We traveled on for two months when we struck an Indian trace that took on our direction, which I was not sorry for we followed that but one week till we got safe to Dolans Vochere where we stopped when going up the river. We then felt ourselves nearly home. It was only 75 miles from Nachitoches.

We stayed there one night and then took our directions which we got from Dolan. We had then a very good path all the way through a most delightful country of land. We had several difficult water courses to cross which kept us back. In one week from Dolans, we arrived safe at Nachitoches on the 10th

26. Flores, *Journal of an Indian Trader*, 37–46.

day of November, which was 8 months from the time we started. We had to start right on with our mules down the river to see them which happened to be a very good time. We found very ready sale for them, it being in time for ginning cotton which they make use of mules for altogether. I was not long in selling them for a very fair price. After selling them, I started down the river to Natchez to take winter quarters there. Arrived safe at Natchez and there made preparations for another Red River voyage. I got plenty that offered there service to go on the same expedition, but when spring came they were not all ready to start.

CHAPTER 10 ❦ *1813*

Robbed by the Osage

I then concluded to go with my old hands and go by land that they might come on when they were ready, they to come all the way by water. We had everything provided that they had to take up for mining and washing of gold. I laid in 1500 dollars worth in goods to take up with us for the Pawnees. Got the goods taken by water to Nachitoches, and there purchased 6 cheap Spanish horses and packed three of them with my goods and we rode one apiece. We started from Nachitoches the 3rd of March, 1813. We took our old road again to Dolans Vacherie and so on the path again till where we struck it when coming down the river. Then I concluded to take a nigher cut. I laid a straight course for the Pawnees, traveled on in a poor country of land for several weeks until we got to the praries where we fell in with three hunters that were there to spend the season in killing buffalo, drying their tongues and hunting bees and saving the wax. They told us that it was dangerous that season of the year to meet the Osages on that route, that we had best keep more on to the left hand although it was out of the way.

I thought that I would risk the nearest course, but it was an unlucky thing to me. We started on through this extensive prarie and found no water at all and the weather excessive warm. We were almost perished the first day. Buffalo were so plenty that they were in solid columns before us. We then shot a buffalo, cut its throat held our cups and caught the blood and drank it warm out of his throat. If it had not been for that, we must inevitably have perished. All the way we had to cook our meat was to gather some turf and dry buffalo dung and scorch it in the blaze. We traveled on till the third day a little after the middle of the day we saw a number of Indians all on horseback making right towards us. We did not know whether they were friends or foes, but they rode up to us, all well-armed with good rifles. They dismounted and immediately pulled us off our horses, took our rifles and then took off the goods. They cried ozaazee to let us know they were of the Osage nation. I knew then that I was undone. We did not know but our lives was a going to be taken next, but they were then so engaged about opening and looking at the goods which was the greatest prize they had ever got at one time.

When they were all seated round the goods a viewing of them, they appeared to be entirely harmless in my opinion. I stepped up to them and tapped one on the shoulder, offered him my hand to shake hands with him calling him brother and making signs to him that I meant to go among them to trade. But one of them jumped up in great rage and knocked me down by striking me on the breast which took my breath from me, left me senseless sprawling on the ground. I laid there several minutes before I came to. My companions took me up for dead, but fortunately recovered. I said no more but stood and looked on till they packed all the goods on the horses again and left us there standing at the mercy of providence to provide for us. They did not search our bodies as we were but meanly dressed in deer skin. They had no thought of obtaining anything more.

All we saved was our knives and I my pocket book, still of some value if ever we should get back but only think of the gloomy prospect we had. We were then 600 miles from any white inhabitants that we knew of although we were but three days journey from hunters that we left at the edge of the prarie. But how could we have got there had it not been for our rifles, even to support us in drink. There we were then and nothing but death before our eyes. If that was our lot, consider what was the sufferings to be before it would take place. We had to make the best of our way and improve our time whilst we were yet strong. We struck our course as straight as we could for the edge of the prarie to find these hunters. We traveled on all that night, steered our course by the north pole but the next day we were so fatigued and in want of water that we could scarcely go any more, but this was only a beginning for it took us till the fourth day after the middle of it before we got through to these hunters.

Therefore, I leave it to the reader to judge what trials we had for our lives, nothing in four days to moisten our throats or satisfy a once craving stomach. But we cared nothing more for anything to eat, drought overpowered it, but the merciful hand of providence brought us through with our lives saved. The hunters were astonished to see us so soon. They made us some turkey soup which we drank very moderately and in a few days we got smart. We then provided for our journey back the nearest route we could take to find white inhabitants as I was then entirely disheartened. We dried as much buffalo meat as we could each of us carry. The hunters gave us a kettle to make soup in and also they had a spare hatchet they let us have.

Return to Civilization

We then concluded our best way was to get to the Ouachitta River, which was our nearest water course, and then to make a raft and drift down the river till we got to the inhabitants which we thought would be easier that walking all the way. So we started on that intent, struck our course into the wild wilderness not knowing what was a going to become of us. We had not our main friend with us, that was our rifles. As long as we had them, we were always at home. We started and took a NE direction as I was well acquainted with the geography of the country. I was convinced that we should strike the river soonest in that direction. We traveled on as expeditiously as possible, lost no time, neither rain nor shine laid us up. We traveled 10 days through a broken piney country until we got into the bottom lands of the Ouattchitta River. We then picked up courage thinking we would soon come to the river, where we could ride down at our ease; even if our provisions were scarce, we had not to walk, but we found our mistake to our sorrow.

After travelling three days through swamps and low grounds, cane brakes and crossing bayous, we at last found ourselves completely surrounded by water. Tried in every direction to find a passage but all in vain. We got beknighted in a most miserable situation, had not a dry spot to lay ourselves down. Next we had to take our track back again for the higher grounds. Our provisions were now as good as gone. What now will become of us, God only knows. We traveled lower down, thinking that we might find high ground after a while to take us to the river. We now had a most beautiful country, the land very fertile and fine for range, very handsomely timbered with different kinds of oak and hickory. These higher grounds were beautiful to travel in, no underbrush to interfere, but we still keep making attempts to get to the river but proved unsuccessful.

Now we had nothing more to eat. Now we have to try every root, herb and bark to try to keep ourselves alive. After a few days, we found something that was a kind of substitute to keep us alive or otherwise must have perished, which was a beech bark, to peel it then scrape the inside till it gets to the outside bark. This bark we could only find in places. It was not a general growth of this country. We held many a court martial over a rattlesnake whom were very numerous there. This way we spent our time in making attempts to get to the river and then had to retreat back. It now began to be serious times with us. We could scarcely rise where we were down.

It was on the 9th day that one of our men got bit by a copperhead snake, which is worse that the bite of a rattlesnake. He was taken very bad. Immediately his leg swelled ready to burst in a few hours. The bite was just above the heel. This was Cox, whom I got on the River Currents. He was an old hunter and well acquainted with herbs such as were cures for snake bites but he did not find those immediately, at least such herbs as he said was good. We were then in the low swamps and found ourselves in a miserable situation. Nothing but cypress swamps and them alive with alligators. Not even a comfortable place to lay down and die for surely we expected nothing else. Cox could hardly walk any more and we not much better. He would often lay down and tell us for God's sake to go on and make the best of our way, that he would lay there and die. This still increased our misery. If we stayed there, we had certainty to perish for we could find nothing there to nourish us.

We stayed with him a while. He made several attempts to get up and walk but could not and we were not able to assist him for it was as much as we could do to get up ourselves. This was the 10th day without anything to eat but our barks and roots. We then concluded to leave him to the mercy of God, left him behind with weeping eyes and a broken heart. After leaving him a few rods, we heard him make the most lamentable moans and cries for God to have mercy on him. It struck me with the most tenderest feelings of affection thinking that he had been such a hero as to stick to me till the last, notwithstanding all the difficulties that we had. He was a man of great fortitude and an undaunted spirit. Thinking of this put me to a stand almost ready to resign myself to the same fate, lay down beside him and see one another last. Whilst we were standing thinking what to do, he had got up and was coming towards us. After walking a little, he began to come to and walked on that day without sitting down much as sitting was not good for him to let the blood settle in his leg. That made it bad to start again. The only way he rested himself was by holding fast by the saplings and support himself. That way we found a fine place of beech timber where we stopped several hours to feed and stayed all night where we had plenty of it next morning.

The 11th day of starvation, Cox's leg was not quite so bad. We still keep crawling along and feeding where ever we could find our beech bark. Next morning, the 12th day, we were traveling on for the river. About the middle of the day, we came to an Indian trace, which I was much pleased to see, thinking that might lead us to some inhabitants but we did not know which end of the path to take. We followed it on toward the river, but soon had to turn back. The river still had the bottom overflowed, so we took the other way, which appeared by the course to take us right back again the way we came from. This discouraged us very much thinking it to be a path that went on to the waters of Red River that we would have to leave it and take our own course again through the woods. But after we got out of the low grounds, we saw that it took more on our course so we kept on it till we got in a most beautiful country and so we traveled on the path winding more towards the river; it kept on a ridge. We at last saw fresh horse track in the path. This revived us much.

Not long after, we saw a smoke rise not far before us, then we were overjoyed and when we came to it, behold, it was two Indians who had come that very day to hunt deer. One of them had just brought in a deer. Think what a sight this was to us. These were Choctaws. I could talk some of their language. I soon told of our distress and showed the man bit by the snake. One of them ran with great speed and was back in a few minutes with a handful of plaintain leaves which grew along the path. He pounded them and put them to the bite. We were now only 15 miles from their village and thirty miles from the Post of Ouachitta on the river where there were white inhabitants. They had some corn with them. They pounded some hominy and made us some good soup, telling us to eat a little at a time. Supping the soup occasionally, we stayed with them three days and then took a start for their village, taking some dried venison to live on by the way. We were still very weak but felt better at heart.

We started early in the morning, thinking to get to their town the first day but we felt too weak to travel fast. About the middle of the afternoon, we saw honey bees in great abundance in the path sucking on the mud. We made a halt there and coursed the bees and found two trees with bees in. We cut them down with our hatchet and got a great deal of honey. I eat too free of the honey which made me so sick that I laid down to die, thinking I could not live an hour the situation I was in. I swelled up as tight as a drum but I laid down on my back and they got some water for me and I drank some, which caused me to vomit and recovered immediately. After that, we then went to the path and struck camp for that night. We got our kettle full of honey which we took with us next morning and in about two hours travel, we got to the Indian town.

The country that we traveled through appeared to be but a light poor soil of land, the timber chiefly pine, some mixed with oak and hickory. But when I came to the Indian village, there I saw the productiveness of this kind of land. Only cultivated by the squaws, the produce of vegetation was beyond my expectation. Corn as rank as any on the river bottoms, sweet potatoes in the greatest abundance, squashes, pumpkins, beans, cucumbers, watermelons and almost every kind of vegetable that we raise in the eastern states. When we came to this village, it was about 9 o'clock in the morning. The squaws were all in the fields at work. At the sight of us, they all run to their wigwams. The sight of an Indian I could not get. They were all out a hunting, only the chief, who they sent for immediately. The chief was a very intelligent man and spoke some English and French. They treated us with all the hospitality that human nature could bestow. They brought us plenty to eat such as shelled beans, squashes, Indian dumplings and all kinds of vegetables. Meat was a scarce article among them as they depend altogether on the woods for that and the men all out at this time. We stayed there that day and night. Next morning, we started for the Post of Ouattchitta, which was 15 miles only where we once more might enjoy ourselves among our own country people.

Maley's Return from Oklahoma Plains to Ouachita Post, 1813

It is difficult to reconcile Maley's narrative of where he traveled in 1813. According to his account, he departed Natchitoches on horseback on March 3, traveled to somewhere on the plains of southern Oklahoma, was robbed by the Osage, and staggered back to Ouachita Post (present-day Monroe, Louisiana) on August 16. However, August would be an unlikely time of year to encounter flooded bottomlands on the Ouachita. Furthermore, according to these dates, the journey took five and a half months, which is much longer than implied by his narrative. Similarly, Maley later stated that he departed Ouachita Post for a journey up the Ouachita River at the end of August, returned to the post, and traveled on to Natchez, arriving there on October 10. Yet this is only forty days, while according to his account, Maley's activities would have required at least two and a half months. One suspects that Maley misinterpreted his own notes. It seems more likely that he first arrived at Ouachita Post in May or early June 2013, and August 16 was the date he returned to the post from his journey up the Ouachita River. While this sort of inconsistency adds to the challenge of reconstructing Maley's travels, in a perverse way it reassures the reader that his account is genuine—anyone fabricating this journal would surely have been more careful in reconciling these details.

Notwithstanding the inconsistencies, it appears Maley was robbed by the Osage on the prairies of southern Oklahoma, some distance north of the Red River, perhaps somewhere between Hugo and Ardmore, Oklahoma. It took the group four days to walk back to the hunters, and from there, ten days through a broken, piney country to hike to the Ouachita River. On first reading Maley's account, his decision to head for the Ouachita River and to float down it to Ouachita Post seems an odd choice. On review, however, it wasn't a bad plan. For example, returning by the route they came would have required the group to hike east to the great bend of the Red River, near current Fulton, Arkansas, then perhaps another 175 miles south to Natchitoches. By comparison, by continuing east from the great bend, they could have reached the Ouachita River in sixty to seventy miles.

His decision may have been influenced, as well, by inaccurate maps, which placed the Ouachita River closer to the Red River than its actual location. The Dunbar and Hunter expedition of 1804–5 produced an accurate map of the Ouachita River, and determined the location of the Hot Springs to be at 36°36'04" North Latitude and 92°50'43" West Longitude.[1] *Two of the most widely published maps available at the time, the Arrowsmith Map of 1808, and the 1810 map by Alexander von Humboldt, replicated the details of the Ouachita River from*

1. Berry et al., *The Forgotten Expedition, 1804–1805*, 2–3, Nicholas King Map of the Washita River of Louisiana.

Hunter and Dunbar. However, they placed Hot Springs a full degree of longitude further west, possibly due to a copying error.[2] *The result was that the best maps that Maley might have had access to at the time showed the Ouachita River to be only about twenty-five miles east of the great bend of the Red River, whereas the actual distance is more than twice that.*

Maley's claim that he struck a northeast direction in his travel to the Ouachita is also confusing. If he had traveled northeast from the great bend of the Red, he would have come to the Little Missouri, a tributary of the Ouachita. Even heading due east would have taken him to the major Caddo trading path, which crossed the Ouachita at Ecore Fabré, present-day Camden, Arkansas. High bluffs there would have made the river accessible from the west, even during flood stage. It seems more likely that Maley traveled east-southeast, striking the river somewhere south of Ecore Fabré, where there are only a few points where the river could be reached without traversing a flooded forest. Further south, where the Ouachita is joined by the Saline River west of current day Crossett, Arkansas, the flooded bottomland would have been as much as ten miles across.

Ultimately, Maley and his companions stumbled onto two Choctaw Indians, who directed the travelers to their village, reportedly fifteen miles from Ouachita Post. William Darby's 1816 map of Louisiana[3] *shows a Choctaw village on South Cheniere Creek, perhaps twelve miles southwest of current Monroe, and it seems likely this was the village mentioned by Maley. From that point, the group could have reached Ouachita Post in a few hours.*

Ouachita Post

We got to the river about two o'clock in the afternoon and crossed over into the town on the 16th day of August, 1813. The settlers here are chiefly French, but we found some from the state of Georgia. Them we put up with.

2. Maps at David Rumsey Historical Map Collection, accessed May 31, 2016 (Arrowsmith Map of 1808) https://www.davidrumsey.com/luna/servlet/detail/RUMSEY~8~1~938~50017:A-Map-Of-The-United-States-Of-North; (Humboldt Map of 1810) https://www.davidrumsey.com/luna/servlet/detail/RUMSEY~8~1~936~50015:A-New-Map-of-Mexico-and-Adjacent-Pr.

3. Map at David Rumsey Historical Map Collection, accessed May 26, 2016, (Darby Map of 1816) https://www.davidrumsey.com/luna/servlet/detail/RUMSEY~8~1~2384~220056:A-Map-of-the-State-of-Louisiana-Wit.

They much pitied our case and gave us good usage, tried to nourish us all they could. We recruited very fast. Cox got better of his snake bite and we continued there about one week and I took much notice of the advantages of that place. It is the highest settlement on that river. There is but one store, these goods retail very high for the county is so productive that planters are generally very wealthy. Their staple is cotton although they raise Indian corn, wheat, etc. Stock in abundance. Leather here is very high. It is for the want of tannin. Hides may be bought for 75 cents the best of cow hides, bark for tanning very convenient. It only wants the mechanic to come and make his fortune in a few years.

Four miles from the post is that delightful settlement called Bayou Saird,[4] a stream that is navigable for 30 miles or upwards. It empties into the river four miles above the post and it extends up to Prarie Marouze,[5] a flourishing settlement chiefly from Kentucky. The lands belong to Abraham Morehouse, originally from the state of New York. He made a purchase there of 30 miles square of Baron de Bast Robe [Bastrop]. The land is excellent. Cotton grows well. They raise abundance of corn and wheat. They are a great deal troubled with the weevil. Unless they grind it soon, corn they don't husk at all. Land may be bought for one, and one and a half dollars an acre. You can take your produce down Bayou Saird into the river. I view this country myself; there is a great chance in this country for men such as accomptants [accountants?], managers, overseers at these extensive cotton plantations. They work negroes. Chiefly there is a great quantity of furs that comes down this river.

Ouachita Post and Northeast Louisiana

The area around Ouachita Post had been explored as early as 1700 by French explorer Jean Baptiste LeMoyne, the Sieur de Bienville, and the Prairie de Canots (Prairie of the Canoes) near present-day Monroe, Louisiana, had been used intermittently by French traders. However, there was little settlement in the Ouachita River valley until after France ceded Louisiana to Spain following the French

4. Now commonly referred to as Bayou Desiard.
5. Prairie Mer Rouge, now known as Mer Rouge, Louisiana, east of Bastrop.

and Indian War.[6] *The earliest known permanent settler was a French Indian trader, Francois Bonaventure. In about 1775 he built a house and established a 2,000-acre plantation at Point Pleasant on Bayou Bartholomew, approximately eighteen miles northeast of Monroe.*[7]

In the 1770s Spain grew concerned over American encroachment from the Natchez country into the Ouachita District, which encompassed most of northern Louisiana and southern Arkansas.[8] *In 1782 Jean Baptiste "Don Juan" Filhiol was given a commission by provisional governor Esteban Miro to establish a Spanish outpost on the Ouachita River.*[9] *Filhiol's mission included organizing settlements in the district, preventing immigration into the area by Americans and English, and maintaining relations with the native tribes. In 1783 Filhiol settled at Ecore Fabré, current Camden, Arkansas, but relocated to Prairie de Canots in 1785. The total non-Indian population of the Ouachita District at the time was estimated to be 207. Filhiol built a palisaded fort at the site, using largely his own money, and named it Fort Miro. He served as commandant of the post until 1800, remaining on his plantation in present-day West Monroe until his death in 1821.*[10]

When Maley arrived at Ouachita Post, the territory was witnessing an influx of Americans. The immigration had begun prior to the Louisiana Purchase, when, in 1796, the Spanish governor-general of Louisiana, Francisco Luis Héctor de Carondelet, provided an enormous land grant in northeastern Louisiana to the Baron de Bastrop. Bastrop, one of the more colorful figures in American history, was born Philip Hendrik Nering Bogel in Dutch Guiana, but after fleeing embezzlement charges in Holland, he changed his name to Felipe Enrique Neri and gave himself the title of Baron de Bastrop. He petitioned Spanish officials to give him a land grant twelve leagues (approximately 31.5 miles) square and ultimately received a block bordering the Ouachita River, Bayou Desiard, and Bayou Bartholomew. In return for the land, Spanish officials expected Bastrop to bring five hundred families to settle on the land. Bastrop did bring in some families from Pennsylvania and Kentucky, but he fell short of expectations and sold his grant to Abraham Morehouse, originally from New York, in 1800.

Following Maley's visit, the region continued to prosper with the boom in

6. "Ouachita Parish Police Jury," accessed June 1, 2016, http://oppj.org/residents/index.php.

7. Helbling, "Beside the Point."

8. Helbling, "Life and Times of the Baron de Bastrop."

9. Filhiol was born Jean Baptiste in 1740 in Eymet, France, but known as Don Juan to Spanish officials. Ouchley, "Don Juan Filhiol."

10. Ibid.

cotton production across the South. Fort Miro was renamed Monroe in 1819, after the first steamboat to visit the town, and is currently the eighth largest town in Louisiana. Abraham Morehouse died in 1813. Bastrop, who left Louisiana for Texas in 1805, was instrumental in securing the 1820 Spanish land grant to Moses and Stephen F. Austin, and served as commissioner of the Austin colonies. He died in 1827.[11] *A visitor to the region today will find little evidence of the region's early history, aside from place names. Present-day Bastrop, Louisiana, named after the baron, is the parish seat of Morehouse Parish, named after Abraham Morehouse. Prairie Mer Rouge, the community that so excited Maley, is today the small agricultural community of Mer Rouge, seven miles east of Bastrop.*

Up the Ouachita

After taking all necessary observations, I saw a chance for a conveyance higher up the river which pleased me well, for this would complete my journey, but my two companions resigned and left me. This boat that I went up with was from N Orleans with a man, a cripple with the rheumatic pains. They were then a going to take him to the hot springs 300 miles up the river, which they said was a certain cure for such diseases. They were well provided with guns and ammunition, for I had none. I started the last of August up the Ouattchitta River, which was the only river west of the Mississippi I did not know the source of. Going up this river, I find the bottoms to overflow sometimes 30 miles from the river. There are very extensive cypress swamps on the river, the timber very tall and large in circumference. There are men that make a great deal of money by cutting cypress logs and rafting them down to N Orleans where they saw them at their steam mills. The manner in which they manage, they cut their logs when the bottoms are not overflowed and in time of a fresh, they float them. They go in with canoes and gather them and raft them together and so go down with very large rafts. This is a general thing up this river. The bottoms generally overflow and cypress swamps very frequent.

About 170 miles up comes in the Little Missouri from the SW. Then comes in a good country of land in between the two rivers. It is getting hilly

11. Helbling, "Life and Times of the Baron de Bastrop."

on the east side of the river. The land was nearly one thing till we got to the hot springs which they call 300 miles from the Post of Ouattchitta. We were three weeks coming from the post. We landed at a convenient place and had to pack out this cripple three miles to the hot spring from the river. We got him and all the baggage there safe and then built a snug cabin that we could lodge comfortable and keep out of the rain. This spring is worth a man's observation. A bold running stream almost sufficient to turn an overshot mill comes out of the foot of a small, stony ridge that is as hot as a boiling pot of water. I was an unbeliever until I had seen and felt it. It will cook a leg of venison or turkey sufficiently to eat by putting it into the spring. It is very stony about the spring and them crusted over with a red iron rust. It smelt very much like unto sulfur. They had to dip up the water in a stone jug and stop it very close so that it should not lose its virtue. So it must stand till it is cool enough to drink. It phisicks a person in a short time. They have a place made to bathe in.

After staying there a few days, I was for taking a tramp further up the river to see the country, but I could get none of those men with me for company. But they let me have a gun and ammunition, which was my best companion. As for wild vermin, I was hardened to them. I took them as company when I had nothing else, especially the wolves for they make such music. I traveled on by myself up the river through a very poor broken country, although game was plenty such as deer and turkey. The river now is getting small. I crossed several large creeks which are all full of beaver. They have not hunted at this place. As I was walking on the river bank, I saw a place where there was much copperas dryed on the bank and also several trees that were petrified. I took off from the river, but found no good land there. I got onto high barren ridges, got so far that I could see the highlands between me and the Keyadamish where I had been before.

I then shifted my course to the southward which in a few days brought me on the waters of Little Missouri. Crossed the Ouattchitta in small branches in a very barren, broken country. There is no good land; it is for hunting. The creeks are very full of beaver. I then shifted my course down the river again between Little Missouri and Ouattchitta. I travelled several days in a poor country till I got nearly to the springs. The land gets better. When I got opposite to the springs, I had to make me a raft to get over the river. I then went on to the springs. They were glad to see me. They thought I would never return. They did not think that I would venture so far by myself. I had been gone 21 days. The cripple could walk by himself. We stayed but one week longer then we all started down the river and in fifteen days got safe at the Post of Ouattchitta again. By this time, this man that had the rheumatism was almost as well as ever he had been.

The Hot Springs

The hot springs visited by Maley, at current day Hot Springs, Arkansas, were well known to Indian tribes in the region. Indigenous groups had been quarrying novaculite, a hard rock used for arrowheads,[12] *for perhaps three thousand years in the vicinity. It is also popularly asserted that various Indian tribes used the springs, but there is no archaeological evidence of settlements at the springs themselves. The Caddo had lived in the area for centuries, and at the time of Maley's visit, the Natchitoches confederation of the Caddo still lived in the area. Also associated with the springs were the Quapaw, who formally conveyed the territory to the United States in 1818.*[13] *However, the area was not frequented by the Osage, as the Ouachita Mountains formed a rugged barrier between the hot springs and Osage hunting grounds to the north. As noted by Dunbar, this permitted whites and other Indians to visit the springs without being attacked.*[14]

While the springs were well known to the Indians, it is not clear who were the first Europeans to visit the site. It has been widely claimed that Spanish explorer Hernando De Soto visited the hot springs in 1541, but more recent studies have questioned that claim.[15] *Prior to Maley's visit, the springs had been known to the French for at least a hundred years: the 1718 map of Louisiana by cartographer Guillaume Delisle shows it as "Caligoa" on the route traveled by De Soto. By the end of the eighteenth century, the springs apparently were receiving regular visitors. The 1804–5 expedition of William Dunbar and George Hunter*

12. Featherstonhaugh reported finding several large pits, twenty to thirty feet deep, where stone for arrowheads had been mined. Featherstonhaugh, *Excursion through the Slave*, 110–11.

13. "American Indians at Hot Springs National Park," National Park Service, Hot Springs National Park Arkansas, accessed June 2, 2016, https://www.nps.gov/hosp/learn/history culture/upload/american_indians.pdf.

14. Berry et al., *The Forgotten Expedition, 1804–1805*, 119.

15. Mitchem, "Route of the De Soto Expedition," accessed June 3, 2016, http://www.encyclopediaofarkansas.net/encyclopedia/entry-detail.aspx?entryID=7679.

found a "log Cabbin and several sheds of split boards, bark, etc." at the springs,[16] *and on their descent of the Ouachita, the group met a boat carrying an elderly Frenchman upstream for treatment there.*[17]

It is also unclear when the first settlers moved to the springs. Some settlers claimed to have established homes there as early as 1807,[18] *but Maley makes no mention of existing structures in his 1813 visit, and his group built a cabin to house themselves. Whenever settlement occurred, development at the springs remained modest for a number of years. In his 1834–35 tour, Featherstonhaugh noted that the area contained only "four wretched-looking log cabins, in one of which was a small store."*[19]

In 1832 Congress designated the area as a federal reserve, arguably making it the country's first national park. However, it wasn't until land disputes were settled in the 1870s that significant development took place at the hot springs. By the 1880s a row of bathhouses had been completed and the area boomed as a health resort through the 1950s.[20] *Today, Hot Springs, Arkansas has a population of approximately 35,000, making it the eleventh-largest city in the state.*

Return to Natchez and Nashville

They went on for N Orleans and I stayed there to get a passage for Natchez, which I soon got with two men that were a going in a pirogue by water the nigh way. We started down the Ouattchitta 150 miles, passing some beautiful settlements on the river till we got to a small river called the Tensaw.[21] Then it takes its name of Black River until it enters into Red River 30 miles from its confluence. After passing the Tensaw, we took out to the left hand through narrow brushy bayou not more than ten yards wide. In a few miles, got into

16. Berry et al., *The Forgotten Expedition, 1804–1805*, 106.

17. Ibid., 188.

18. Cunning, "Garland County," accessed June 6, 2016, http://www.encyclopediaofarkansas.net/encyclopedia/entry-detail.aspx?entryID=770.

19. Featherstonhaugh, *Excursion through the Slave States*, 108.

20. Shugart, "Hot Springs National Park," accessed June 6, 2016, http://www.encyclopediaofarkansas.net/encyclopedia/entry-detail.aspx?entryID=2547.

21. The Tensas River, which joins the Ouachita near current day Jonesville, Louisiana, to form the Black River.

an extensive lake.[22] It was not more than 5 miles wide but the length I can not tell as we took out of it to the left again through a bayou right through heavy timbered country. Alligators were here very numerous and large. They were very dangerous. We had to keep a watch for them at night least they might devour us. One stood sentry whilst the other two slept and so took it turn about. Fish also appeared to be very plenty. The lands here are very strong. The timber grows very tall, which is all poplar, cottonwood and sweet gum.

We at last got into that beautiful lake called Concordia Lake.[23] It is about ten miles in length, and an island in the middle of it which is the property of General Wade Hampton. There can be no better land. It is only five miles from Natchez. The main share of this lake is handsomely settled by Americans who make a business of raising cotton. Their buildings are very elegant and make a fine appearance off of the water. Fish in this lake is beyond any thing ever seen. The whole lake seems to be in a continual motion, even in a calm, only by the fish. They come from Natchez and all parts of the country on parties of pleasure for fishing. They angle them altogether.[24] We left this lake immediately below the east end of this island and took into a bayou that supports this lake from the Mississippi River and so makes a passage through from that to Black River. After leaving this lake about five miles, we got into the Mississippi River about five miles above Natchez, then took down the river and landed safe on the levy on the 10th of October, 1813.

This ended my travels. Here I tarried a few weeks and was sickly at the time. I wished to try a more northern climate for my health, but let not this discourage any person from going to that country, for this was the first day's sickness that I had in four years to lay me one day in bed itself. It is all in a man knowing how to be prudent enough to take care of himself. I bought me a Spanish horse and joined in a company that were going into Kentucky. We then had to go 500 miles of a wilderness and through Indian territories before we got into Nashville in the state of Tennessee. We started five in

22. Their route appears to have been via Bayou Cocodrie; this lake was probably Cocodrie Lake, about ten miles southeast of Jonesville, Louisiana.

23. East of present-day Ferriday, Louisiana.

24. Lake Concordia is still a popular site for fishermen.

Remnants of the Natchez Trace near Port Gibson, Mississippi.
Photograph by the editor.

company, went on 75 miles to Bayou Piere, which is a navigable stream at all seasons of the year 30 miles up from the Mississippi, with the most productivest country in the world for cotton, although it is subject to fever and agues. On this bayou stands the flourishing town of Gibson Port,[25] all settled by Americans. It is in an extensive, fertile country but 40 miles from the Indian territories.

❦ ❦ ❦

The Natchez Trace

Maley reached the Natchez Trace, at Colbert's Ferry, in his 1810 trip up the Tennessee River, and in 1813, traveled from Natchez to Nashville via the roadway. The trace is considered to be the most significant highway in the Old Southwest.[26] *Originally an Indian path, it followed relatively high ground to link Natchez, Mississippi, with Nashville, Tennessee. President Jefferson designated the Trace as a postal road in 1801, and in the first decade of the nineteenth century, the United States negotiated with the Chickasaw and Choctaw tribes to expand the path to a wagon road. During the War of 1812, Andrew Jackson moved his Tennessee militia down the Trace to fight the British at the Battle of New Orleans.*[27]

At the time of Maley's travels, the key role for the Natchez Trace was to facilitate the return of boatmen from Natchez to their homes upriver. Settlers in Kentucky and Tennessee and on the Ohio River shipped agricultural products, livestock, and other goods down river on flatboats. The goods, as well as the timber composing the boats, was typically sold in Natchez or New Orleans, and the boatmen found it easier to return by land via the Trace than to try to row back up the river. Beginning in the 1820s, however, it became more expedient to return upriver by steamboat, and traffic on the Natchez Trace fell substantially. In the 1930s, in recognition of the historic role the trail played in American history, the federal government began construction of a modern road along the trace. Today, the Natchez Trace Parkway, maintained by the U.S. National Park

25. Port Gibson, Mississippi.

26. National Park Service, *Natchez Trace Parkway*, brochure provided by National Park Service, U.S. Department of the Interior, Natchez Trace Parkway, Tupelo, Mississippi 38814 (updated 2014).

27. Discover America, *Explore the Natchez Trace*, visitor guide brochure, obtained March 2016, published by www.scenictrace.com.

Service, provides a 444-mile scenic route from central Tennessee to the bluffs on the lower Mississippi River.

ON TOWARDS the north comes in the Choctaw tribe. I traveled through this nation and found them very hospitable. Some of them are very wealthy and own a number of slaves. There are a great number of white men married among them. They generally live on the road to keep entertainment. This now is a great road but I say it will become of the greatest in the world. After leaving the Choctaws, we get into the Chickasaws. There we find nearly the same as among the Choctaws, whites mixed among them. Congress is endeavoring to bring to a naturalized state. They have an agent among them appointed by the United States who sees that they are supported in forming utensiels and every thing that would bring them to become fitting for society. Hunting among these natives is chiefly out of fashion for game is getting scarce and cattle they can raise in any quantity. These nations have ever been peaceable; it is not their design to shed blood. They are much attached to white people on account of bringing them in a way of cultivating their lands but they still hold to it that white people are rogues. They say that they will tell so many lies which they were not acquainted with before they knew white people, but they will act with a great deal of respect unto travelers if they are civil.

So we traveled safe among them till we got George Colberts on the Tennessee River where I had been before, which closes my journal. After going to Nashville, there I took my residence till I recruited.

Finis.

Epilogue

THUS ENDS MALEY'S ACCOUNT. While his journal is relatively short, it records a remarkable achievement. In reconstructing Maley's travels, the editor calculates that over a period of six years, he traveled more than sixteen thousand miles, crossing parts of what are now thirteen states.[1] More than ten thousand miles was covered by boat, half of that by pirogue, traveling on sixteen rivers. Maley also covered an estimated thirty-five hundred miles on horse or mule-back, and walked more than two thousand miles on his various explorations. Some of Maley's travels took place in settled territories, like Illinois, Kentucky, Tennessee, and Louisiana, but more than half the miles he covered—including exploration on the Missouri, Current, White, Arkansas, Red, and Ouachita Rivers—were beyond the fringes of white settlements. Furthermore, Maley's journal is among the earliest written records of travel in several of these regions. His travel on the White and Arkansas Rivers, for example, came a decade before they were more fully described by Schoolcraft and Nuttall, respectively. Similarly, the upper Red River would remain relatively unknown for forty years following Maley's travels, until it was mapped by the Marcy expedition.

To cover this much ground required Maley to maintain a frenetic pace. Over the six year period, he spent an estimated forty-eight months on the road, with twenty months of that time sleeping under the stars, or in Indian villages, beyond the bounds of civilization. Maley spent only eighteen months in "quarters," and most of that was a year spent in New Orleans, from January 1811 to January 1812. His other stops for "winter quarters" were brief: perhaps three and a half months in Potosi during the winter of

1. By way of comparison, the Lewis and Clark expedition covered more than eight thousand miles through parts of ten states.

1808–9, less than a month in Shawneetown in the winter of 1809–10, and about two months in Natchez during the winter of 1812–13.

It is not clear what drove Maley. Although he ultimately recorded his experiences in a journal, it seems unlikely that someone with his limited writing skills embarked on a six-year excursion of the frontier to write a book. In fact, the book itself seems something of an afterthought, likely written in 1817 or later, years after his travels had ended. Similarly, while Maley was interested in commercial opportunities along the frontier, he didn't stop his travels to take advantage of them. If Maley was primarily interested in making money, one has to wonder why he didn't buy some of the wonderful farmland he saw, or start a meat-packing or leather-tanning business, or even go into the burgeoning cotton business. Maley even appears to abandon his primary commercial interest—the search for valuable minerals—after being robbed by the Osage. While that incident was undoubtedly a devastating blow, the gold he had discovered in the Wichita Mountains was still there, and Maley could have presumably mounted another expedition to recover it. He also lost interest in what he grandly referred to as "New Potosi," and made no effort to exploit the vein of silver ore he claimed to have found in southeast Missouri.

Although Maley may have begun his travels to identify commercial opportunities, by the end of the period, he seems instead to have become a captive of his own wanderlust. Particularly telling is his 1813 venture up the Ouachita River. Although he had almost starved to death in his recent return from an aborted trip up the Red River, Maley decided to join a group of travelers taking an invalid up the Ouachita River to the hot springs. There don't appear to have been commercial opportunities on this trip—no trapping or trading with the Indians—and neither of his two companions elected to join him. Instead, Maley apparently traveled up the Ouachita simply because it was there. Moreover, after reaching the hot springs, he got bored, borrowed a rifle, and then wandered alone for three weeks in the Ouachita Mountains. Rather than being traumatized by his near-death experience, Maley seems to have become the man described years later by Supreme Court justice William Johnson as "one of those troubled spirits that find rest only in motion."

Very little is known about Maley's later life. Based on references in his journal, he was in New Orleans at a later date, possibly in 1814–15, and may have been a witness to the Battle of New Orleans and subsequent schemes hatched there for the invasion of Mexico. It appears that Maley wrote his journal between 1817 and 1819. There are references in the book to steamboat traffic that didn't develop until 1817, and Isaac Riley, the Philadelphia publisher who purchased Maley's journal, went bankrupt in 1820. Finally, according to an obituary published in Charleston, it appears that John Maley died July 16, 1819, at the age of 43, at Mrs. Horry's plantation, in Goose Creek, South Carolina. The obituary notes that he was a native of New York, had been a "respectable inhabitant" of Charleston for three years, and left behind a widow and a large circle of acquaintances.[2] While we can't be certain that this is the same man, it is the only such notice the editor has been able to find, the date is consistent with Justice William Johnson's observation that Maley died sometime before August 1821,[3] and Maley's presence in Charleston would also help explain his acquaintance with Johnson.[4]

We know even less about Maley's companions, Cox and Bradley. Cox, in particular, seems to have been an extremely capable frontiersman. He accompanied Maley from 1810 to 1813 on his most perilous expeditions—on the Ozark Plateau, in western Arkansas, and up the Red River—and was probably instrumental in Maley returning alive. There is one possible clue as to Cox's identity. According to Benjamin Silliman, he received two letters in 1829 from a Robert Cox, in Sparta, Tennessee, that referred to "a gentleman" who had spent five years in Texas and who had been taken by a group of Comanche Indians to see a metallic mass there.[5] Flores speculated that the author of these letters may have been the man who accompanied Maley.[6] While possible, only one Robert Cox, between fifty and sixty years of age, is recorded in the 1830 census for White County, Tennessee.[7] It seems unlikely that this individual would have been the "old hunter" who accompanied

2. "Obituary, John Maley," *City Gazette (Charleston, S.C.)*, August 10, 1819, accessed August 1, 2016, http://www.genealogybank.com/.

3. Johnson to Silliman, August 18, 1821, Silliman Family Papers.

4. Brown, *Maley, John*, 68. In his notes on the manuscript, Michael Brown, the rare-book dealer who sold the first half of Maley's journal to Southern Methodist University, points out that Mrs. Horry was the sister of Charles Cotesworth Pinckney, under whom Justice William Johnson had read law, and it was likely this connection that led to the acquaintance between Johnson and Maley.

5. Silliman, "Meteoric Iron in Texas," 257.

6. Flores, "The John Maley Journal," 27.

7. U.S. Census, "1830 Federal Census, White Co., Tennessee," *rootsweb*, White Co, Tenn., Census Project, accessed July 20, 2016, http://homepages.rootsweb.ancestry.com/~jmack/tnwhite/1830–23.htm.

Maley twenty years earlier since he would have been between thirty and forty years old at the time—about the same age as Maley. However, Silliman's correspondent may have been a younger relative of the Cox who accompanied Maley, and was relating what he had been told by him.

In following Maley's travels around the country, one can't help but be struck by the fleeting nature of prosperity in American history. Only a few of the sites Maley traveled to, such as St. Louis and Nashville, grew to be major U.S. cities. There are also a handful of charming towns, such as Ste. Genevieve, Natchez, and Natchitoches, that while never becoming large cities, have succeeded in preserving their heritage. It is sobering, however, to stand on deserted sites like Kaskaskia, Arkansas Post, or Old Shawneetown, and realize that, only two hundred years ago, these were among the most important communities on the American frontier. It is also sobering to pass through towns that didn't exist when Maley traveled past, steamboat towns like Cairo, Paducah, and Vicksburg that were founded, prospered, and have subsequently faded in importance. Finally, history has not been kind to the small rural communities that were established by those who followed in Maley's wake. Although agriculture remains an important component of the American economy, many of the communities that were once the pride of small-town residents and businessmen are today characterized by shuttered storefronts, abandoned buildings and deserted streets—mute witnesses to the forces of urbanization that continue to shape the country.

It is not clear what legacy should be accorded to Maley. If Isaac Riley had been able to publish Maley's journal, it would have joined a group of other early nineteenth-century travel journals. His account is less precise than many of his contemporaries, but it describes travel much further into the unknown frontier. Had it been published then, parts of his account, particularly his tales of "New Potosi" and gold in the Wichita Mountains, likely would have stimulated exploration into those regions. Today, two hundred years later, his journal no longer serves as a travel guide to the Louisiana Territory; the world it described has long since vanished. However, it does provide a window into life at a time of transition on the frontier, and documents the travels of one of the more ambitious wanderers in American history.

Bibliography

Anderson, John Q., and Diana J. Kleiner. "Copper Production." In *Handbook of Texas Online*. Texas State Historical Association. Accessed February 27, 2016. https://tshaonline.org/handbook/online/articles/dkc04.

Arnold, Morris S. *Colonial Arkansas, 1686–1804: A Social and Cultural History*. Fayetteville: University of Arkansas Press, 1991.

Association for the Preservation of Historic Natchitoches. "Melrose Plantation History." Association for the Preservation of Historic Natchitoches. Accessed May 1, 2016. http://www.melroseplantation.org/history/.

Barker, Eugene C. "Austin, Stephen Fuller." In *Handbook of Texas Online*. Texas State Historical Association. Accessed April 18, 2016. https://www.tshaonline.org/handbook/online/articles/fau14.

Barnett, James F., Jr. "The Yamasee War, the Bearded Chief, and the Founding of Fort Rosalie." *Journal of Mississippi History* (2012). Accessed June 6, 2017. https://www.mdah.ms.gov/new/wp-content/uploads/2013/07/JMH_Spring2012.pdf.

Bateman, Newton, Paul Selby, and Josiah Seymour Currey, eds. *Historical Encyclopedia of Illinois and History of Hancock County*. Chicago: Munsell Publishing Company, 1921. Accessed December 15, 2015. https://books.google.com/books?id=ri5EAQAAMAAJ.

Beckert, Sven. *Empire of Cotton: A Global History*. New York: Vintage Books, 2014.

Berry, Trey, Pam Beasley, and Jeanne Clements. *The Forgotten Expedition, 1804–1805: The Louisiana Purchase Journals of Dunbar and Hunter*. Baton Rouge: Louisiana State University Press, 2006.

Brackenridge, H. M. *Views of Louisiana: Containing Geographical, Statistical and Historical Notices of that Vast and Important Portion of America*. Baltimore: Schaeffer and Maund, 1817. Accessed March 16, 2016. https://archive.org/details/viewsoflouisiana00brac.

Bradbury, John. *Travels in the Interior of America in the Years 1809, 1810, and 1811*. London: Sherwood, Neely and Jones, 1819. Accessed April 21, 2016. https://archive.org/details/travelsininteri00bywagoog.

Brown, Michael. *Maley, John, Hitherto Unknown Manuscript Account of Western Travel, 1808–1810*. Excerpt from Catalog #47, Manuscripts, Letters, Correspondence, Diaries & Archives. Philadelphia: Michael Brown Rare Books, LLC, 53–68.

Buck, Solon J., and Elizabeth H. Buck. *The Planting of Civilization in Western Pennsylvania*. Pittsburgh: University of Pittsburgh Press, 1976.

Burns, Louis F. *A History of the Osage People*. Tuscaloosa: University of Alabama Press, 2004.

Caldwell, Norman W. "Fort Massac during the French and Indian War." *Journal of the Illinois State Historical Society* 43, no. 2 (Summer 1950): 100–19. Accessed October 28, 2015. http://penelope.uchicago.edu/Thayer/E/Gazetteer/Places/America/United_States/Illinois/_Texts/journals/JIllSHS/43/2/Fort_Massac_during_the_French_and_Indian_War*.html.

———. "Fort Massac: The American Frontier Post, 1778–1805." *Journal of the Illinois State Historical Society* 43, no. 4 (Winter 1950): 265–81. Accessed October 28, 2015. http://penelope.uchicago.edu/Thayer/E/Gazetteer/Places/America/United_States/Illinois/_Texts/journals/JIllSHS/43/4/Fort_Massac_the_American_Frontier_Post*.html.

———. "Shawneetown: A Chapter in the Indian History of Illinois." *Journal of the Illinois State Historical Society (1908–1984)* 32, no. 2 (June 1939). Accessed December 1, 2015. www.jstor.org/stable/40185360.

———. "The Red River Raft." *Chronicles of Oklahoma* 19, no. 3 (September 1941): 253–68. Accessed April 29, 2016. http://digital.library.okstate.edu/Chronicles/v019/v019p253.html.

Catlin, George. *Illustrations of the Manners, Customs, and Condition of the North American Indians*. Vol. 2. London: Chatto & Windus, Piccadilly, 1876. Accessed July 28, 2016. https://archive.org/details/illmannerscust02catlrich.

Chapelle, Howard. *American Small Sailing Craft: Their Design, Development, and Construction*. New York: W. W. Norton and Company, 1951.

Cramer, Zadock. *The Navigator: Containing Directions for Navigating the Monongahela, Allegheny, Ohio, and Mississippi Rivers*. 6th ed. Pittsburgh: Zadok Cramer, 1808. Accessed March 15, 2017. https://archive.org/details/navigatorcontain00cram.

Cuming. "Cuming's Tour to the Western Country (1807–1809)." In *Early Western Travels, 1748–1846, vol. 4*, ed. Ruben Gold Thwaites. Cleveland: Arthur H. Clark, 1904. Accessed December 1, 2015. https://ia902705.us.archive.org/19/items/cumingstourtowes00cumirich/cumingstourtowes00cumirich.pdf.

Cunning, Charles W. "Garland County." In *Encyclopedia of Arkansas History and Culture*. Accessed June 6, 2016. http://www.encyclopediaofarkansas.net/encyclopedia/entry-detail.aspx?entryID=770.

Darby, William. *Geographical Description of the State of Louisiana: Presenting a view of the soil, climate, animal, vegetable, and mineral productions; illustrative of its natural physiognomy, its geographical configuration, and relative situation: with an account of the characters and manners of the inhabitants, being an accompaniment to The Map of Louisiana*. Philadelphia: John Melish, 1816. Accessed October 26, 2017. https://archive.org/stream/geographicaldesc00darb#page/162/mode/2up.

Darst, Maury. "Medicine Mounds." In *Handbook of Texas Online*. Texas State Historical Association. Accessed March 3, 2016. https://tshaonline.org/handbook/online/articles/rjm44.

DeArmond-Huskey, Rebecca. "Bayou Bartholomew." In *Encyclopedia of Arkansas History and Culture*. 2014. Accessed June 14, 2016. http://www.encyclopediaofarkansas.net/encyclopedia/entry-detail.aspx?entryID=2226.

Devera, J. A., W. J. Nelson, J. M. Masters. "Geologic Map of the Mill Creek and McClure Quadrangles, Alexander and Union Counties, Illinois." Champaign: Illinois Department of Energy and Natural Resources, Illinois State Geological Survey, 1994. Accessed April 13, 2016. http://isgs.illinois.edu/maps/isgs-quads/geology/mcclure-mill-creek.

Dixon, Frank Haigh. *A Traffic History of the Mississippi River System*. National Waterways Commission Document No. 11. Washington, D.C.: Government Printing Office, 1909. Accessed June 6, 2017. https://archive.org/details/traffichistoryof00dixo.

Duval, Kathleen. "Arkansas Post." In *Encyclopedia of Arkansas History and Culture*. Accessed November 10, 2015. http://www.encyclopediaofarkansas.net/encyclopedia/entry-detail.aspx?entryID=3.

Eckberg, Carl J. *French Roots in the Illinois Country*. Urbana and Chicago: University of Illinois Press, 1998.

Fay, Robert O. *Bibliography of Copper Occurrences in Pennsylvanian and Permian Red Beds and Associated Rocks in Oklahoma, Texas, and Kansas (1805 to 1996)*. Special Publication. Norman: Oklahoma Geological Survey, 2000. Accessed February 27, 2016. http://ogs.ou.edu/docs/specialpublications/SP2000-1.pdf.

Featherstonhaugh, G. W. *Excursion through the Slave States from Washington on the Potomac to the Frontier of Mexico; with Sketches of Popular Manners and Geological Notices*. New York: Harper & Brothers, 1844. Accessed June 2, 2016. https://archive.org/details/excursionthrough00feat.

Flores, Dan L., ed. *Journal of an Indian Trader: Anthony Glass and the Texas Trading Frontier, 1790–1810*. College Station: Texas A&M University Press, 1985.

———, ed. *Southern Counterpart to Lewis and Clark: The Freeman and Custis Expedition of 1806*. Norman: University of Oklahoma Press, 1984.

———. "The John Maley Journal: Travels and Adventures in the American Southwest, 1810–1813." Master's thesis, Northwestern State University of Louisiana, 1971.

Fort Massac: An Historic Site of Southern Illinois. Unpublished brochure provided by staff of Fort Massac State Park, Illinois, October 2015.

Fort Massac State Park. Brochure, DNR142–3/15. Illinois Department of Natural Resources, 2015.

Garrett, J. K. "Dr. John Sibley and the Louisiana-Texas Frontier, 1803–1814." *The Southwestern Historical Quarterly* 49, no. 3 (January 1946): 399–431. Accessed June 6, 2017. http://www.jstor.org/stable/30240639?seq=1#page_scan_tab_contents.

Gilbert, Charles. "Tors on the Southwestern Side of Elk Mountain." Edited by Christie Cooper. *Oklahoma Geology Notes* (Oklahoma Geological Survey) 47, no. 5 (1987): 202. Accessed March 8, 2016. http://ogs.ou.edu/docs/geologynotes/GN-V47N5.pdf.

The Goodspeed Publishing Company. *History of Gallatin, Saline, Hamilton, Franklin and Williamson Counties, Illinois.* Chicago: Goodspeed, 1887. Accessed December 1, 2015. https://archive.org/details/historyofgallati00chic.

Goetzmann, William H. *Exploration and Empire: The Explorer and Scientist in the Winning of the American West.* Austin: Texas State Historical Association, 2000.

Haggard, J. V. "Neutral Ground." In *Handbook of Texas Online.* Texas State Historical Association. Accessed May 19, 2016. https://tshaonline.org/handbook/online/articles/nbn02.

Harrison, William Henry. *Messages and Letters of William Henry Harrison.* Edited by Logan Esarey. Indianapolis: Indiana Historical Commission, 1922. Accessed October 30, 2015. https://archive.org/details/messageslettersо01harr.

Helbling, Wes. "Life and Times of the Baron de Bastrop." *Bastrop Daily Enterprise,* November 21, 2009. Accessed June 1, 2016. http://www.bastropenterprise.com/article/20091121/NEWS/311219993.

———. "Beside the Point: A Brief History of an Early Community." *Bastrop Daily Enterprise,* August 21, 2010. Accessed June 1, 2016. http://www.bastropenterprise.com/article/20100821/NEWS/308219999.

Hodge, Frederick Webb, ed. *Handbook of American Indians North of Mexico, Part 1.* Washington, D.C.: Smithsonian Institution Bureau of American Ethnology, Bulletin 30, 1907. Accessed June 10, 2016. https://archive.org/details/handbookamindians02hodgrich.

———, ed. *Handbook of American Indians North of Mexico, Part 2.* Washington. D.C.: Smithsonian Institution Bureau of American Ethnology, Bulletin 30,

1910. Accessed June 10, 2016. https://archive.org/details/handbookamindians01hodgrich.

Ingenthron, Elmo. *Indians of the Ozark Plateau*. Point Lookout, Mo.: The School of the Ozarks Press, 1970.

Jackson, Jack. " Menchaca, Jose." In *Handbook of Texas Online*. Texas State Historical Association. June 15, 2010. Accessed May 19, 2016. http://www.tshaonline.org/handbook/online/articles/fme11.

———. "Nolan, Philip." In *Handbook of Texas Online*. Texas State Historical Association. June 15, 2010. Accessed June 22, 2016. https://tshaonline.org/handbook/online/articles/fno02.

Johns, Elizabeth A. H. *Storms Brewed in Other Men's Worlds: The Confrontation of Indians, Spanish and French in the Southwest, 1540–1795*. College Station: Texas A&M University Press, 1975.

Johnson, William. "Letter to Benjamin Silliman, August 18, 1821." Silliman Family Papers. Yale University Library. New Haven, Conn. Microfilm.

Kappler, Charles J. *Treaty with the Osage, 1808*. Vol. 2. Washington, D.C.: Government Printing Office, 1904. Accessed April 19, 2016. http://digital.library.okstate.edu/kappler/vol2/treaties/osa0095.htm.

Lippincott, Isaac. "The Early Salt Trade of the Ohio Valley." *Journal of Political Economy* (University of Chicago Press) 20, no. 10 (1912): 1029–52. Accessed March 18, 2016. http://www.jstor.org/stable/1820548.

Lloyd, James T. *Lloyd's Steamboat Directory and Disasters on the Western Waters*. Cincinnati: James T. Lloyd and Company, 1856. Accessed December 22, 2015. https://archive.org/stream/lloydssteamboatd00lloy#page/n0/mode/2up.

Maley, John. "Journal of John Maley's Wanderings in the Red River Country of the Southwest, 1811–1813." Silliman Family Papers, Yale University Library, New Haven, Conn. Microfilm.

———. "Travels, Hunting Expedition, Trapping Discoveries, Trading, Etc., Etc.," Southern Methodist University, DeGolyer Library. Accessed August 19, 2014. http://digitalcollections.smu.edu/cdm/ref/collection/wes/id/1471.

Marcy, R. B., and McClellan, G. B. *Exploration of the Red River of Louisiana in the Year 1852*. Washington, D.C.: A. O. P. Nicholson, 1854. Accessed September 3, 2015. https://archive.org/details/explorationofred01marc.

Martin, James C., and R. S. Martin. *Maps of Texas and the Southwest, 1513–1900*. Albuquerque: University of New Mexico Press, 1984.

Meredith, Howard. "Caddo (Kadohadacho)." In *Encyclopedia of Oklahoma History and Culture*. 2009. Accessed June 9, 2016. http://www.okhistory.org/publications/enc/entry.php?entry=CA003.

Meyer, William E. *Indian Trails of the Southeast.* Facsimile extract from *42nd Annual Report, Bureau of American Ethnology, 1924–25*. Washington, D.C.: Gustavs Library, 2009.

Miller, Adam. "Georgetown (White County)." In *Encyclopedia of Arkansas History and Culture.* Accessed July 28, 2016. http://www.encyclopediaofarkansas.net/encyclopedia/entry-detail.aspx?entryID=3024.

Mills, Elizabeth Shown. "Mézières, Trichel, Grappe: A Study of Tri-Caste Lineages in the Old South." *The Genealogist,* no. 6 (Spring 1985): 3–84. Accessed May 1, 2016. https://www.historicpathways.com/download/mezieres.pdf.

Missouri Department of Labor. "The Importance of Mining in Missouri's History." Missouri Department of Economic Development. Accessed April 18, 2016. https://www.visitmo.com/missouri-travel/the-importance-of-mining-in-missouris-history.aspx.

Mitchem, Jeffrey M. "Route of the De Soto Expedition." In *Encyclopedia of Arkansas History and Culture.* Accessed June 3, 2016. http://www.encyclopediaofarkansas.net/encyclopedia/entry-detail.aspx?entryID=7679.

National Park Service. *Big Spring.* Park brochure, provided by National Park Service, Ozark National Scenic Riverways, Van Buren, Missouri, 2015, National Park Service, U.S. Department of the Interior.

———. "History of the Cane River Region." National Park Service, U.S. Department of the Interior. Accessed April 29, 2016. https://www.nps.gov/nr/travel/caneriver/history.htm.

Nuttall, Thomas. *A Journal of Travels into the Arkansas Territory during the Year 1819.* Edited by Savoie Lottinville. Norman: University of Oklahoma Press, 1980.

Ouchley, Kelby. "Don Juan Filhiol." Edited by David Johnson. Louisiana Endowment for the Humanities. August 27, 2013. Accessed June 1, 2016. http://www.knowla.org/entry/506.

Parker, W. B. *Notes Taken during the Expedition Commanded by Capt. R. B. Marcy, U.S.A., through Unexplored Texas, in the Summer and Fall of 1854.* Philadelphia: Hayes and Zell, 1856. Accessed June 8, 2017. https://archive.org/details/notestakenduring00parkrich.

Polechla, Paul J. "Fur Trade Records from Arkansas Factory, Arkansas Post, Louisiana Territory, 1805–1810." *Proceedings of the Arkansas Academy of Science* 41 (1987). Accessed November 10, 2015. http://scholarworks.uark.edu/cgi/viewcontent.cgi?article=2366&context=jaas.

Pool, Carolyn Garrett. "Wichita." In *Encyclopedia of Oklahoma History and Culture.* 2009. Accessed June 9, 2016. http://www.okhistory.org/publications/enc/entry.php?entry=WI001.

Reynolds, John. *Reynolds' History of Illinois. My Own Times: Embracing Also the History of my Life*. Chicago: Chicago Historical Society, 1879. Accessed April 14, 2016. https://archive.org/details/reynoldshistoryo00reyn.

Rothert, Otto A. *A History of Muhlenberg County*. Louisville: John P. Morton, 1913. Accessed December 1, 2015. https://ia800306.us.archive.org/6/items/historyofmuhlenb00roth/historyofmuhlenb00roth.pdf.

Royce, Charles C., comp. *Indian Land Cessions of the United States, in the Eighteenth Annual Report of the Bureau of American Ethnology*. Washington, D.C.: Government Printing Office, 1899. Accessed November 4, 2015. https://archive.org/details/annualreportofbu182smit.

Schoolcraft, Henry R. *A View of the Lead Mines of Missouri: Including Some Observations on the Minerology, Geology, Geography, Antiquities, Soil, Climate, Population, and Productions of Missouri and Arkansaw and Other Sections of the Western Country*. New York: Charles Wiley and Son, 1819. Accessed April 15, 2016. https://archive.org/details/viewofleadmineso01scho.

———. *Journal of a Tour into the Interior of Missouri and Arkansaw*. London: Sir Richard Phillips and Co., 1821. Accessed December 2, 2015. https://archive.org/details/journalatourint00schogoog.

Seeger, Cheryl M. "History of Mining in the Southeast Missouri Lead District and Description of Mine Processes, Regulatory Controls, Environmental Effects, and Mine Facilities in the Viburnum Trend Subdistrict." Chapter 1 in *Hydrologic Investigations Concerning Lead Mining Issues in Southeastern Missouri*, edited by Michael J. Kleeschulte. U.S. Department of the Interior, U.S. Geological Survey, 2008. Accessed January 9, 2015. https://pubs.usgs.gov/sir/2008/5140/pdf/Chapter1.pdf.

Shugart, Sharon. "Hot Springs National Park." In *Encyclopedia of Arkansas History and Culture*. Accessed June 6, 2016. http://www.encyclopediaofarkansas.net/encyclopedia/entry-detail.aspx?entryID=2547.

Sibley, John, to Henry Dearborn, April 10, 1805. In *Annals of Congress, 9th Congress, Second Session*, 1088–104. Washington, D.C.: Library of Congress, 1852. Accessed June 11, 2017. https://memory.loc.gov/cgi-bin/ampage?collId=llac&fileName=016/llac016.db&recNum=541.

Silliman, Benjamin. "Meteoric Iron in Texas." Edited by Benjamin Silliman. *American Journal of Science and Arts* 33 (January 1838): 257. Accessed June 8, 2017. https://archive.org/details/americanjournalo33183738newh.

———, ed. "Notice of the Malleable Iron of Louisiana." *The American Journal of Science and Arts* (S. Converse, for the Editor) 8, no. 2 (August 1824). Accessed June 8, 2017. https://archive.org/details/americanjournal081824newh.

Smith, George Washington. *A History of Southern Illinois: A Narrative Account of its Historical Progress, its People, and its Principal Interests.* Vol. 1. New York: The Lewis Publishing Company, 1912. Accessed December 2, 2015. https://archive.org/details/historyofsouther01smit.

Smith, Jeffrey E., ed. *Seeking a Newer World: The Fort Osage Journals and Letters of George Sibley, 1808–1811.* St. Charles, Mo.: Lindenwood University Press, 2003.

Smithey, Emily P. "Transformation of Early Nineteenth-Century Chickasaw Leadership Patterns, 1800–1845." Masters thesis. University of Mississippi, 2015.

State Historical Society of Missouri. "Moses Austin." Historic Missourians, The State Historical Society of Missouri. Accessed April 15, 2016. http://shsmo.org/historicmissourians/name/a/austin/.

Stoddard, Amos. *Sketches, Historical and Descriptive, of Louisiana.* Philadelphia: Matthew Carey, 1812. Accessed March 16, 2016. https://archive.org/details/sketcheshistoric00stod.

Stroud, R. B., et al. *Production Potential of Copper Deposits Associated with Permian Red Bed Formations in Texas, Oklahoma, and Kansas.* Washington, D.C.: U.S. Department of the Interior, Bureau of Mines, 1970. Accessed December 12, 2016. https://digital.library.unt.edu/ark:/67531/metadc38718/m1/1/.

Taibi, Richard. "The Early Years of Meteor Observations in the USA." American Meteor Society. Accessed May 24, 2016. http://www.amsmeteors.org/about/ams-history/the-early-years-of-meteor-observations-in-the-usa/.

Thomassy, R. *Geologie Pratique de la Louisiane.* New Orleans and Paris: Author, and Lacroix and Baudry, 1860. Accessed May 3, 2016. https://archive.org/stream/gologiepratique00thomgoog#page/n7/mode/2up.

Townes, J. Edward "The Neutral Strip." In *knowlouisiana.org Encyclopedia of Louisiana,* edited by David Johnson. Louisiana Endowment for the Humanities, 2010–. Article published July 12, 2011. Accessed May 16, 2016. http://www.knowlouisiana.org/entry/the-neutral-strip.

Tyson, Carl Newton. *The Red River in Southwestern History.* Norman: University of Oklahoma Press, 1981.

U.S. Geological Survey. "National Mineral Assessment Tract GP03 (Sediment-hosted Cu, redbed)." 1998. U.S. Geological Survey. Accessed February 29, 2016. https://mrdata.usgs.gov/nmra/show-nmra.php?tract=GP03.

Veatch, A. C. *Geology and Underground Water Resources of Northern Louisiana and Southern Arkansas.* U.S. Geological Survey, Professional Paper No. 46. Washington, D.C.: Department of the Interior, United States Geological Survey, 1906. Accessed June 8, 2017. https://pubs.usgs.gov/pp/0046/report.pdf.

Wallace, Anthony F. C. *Jefferson and the Indians.* Cambridge, Mass., and London, England: The Belknap Press of Harvard University Press, 1999.

Warren, Harris Gaylord. *The Sword Was Their Passport: A History of American Filibustering in the Mexican Revolution.* Port Washington, N.Y., and London: Kennikat Press, 1972.

Wilson, Steve. *Oklahoma Treasures and Treasure Tales.* Norman: University of Oklahoma Press, 1976.

Index

Page numbers in *italic* type indicate illustrations. *Also appears as* indicates Maley's term differs from the modern or accepted term, unless it is readily apparent in the text.